SOUND AND SENSE

AN INTRODUCTION TO POETRY

SEVENTH EDITION

True ease in writing comes from art, not chance,
As those move easiest who have learned to dance.
'Tis not enough no harshness gives offense,
The sound must seem an echo to the sense.

ALEXANDER POPE from *An Essay on Criticism*

Relationships
Conflicts
Person vs. Person
person vs. society
person vs. god
person vs. nature
person vs. self

satire   nasty intent

Irony
verbal   said vs. meant
dramatic   speaker vs. knowledge
situational   expectations should be

SOUND AND SENSE

AN INTRODUCTION TO POETRY

SEVENTH EDITION

Laurence Perrine

with the assistance of
Thomas R. Arp
Southern Methodist University

Harcourt Brace Jovanovich, Publishers
San Diego   New York   Chicago   Austin   Washington,D.C.
London   Sydney   Tokyo   Toronto

ISBN: 0-15-582608-5
Library of Congress Catalog Card Number: 86-80755
Printed in the United States of America

Copyrights and Acknowledgments appear on pages 325–31, which constitute a continuation of the copyright page.

Preface

The seventh edition of *Sound and Sense*, like the earlier editions, is written for the college student who is beginning a serious study of poetry. It seeks to give that student a sufficient grasp of the nature and variety of poetry, some reasonable means for reading it with appreciative understanding, and a few primary ideas of how to evaluate it. The separate chapters gradually introduce the student to the elements of poetry, putting the emphasis always on *how* and *why: How* can the reader use these elements to get at the meaning of the poem, to interpret it correctly, and to respond to it adequately? *Why* does the poet use these elements? What values have they for the poet and reader?

In matters of theory, some issues are undoubtedly oversimplified, but I hope none seriously. The purpose has always been to give the beginning student something to understand and use. The first assumptions of *Sound and Sense* are that poetry needs to be read carefully and thought about considerably and that, when so read, poetry gives its readers continuing rewards in experience and understanding.

Each chapter is divided into two parts: a discussion of the topic indicated by the chapter title, with illustrative poems, and a relevant selection of poems, with study questions, for further reading. The division between the two parts is visually indicated by a row of asterisks. The whole book is similarly divided into two parts: Part One consists of the sixteen discussion chapters; Part Two of poems, without study questions, for further reading.

The seventh edition differs from the sixth chiefly in the following respects: (a) Approximately twenty-seven of the poems are new. Among the new poems, more than a dozen were first published in the 1980s. (b) John Donne has replaced A. E. Housman as one of the three poets who are represented by a sufficient number of poems to support study of them as individual artists. (c) The number of poems by women (and the number of woman poets) has been increased. (d) Each poem has been assigned a number. This feature has been introduced to facilitate the making of assignments and syllabuses by instructors who wish to depart from the strict ordering of the Table of Contents.

A book of this kind inevitably owes something to all who have thought and written about literature. It would be impossible to express all indebtedness, but for personal advice, criticism, and assistance I wish especially to thank my wife, Catherine Perrine; Maynard Mack, Yale University; Willis Glover, Mercer University; James W. Byrd, East Texas State University; Paul T. Hopper, Washington, D.C.; Margaret Rusk White, Keene State University; and the late Margaret Morton Blum, Southern Methodist University.

I would also like to thank the following instructors, who have sent me helpful reactions and suggestions for this seventh edition of *Sound and Sense:* Barbara Adams, Pace University; Gail Albracht, Oakton Community College; Linda Rae Andrews, University of Illinois, Chicago; Marion Baily, North Shore Community College; Thomas H. Barthel, Herkimer County Community College; Wilma Beard, Arkansas State University; Harry Brown, Midwestern State University; Carolyn Bruder, University of Southwestern Louisiana; James Byrd, East Texas State University; Linda Caruthers, Kishwaukee College; Frank Chiarenza, University of Hartford; Betty Clement, Paris Junior College; Robert Coard, St. Cloud State University; Mattie Collins, Angelina College; James Cotter, Mount Saint Mary College; Carmen Cramer, University of Southwestern Louisiana; Henry Crooke, Suffolk County Community College, Selden Campus; Elizabeth Davis, Southern Arkansas University; Henry Davis, Spring Hill College; Robert Diebold, Husson College; Philip Dillard, Floyd Junior College; Joyceann Ditka, Community College of Allegheny County, North Campus; John Duffy, University of Connecticut; Joyce Erickson, Warner Pacific College; Gabriel Fagan, St. Mary's College; Francis Fike, Hope College; Rosemary Fithian, Friends University; Arthur Flodstrom, St. Mary's College; Skip Fox, University of Southwestern Louisiana; Constance Franz, St. John's University, Staten Island Campus; Paula Friedman, Cardinal Stritch College; Beverly Furlow, Pima

Community College; Elsa A. Gaines, North Georgia College; Jane Gardner, Hastings College; Gary Grassinger, Community College of Allegheny County, North Campus; James Grimshaw, East Texas State University; James Harcharik, Kishwaukee College; Eleanor Harris, University of Illinois, Chicago; Robert Harwick, Hastings College; Walter Herrscher, University of Wisconsin, Green Bay; Gillian Hettinger, Montclair State College; Judith Hiltner, Christian Brothers College; Myra Hinman, University of Kansas; James Hoggard, Midwestern State University; Karla Holloway, Western Michigan University; Ralph Hoppe, Concordia College; Ann Hostetler, Golden West College; Wayne Hubert, Chaffey College; Bob Huff, Western Washington University; Constance Hunting, University of Maine, Orono; Frederick Ivor-Campbell; Dorothy Jacobs, University of Rhode Island; Ronald Janssen, Hofstra University; Elwood Johnson, Western Washington University; William C. Johnson, Northern Illinois University; James Jolly, Shelton State Community College; Janet Jones, Middlesex Community College; Harriet Joseph, Pace University, Westchester; William Joyce, Fulton-Montgomery Community College; James Keech, SUNY, Buffalo; Sue Kelley, Snead State Junior College; Nancy Kelly, Fitchburg State College; Dolores Keranen, University of Illinois, Chicago; William Kessel, Erie Community College, South; Herb Kjos, Lakewood Community College; Carole Brown Knuth, SUNY, Buffalo; Mary Kramer, University of Lowell; Bette Burnette Lansdown, Cameron University; Deborah Lethbridge, Union College; Kenneth Lewars, Southern Connecticut State University; Cheng Lok Chua, Moorhead State University; Woodley Lott, Mississippi Gulf Coast Junior College; Dennis Loyd, David Lipscomb College; Thomas Luddy, Salem State College; Richard Lyttle, Northland Community College; Robin McAllister, Sacred Heart University; Robert McCarty, Saint Peter's College; Mary McCauley, Dyersburg State Community College; Marcia Ann McDonald, Belmont College; Joy Ellis McLemore, University of Texas, Tyler; Helen Maloney, Tidewater Community College; J. Ron Medlin, Belmont College; Dr. Michael Mikolajczak, Marquette University; Albert Millar, Christopher Newport College; Robert Morsberger, California State Polytechnic University; Walter Mullen, Mississippi Gulf Coast Junior College; James Nazen, University of Nevada, Las Vegas; Pearl Ostrow, New York Institute of Technology; Rosemary Palms, Pratt Institute; Linda Plagman, Cardinal Stritch College; Gloria Debble Pond, Mattatuck Community College; Joseph Popson, Macon Junior College; Marion J. Reis, College of Du Page; Patricia Robertson, University of Southwestern Louisiana; Cora Robey,

Tidewater Community College; Douglas Roycraft, Erie Community College, North; Mary Russell, Bunker Hill Community College; Alan Shaw, Monroe Community College; Michael Sita, Pima Community College; Fred Sokol, Asnuntuck Community College; Daniel Speca, Community College of Allegheny County, South Campus; Kenneth Sroka, Canisius College; Catherine Stevenson, University of Hartford; Peggy Stiffler, Chaffey College; Edward Stone, University of Arkansas; John Sweney, Colby College; David Toor, SUNY, Cortland; Robbie Townson, Snead State Junior College; Peter Ulisse, Housatonic Regional Community College; Lyle Van Pelt, St. Cloud State University; Agnes Vardy, Robert Morris College; Bernard Verniel, Triton College; Vianney Vormwald, Siena College; Carolyn Wall, Spokane Community College; Leon Ward, Grayson County College; Terri Whitney, North Shore Community College; Joyce Williams, Jefferson State Junior College; Mike Williams, Angelina College; Mary Wood, Santa Ana College; Charles Workman, Samford University; Valree Wynn, Cameron University; George Zimmer, College of Lake County.

L.P.

Contents

Preface   v

Part 1   **The Elements of Poetry**   1

Chapter One   What Is Poetry?   3

1. *Alfred, Lord Tennyson*   The Eagle   5
2. *William Shakespeare*   Winter   6
3. *Wilfred Owen*   Dulce et Decorum Est   8

* * *

4. *Lawrence Ferlinghetti*   Constantly risking absurdity   11
5. *Emily Dickinson*   A bird came down the walk   12
6. *John Donne*   The Triple Fool   13
7. *William Carlos Williams*   The Red Wheelbarrow   14
8. *A. E. Housman*   Terence, this is stupid stuff   14

Chapter Two   Reading the Poem   17

9. *Thomas Hardy*   The Man He Killed   19
10. *A. E. Housman*   Is my team ploughing   21
GENERAL QUESTIONS FOR ANALYSIS AND EVALUATION   24

* * *

11. *Robert Frost*   Mowing   25
12. *John Donne*   Break of Day   26
13. *Emily Dickinson*   There's been a death in the opposite house   27
14. *Mari Evans*   When in Rome   28
15. *George Gascoigne*   And if I did what then?   29
16. *Edwin Arlington Robinson*   The Mill   30
17. *Sylvia Plath*   Mirror   31
18. *Philip Larkin*   A Study of Reading Habits   31
EXERCISE   32

Chapter Three   Denotation and Connotation   33

19. *Emily Dickinson*   There is no frigate like a book   34
20. *William Shakespeare*   When my love swears that she is made of truth   35
21. *Robert Graves*   The Naked and the Nude   36
EXERCISES   38

* * *

22. *Edwin Arlington Robinson*   Richard Cory   39
23. *Henry Reed*   Naming of Parts   40
24. *Ezra Pound*   Portrait d'une Femme   41
25. *Langston Hughes*   Cross   42
26. *William Wordsworth*   The world is too much with us   43
27. *John Donne*   A Hymn to God the Father   44
28. *Siegfried Sassoon*   Base Details   45
EXERCISES   45

Chapter Four   Imagery   46

29. *Robert Browning*   Meeting at Night   47
30. *Robert Browning*   Parting at Morning   48

* * *

31. *Richard Wilbur*   A Late Aubade   49
32. *Robert Frost*   After Apple-Picking   50
33. *Emily Dickinson*   A narrow fellow in the grass   52
34. *Adrienne Rich*   Living in Sin   53
35. *Robert Hayden*   Those Winter Sundays   54
36. *Thomas Hardy*   The Darkling Thrush   54

37. *Gerard Manley Hopkins* Spring 56
38. *John Keats* To Autumn 56

Chapter Five **Figurative Language 1**
Metaphor, Personification,
Metonymy 58

39. *Frances Cornford* The Guitarist Tunes Up 59
40. *Robert Francis* The Hound 60
41. *Robert Frost* Bereft 60
42. *Emily Dickinson* It sifts from leaden sieves 61
43. *George Herbert* The Quip 63
44. *Edwin Arlington Robinson* The Dark Hills 64
45. *Emily Dickinson* A Hummingbird 66
EXERCISE 68

* * *

46. *Thomas Campion* There is a garden in her face 69
47. *Robert Frost* The Silken Tent 70
48. *Sylvia Plath* Metaphors 70
49. *Philip Larkin* Toads 71
50. *John Donne* A Valediction: Forbidding Mourning 72
51. *Andrew Marvell* To His Coy Mistress 74
52. *John Keats* To Sleep 76
53. *A. E. Housman* Loveliest of trees 76
54. *Langston Hughes* Dream Deferred 77

Chapter Six **Figurative Language 2**
Symbol, Allegory 78

55. *Robert Frost* The Road Not Taken 78
56. *Dorothy Lee Richardson* At Cape Bojeador 80
57. *William Blake* The Sick Rose 81
58. *Archibald MacLeish* You, Andrew Marvell 83
59. *Robert Herrick* To the Virgins, to Make Much of Time 86
60. *George Herbert* Redemption 88

* * *

61. *Robert Frost* Fire and Ice 88
62. *Rupert Brooke* The Dead 89
63. *Alfred, Lord Tennyson* Ulysses 90

64. *Alastair Reid*   Curiosity   92
65. *Alan Dugan*   Love Song: I and Thou   93
66. *John Donne*   Hymn to God My God, in My Sickness   95
67. *Christina Rossetti*   Uphill   96
68. *Robert Frost*   Dust of Snow   97
69. *William Blake*   Soft Snow   97

**Chapter Seven   Figurative Language 3
Paradox, Overstatement,
Understatement, Irony   98**

70. *Emily Dickinson*   My life closed twice   99
71. *John Donne*   The Sun Rising   100
72. *Countee Cullen*   Incident   101
73. *Alexander Pope*   On a Certain Lady at Court   103
74. *William Blake*   The Chimney Sweeper   105
75. *Percy Bysshe Shelley*   Ozymandias   106
EXERCISE   107

* * *

76. *John Donne*   Batter my heart, three-personed God   108
77. *John Frederick Nims*   Love Poem   109
78. *Sir John Harington*   On Treason   110
79. *Donald W. Baker*   Formal Application   110
80. *W. H. Auden*   The Unknown Citizen   111
81. *Robert Frost*   Departmental   112
82. *M. Carl Holman*   Mr. Z   113
83. *Robert Browning*   My Last Duchess   114
EXERCISE   116

Chapter Eight   Allusion   117

84. *Robert Frost*   "Out, Out—"   118
85. *William Shakespeare*   From *Macbeth:* She should have died
     hereafter   120
86. *e. e. cummings*   in Just-   121
87. *John Milton*   On His Blindness   122
88. *John Donne*   Hero and Leander   122
89. *Keith Jennison*   Last Stand   123
90. *Edwin Arlington Robinson*   Miniver Cheevy   123
91. *William Butler Yeats*   Leda and the Swan   124

92. *T. S. Eliot*   Journey of the Magi   125
93. *Emily Dickinson*   Abraham to kill him   127
94. *Emily Dickinson*   Belshazzar had a letter   127
95. *Anonymous*   In the Garden   128
EXERCISE   128

Chapter Nine   Meaning and Idea   129

96. *Anonymous*   Little Jack Horner   129
97. *Sara Teasdale*   Barter   131
98. *Robert Frost*   Stopping by Woods on a Snowy Evening   131

* * *

 99. *William Cullen Bryant*   To a Waterfowl   133
100. *Robert Frost*   Design   134
101. *John Donne*   The Indifferent   135
102. *John Donne*   Love's Deity   136
103. *Gerard Manley Hopkins*   The Caged Skylark   137
104. *Philip Larkin*   Aubade   138
105. *Archibald MacLeish*   Ars Poetica   140

Chapter Ten   Tone   141

106. *W. H. Davies*   The Villain   143
107. *Emily Dickinson*   Apparently with no surprise   143

* * *

108. *William Butler Yeats*   The Coming of Wisdom with Time   145
109. *Michael Drayton*   Since there's no help   146
110. *Robert Frost*   The Telephone   146
111. *John Wakeman*   Love in Brooklyn   147
112. *Emily Dickinson*   One dignity delays for all   148
113. *Emily Dickinson*   'Twas warm at first like us   149
114. *Alfred, Lord Tennyson*   Crossing the Bar   149
115. *Thomas Hardy*   The Oxen   150
116. *John Donne*   The Apparition   151
117. *John Donne*   The Flea   152
118. *Alexander Pope*   Engraved on the Collar of a Dog Which I
        Gave to His Royal Highness   153
119. *Anonymous*   Love   154
EXERCISE   154

Chapter Eleven Musical Devices 155

120. *Ogden Nash* The Turtle 156
121. *W. H. Auden* That night when joy began 158
122. *Gerard Manley Hopkins* God's Grandeur 160

* * *

123. *A. E. Housman* With rue my heart is laden 161
124. *Gwendolyn Brooks* We Real Cool 162
125. *Emily Dickinson* As imperceptibly as grief 162
126. *Carl Sandburg* The Harbor 163
127. *John Crowe Ransom* Parting, Without a Sequel 164
128. *Ralph Pomeroy* Row 165
129. *Edna St. Vincent Millay* Counting-Out Rhyme 166
130. *William Stafford* Traveling Through the Dark 166
131. *Robert Frost* Nothing Gold Can Stay 167

Chapter Twelve Rhythm and Meter 168

132. *George Herbert* Virtue 170
EXERCISES 179

* * *

133. *William Blake* "Introduction" to *Songs of Innocence* 180
134. *Robert Frost* It takes all sorts 181
135. *A. E. Housman* Epitaph on an Army of Mercenaries 181
136. *e. e. cummings* if everything happens that can't be done 182
137. *A. E. Housman* Oh who is that young sinner 184
138. *William Butler Yeats* Down by the Salley Gardens 185
139. *Walt Whitman* Had I the Choice 186
140. *Robert Frost* The Aim Was Song 186
141. *Samuel Taylor Coleridge* Metrical Feet 187
EXERCISE 187

Chapter Thirteen Sound and Meaning 188

142. *Anonymous* Pease porridge hot 188
143. *William Shakespeare* Song: Hark, hark! 189
144. *Carl Sandburg* Splinter 190
145. *Robert Herrick* Upon Julia's Voice 191
146. *Robert Frost* The Span of Life 195
EXERCISE 196

* * *

147. *Alexander Pope*   Sound and Sense   198
148. *Emily Dickinson*   I like to see it lap the miles   198
149. *Ted Hughes*   Wind   199
150. *Gerard Manley Hopkins*   Heaven-Haven   200
151. *Wilfred Owen*   Anthem for Doomed Youth   201
152. *A. E. Housman*   Eight O'Clock   201
153. *James Joyce*   All day I hear   202
154. *Emily Dickinson*   I heard a fly buzz when I died   203
155. *William Carlos Williams*   The Dance   203
EXERCISE   204

Chapter Fourteen   Pattern   205

156. *e. e. cummings*   the greedy the people   207
157. *Anonymous*   I sat next the Duchess at tea   208
158. *John Keats*   On First Looking into Chapman's Homer   209
159. *William Shakespeare*   That time of year   210
EXERCISES   212

* * *

160. *Anonymous, Carolyn Wells,*
     Anonymous, Martin Bristow
     Smith, Anonymous, David
     McCord   A Handful of Limericks   212
161. *Dylan Thomas*   Poem in October   214
162. *Matsuo Bashō/Moritake*   Two Japanese Haiku   216
163. *William Shakespeare*   From *Romeo and Juliet:* If I profane
     with my unworthiest hand   216
164. *John Donne*   Death, be not proud   217
165. *Martha Collins*   The Story We Know   218
166. *Randolph Stow*   As he lay dying   219
167. *Anonymous*   Edward   219
168. *Maxine Kumin*   400-Meter Freestyle   221
169. *William Burford*   A Christmas Tree   223
EXERCISES   223

Chapter Fifteen   Bad Poetry and Good   224

170. God's Will for You and Me   229
171. Pied Beauty   229

172. Pitcher   229
173. The Old-Fashioned Pitcher   230
174. Come Up from the Fields Father   230
175. The Faded Coat of Blue   232
176. A Poison Tree   233
177. The Most Vital Thing in Life   233
178. On a Dead Child   234
179. Bells for John Whiteside's Daughter   234
180. Some keep the Sabbath going to church   235
181. My Church   235
182. The Long Voyage   236
183. Breathes there the man   236
184. Little Boy Blue   237
185. The Toys   238

Chapter Sixteen   Good Poetry and Great   239

186. *John Donne*   The Canonization   241
187. *Robert Frost*   Home Burial   243
188. *T. S. Eliot*   The Love Song of J. Alfred Prufrock   247

Part 2   **Poems for Further Reading**   253

189. *Joan Aleshire*   Slipping   255
190. *A. R. Ammons*   Providence   255
191. *Matthew Arnold*   Dover Beach   256
192. *W. H. Auden*   Musée des Beaux Arts   257
193. *D. C. Berry*   On Reading Poems to a Senior Class at South High   257
194. *Elizabeth Bishop*   One Art   258
195. *William Blake*   The Garden of Love   259
196. *William Blake*   The Lamb   259
197. *William Blake*   The Tiger   260
198. *Lucille Clifton*   Good Times   260
199. *Samuel Taylor Coleridge*   Kubla Khan   261
200. *Emily Dickinson*   Because I could not stop for Death   262
201. *Emily Dickinson*   I taste a liquor never brewed   263
202. *Emily Dickinson*   In winter in my room   264
203. *John Donne*   The Good-Morrow   265

204. *John Donne*   Song: Go and catch a falling star   266
205. *Keith Douglas*   Vergissmeinnicht   266
206. *Carolyn Forché*   The Colonel   267
207. *Robert Frost*   Acquainted with the Night   268
208. *Robert Frost*   Mending Wall   268
209. *Isabella Gardner*   Gimboling   269
210. *Christopher Gilbert*   Pushing   270
211. *Robert Graves*   Down, Wanton, Down!   270
212. *Thomas Hardy*   Channel Firing   271
213. *A. E. Housman*   Bredon Hill   272
214. *A. E. Housman*   To an Athlete Dying Young   273
215. *Randall Jarrell*   The Death of the Ball Turret Gunner   274
216. *Ellen Kay*   Pathedy of Manners   274
217. *John Keats*   La Belle Dame sans Merci   275
218. *John Keats*   Ode on a Grecian Urn   277
219. *John Keats*   Ode to a Nightingale   278
220. *Galway Kinnell*   Blackberry Eating   280
221. *Etheridge Knight*   The warden said to me   281
222. *George MacBeth*   Bedtime Story   281
223. *Naomi Long Madgett*   Midway   282
224. *Andrew Marvell*   A Dialogue Between the Soul and Body   283
225. *Cleopatra Mathis*   Getting Out   284
226. *Marianne Moore*   Nevertheless   285
227. *Ogden Nash*   I Do, I Will, I Have   286
228. *Howard Nemerov*   Grace to Be Said at the Supermarket   287
229. *Naomi Shihab Nye*   Famous   287
230. *Sharon Olds*   The Connoisseuse of Slugs   288
231. *P. K. Page*   The Landlady   288
232. *Linda Pastan*   Ethics   289
233. *Dudley Randall*   Ballad of Birmingham   290
234. *Alberto Ríos*   Nani   291
235. *Edwin Arlington Robinson*   Mr. Flood's Party   292
236. *Theodore Roethke*   I Knew a Woman   294
237. *Theodore Roethke*   The Waking   295
238. *William Shakespeare*   Fear no more   295
239. *William Shakespeare*   Let me not to the marriage of true minds   296
240. *William Shakespeare*   My mistress' eyes   296
241. *Gary Soto*   Small Town with One Road   297
242. *Wallace Stevens*   The Death of a Soldier   298
243. *Wallace Stevens*   The Snow Man   298

244. *May Swenson*   Question   298
245. *Jonathan Swift*   A Description of the Morning   299
246. *Dylan Thomas*   Do Not Go Gentle into that Good Night   300
247. *Dylan Thomas*   Fern Hill   300
248. *Jean Toomer*   Reapers   302
249. *John Updike*   Ex-Basketball Player   302
250. *David Wagoner*   Return to the Swamp   303
251. *Derek Walcott*   The Virgins   304
252. *Marilyn Nelson Waniek*   Old Bibles   305
253. *Robert Penn Warren*   Boy Wandering in Simms' Valley   306
254. *Walt Whitman*   A Noiseless Patient Spider   306
255. *Walt Whitman*   There Was a Child Went Forth   307
256. *Walt Whitman*   When I Heard the Learn'd Astronomer   308
257. *Richard Wilbur*   The Mill   309
258. *Nancy Willard*   A Wreath to the Fish   310
259. *Miller Williams*   A Poem for Emily   310
260. *William Wordsworth*   I wandered lonely as a cloud   311
261. *William Wordsworth*   The Solitary Reaper   312
262. *William Butler Yeats*   Sailing to Byzantium   313
263. *William Butler Yeats*   The Second Coming   314
264. *William Butler Yeats*   The Wild Swans at Coole   315

Glossary of Poetic Terms   316

Index of Authors, Titles, and First Lines   332

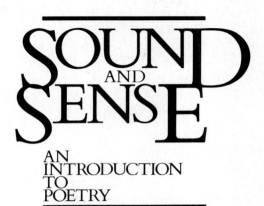

SOUND AND SENSE

AN INTRODUCTION TO POETRY

SEVENTH EDITION

part 1
THE ELEMENTS OF POETRY

Chapter one
What Is Poetry?

Poetry is as universal as language and almost as ancient. The most primitive peoples have used it, and the most civilized have cultivated it. In all ages, and in all countries, poetry has been written—and eagerly read or listened to—by all kinds and conditions of people, by soldiers, statesmen, lawyers, farmers, doctors, scientists, clergy, philosophers, kings, and queens. In all ages it has been especially the concern of the educated, the intelligent, and the sensitive, and it has appealed, in its simpler forms, to the uneducated and to children. Why? First, because it has given pleasure. People have read it, listened to it, or recited it because they liked it—because it gave them enjoyment. But this is not the whole answer. Poetry in all ages has been regarded as important, not simply as one of several alternative forms of amusement, as one person might choose bowling, another chess, and another poetry. Rather, it has been regarded as something central to existence, something having unique value to the fully realized life, something that we are better off for having and spiritually impoverished without. To understand the reasons for this, we need to have at least a provisional understanding of what poetry is—provisional, because people have always been more successful at appreciating poetry than at defining it.

Initially, poetry might be defined as a kind of language that says *more* and says it *more intensely* than does ordinary language. To understand this fully, we need to understand what poetry "says." For language is employed on different occasions to say quite different kinds of things; in other words, language has different uses.

3

Perhaps the commonest use of language is to communicate *information*. We say that it is nine o'clock, that we liked a certain movie, that George Washington was the first president of the United States, that bromine and iodine are members of the halogen group of chemical elements. This we might call the *practical* use of language; it helps us with the ordinary business of living.

But it is not primarily to communicate information that novels, short stories, plays, and poems are written. These exist to bring us a sense and a perception of life, to widen and sharpen our contacts with existence. Their concern is with *experience*. We all have an inner need to live more deeply and fully and with greater awareness, to know the experience of others, and to understand our own experience better. Poets, from their own store of felt, observed, or imagined experiences, select, combine, and reorganize. They create significant new experiences for their readers—significant because focused and formed—in which readers can participate and from which they may gain a greater awareness and understanding of their world. Literature, in other words, can be used as a gear for stepping up the intensity and increasing the range of our experience and as a glass for clarifying it. This is the *literary* use of language, for literature is not only an aid to living but a means of living.*

Suppose, for instance, that we are interested in eagles. If we want simply to acquire information about eagles, we may turn to an encyclopedia or a book of natural history. There we find that the family Falconidae, to which eagles belong, is characterized by imperforate nostrils, legs of medium length, a hooked bill, the hind toe inserted on a level with the three front ones, and the claws roundly curved and sharp; that land eagles are feathered to the toes and sea-fishing eagles halfway to the toes; that their length is about three feet, the extent of wing seven feet; that the nest is usually placed on some inaccessible cliff; that the eggs are spotted and do not exceed three; and perhaps that the eagle's "great power of vision, the vast height to which it soars in the sky, the

---

*A third use of language is as an instrument of persuasion. This is the use we find in advertisements, propaganda bulletins, sermons, and political speeches. These three uses of language—the practical, the literary, and the hortatory—are not sharply divided. They may be thought of as three points of a triangle; most actual specimens of written language fall somewhere within the triangle. Most poetry conveys some information, and some poetry has a design on the reader. But language becomes *literature* when the desire to communicate experience predominates.

wild grandeur of its abode, have . . . commended it to the poets of all nations."*

But unless we are interested in this information only for practical purposes, we are likely to feel a little disappointed, as though we had grasped the feathers of the eagle but not its soul. True, we have learned many facts about the eagle, but we have missed somehow its lonely majesty, its power, and the "wild grandeur" of its surroundings that would make the eagle a living creature rather than a mere museum specimen. For the living eagle we must turn to literature.

1. THE EAGLE

He clasps the crag with crooked hands;
Close to the sun in lonely lands,
Ringed with the azure world, he stands.

The wrinkled sea beneath him crawls;
He watches from his mountain walls,
And like a thunderbolt he falls.

Alfred, Lord Tennyson (1809–1892)

QUESTIONS

1. What is peculiarly effective about the expressions "crooked hands," "close to the sun," "ringed with the azure world," "wrinkled," "crawls," and "like a thunderbolt"?
2. Notice the formal pattern of the poem, particularly the contrast of "he stands" in the first stanza and "he falls" in the second. Is there any other contrast between the two stanzas?

When "The Eagle" has been read well, readers will feel that they have enjoyed a significant experience and understand eagles better, though in a different way, than they did from the encyclopedia article alone. For if the article *analyzes* man's experience with eagles, the poem in some sense *synthesizes* such an experience. Indeed, the two approaches to experience—the scientific and the literary—may be said to complement each other. And it may be contended that the kind of

Encyclopedia Americana (1955), IX, 473–74.

understanding we get from the second is at least as valuable as the kind we get from the first.

Literature, then, exists to communicate significant experience—significant because concentrated and organized. Its function is not to tell us *about* experience but to allow us imaginatively to *participate* in it. It is a means of allowing us, through the imagination, to live more fully, more deeply, more richly, and with greater awareness. It can do this in two ways: by *broadening* our experience—that is, by making us acquainted with a range of experience with which, in the ordinary course of events, we might have no contact—or by *deepening* our experience—that is, by making us feel more poignantly and more understandingly the everyday experiences all of us have.

Two false approaches often taken to poetry can be avoided if we keep this conception of literature firmly in mind. The first approach always looks for a lesson or a bit of moral instruction. The second expects to find poetry always beautiful. Let us consider a song from Shakespeare's *Love's Labor's Lost* (V, ii).

2. WINTER

When icicles hang by the wall,
And Dick the shepherd blows his nail,
And Tom bears logs into the hall,
And milk comes frozen home in pail,
When blood is nipped and ways be foul,   5
Then nightly sings the staring owl,
"Tu-whit, tu-who!"
    A merry note,
    While greasy Joan doth keel° the pot.   skim

When all aloud the wind doth blow,   10
And coughing drowns the parson's saw,
And birds sit brooding in the snow,
And Marian's nose looks red and raw,
When roasted crabs° hiss in the bowl,   crab apples
Then nightly sings the staring owl,   15
"Tu-whit, tu-who!"
    A merry note,
    While greasy Joan doth keel the pot.

William Shakespeare (1564–1616)

QUESTIONS

1. What are the meanings of "nail" (2) and "saw" (11)?
2. Is the owl's cry really a "merry" note? How are this adjective and the verb "sings" employed?
3. In what way does the owl's cry contrast with the other details of the poem?

In the poem "Winter" Shakespeare communicates the quality of winter life around a sixteenth-century English country house. But he does not do so by telling us flatly that winter in such surroundings is cold and in many respects unpleasant, though with some pleasant features too (the adjectives *cold, unpleasant,* and *pleasant* are not even used in the poem). Instead, he provides a series of concrete homely details that suggest these qualities and enable us, imaginatively, to experience this winter life ourselves. The shepherd blows on his fingernails to warm his hands; the milk freezes in the pail between the cowshed and the kitchen; the roads are muddy; the folk listening to the parson have colds; the birds "sit brooding in the snow"; and the servant girl's nose is raw from cold. But pleasant things are in prospect. Logs are being brought in for a fire, hot cider or ale is being prepared, and the kitchen maid is making a hot soup or stew. In contrast to all these homely, familiar details of country life is the mournful, haunting, and eerie note of the owl.

Obviously the poem contains no moral. Readers who always look in poetry for some lesson, message, or noble truth about life are bound to be disappointed. Moral-hunters see poetry as a kind of sugar-coated pill—a wholesome truth or lesson made palatable by being put into pretty words. What they are really after is a sermon—not a poem, but something inspirational. Yet "Winter," which has appealed to readers now for nearly four centuries, is not inspirational and contains no moral preachment.

Neither is the poem "Winter" beautiful. Though it is appealing in its way and contains elements of beauty, there is little that is really beautiful in red raw noses, coughing in chapel, nipped blood, foul roads, and greasy kitchen maids. Yet some readers think that poetry deals exclusively with beauty—with sunsets, flowers, butterflies, love, God—and that the one appropriate response to any poem is, after a moment of awed silence, "Isn't that beautiful!" For such readers poetry is a precious affair, the enjoyment only of delicate souls, removed from the heat and sweat of ordinary life. But theirs is too narrow an approach to poetry. The function of poetry is sometimes to be ugly rather than beautiful. And poetry may deal with common colds and greasy kitchen maids as legitimately as with sunsets and flowers. Consider another example:

3. DULCE ET DECORUM EST

Bent double, like old beggars under sacks,
Knock-kneed, coughing like hags, we cursed through sludge,
Till on the haunting flares we turned our backs,
And towards our distant rest began to trudge.
Men marched asleep. Many had lost their boots,   5
But limped on, blood-shod. All went lame, all blind;
Drunk with fatigue; deaf even to the hoots
Of gas-shells dropping softly behind.

Gas! GAS! Quick, boys!—An ecstasy of fumbling,
Fitting the clumsy helmets just in time,   10
But someone still was yelling out and stumbling
And flound'ring like a man in fire or lime.—
Dim through the misty panes and thick green light,
As under a green sea, I saw him drowning.

In all my dreams before my helpless sight   15
He plunges at me, guttering, choking, drowning.

If in some smothering dreams, you too could pace
Behind the wagon that we flung him in,
And watch the white eyes writhing in his face,
His hanging face, like a devil's sick of sin,   20
If you could hear, at every jolt, the blood
Come gargling from the froth-corrupted lungs
Bitter as the cud
Of vile, incurable sores on innocent tongues,—
My friend, you would not tell with such high zest   25
To children ardent for some desperate glory,
The old lie: *Dulce et decorum est*
Pro patria mori.

Wilfred Owen (1893–1918)

QUESTIONS

1. The Latin quotation, from the Roman poet Horace, means "It is sweet and becoming to die for one's country." (Wilfred Owen died fighting for England in World War I, a week before the armistice.) What is the poem's comment on this statement?

2. List the elements of the poem that seem not beautiful and therefore "un-poetic." Are there any elements of beauty in the poem?
3. How do the comparisons in lines 1, 14, 20, and 23–24 contribute to the effectiveness of the poem?

Poetry takes all life as its province. Its primary concern is not with beauty, not with philosophical truth, not with persuasion, but with experience. Beauty and philosophical truth are aspects of experience, and the poet is often engaged with them. But poetry as a whole is concerned with all kinds of experience—beautiful or ugly, strange or common, noble or ignoble, actual or imaginary. One of the paradoxes of human existence is that all experience—even painful experience—is, for the good reader, enjoyable when transmitted through the medium of art. In real life, death and pain and suffering are not pleasurable, but in poetry they may be. In real life, getting soaked in a rainstorm is not pleasurable, but in poetry it can be. In actual life, if we cry, usually we are unhappy; but if we cry in a movie, we are manifestly enjoying it. We do not ordinarily like to be terrified in real life, but we sometimes seek movies or books that will terrify us. We find some value in all intense living. To be intensely alive is the opposite of being dead. To be dull, to be bored, to be imperceptive is in one sense to be dead. Poetry comes to us bringing life and therefore pleasure. Moreover, art focuses and orga-nizes experience so as to give us a better understanding of it. And to understand life is partly to be master of it.

There is no sharp distinction between poetry and other forms of imaginative literature. You may have been taught to believe that poetry can be recognized by the arrangement of its lines on the page or by its use of rime and meter. Such superficial tests are almost worthless. The Book of Job in the Bible and Melville's *Moby Dick* are highly poetical, but the familiar verse that begins: "Thirty days hath September, / April, June, and November . . . " is not. The difference between po-etry and other literature is one only of degree. Poetry is the most con-densed and concentrated form of literature, saying most in the fewest number of words. It is language whose individual lines, either because of their own brilliance or because they focus so powerfully what has gone before, have a higher voltage than most language. It is language that grows frequently incandescent, giving off both light and heat.

Ultimately, therefore, poetry can be recognized only by the re-sponse made to it by a good reader, someone who has acquired some sensitivity to poetry. But there is a catch here. We are not all good readers. To a poor reader, poetry will often seem dull and boring, a fancy way of writing something that could be said more simply. So might a colorblind man deny that there is such a thing as color.

The act of communication involved in reading poetry is like the act of communication involved in receiving a message by radio. Two factors are involved: a transmitting station and a receiving set. The completeness of the communication depends on both the power and clarity of the transmitter and the sensitivity and tuning of the receiver. When a person reads a poem and no experience is transmitted, either the poem is not a good poem or the reader is a poor reader or not properly tuned. With new poetry, we cannot always be sure which is at fault. With older poetry, if it has acquired critical acceptance—has been enjoyed by generations of good readers—we may assume that the receiving set is at fault. Fortunately, the fault is not irremediable. Though we cannot all become expert readers, we can become good enough to find both pleasure and value in much good poetry, or we can increase the amount of pleasure we already find in poetry and the number of kinds of poetry we find it in. To help you increase your sensitivity and range as a receiving set is the purpose of this book.

Poetry, finally, is a kind of multidimensional language. Ordinary language—the kind that we use to communicate information—is one-dimensional. It is directed at only part of the listener, his understanding. Its one dimension is intellectual. Poetry, which is language used to communicate experience, has at least four dimensions. If it is to communicate experience, it must be directed at the *whole* person, not just at his understanding. It must involve not only his intelligence but also his senses, emotions, and imagination. Poetry, to the intellectual dimension, adds a sensuous dimension, an emotional dimension, and an imaginative dimension.

Poetry achieves its extra dimensions—its greater pressure per word and its greater tension per poem—by drawing more fully and more consistently than does ordinary language on a number of language resources, none of which is peculiar to poetry. These various resources form the subjects of a number of the following chapters. Among them are connotation, imagery, metaphor, symbol, paradox, irony, allusion, sound repetition, rhythm, and pattern. Using these resources and the materials of life, the poet shapes and makes a poem. Successful poetry is never effusive language. If it is to come alive it must be as cunningly put together and as efficiently organized as a tree. It must be an organism whose every part serves a useful purpose and cooperates with every other part to preserve and express the life that is within it.

*   *   *

4. CONSTANTLY RISKING ABSURDITY*

<pre>
    Constantly risking absurdity
                          and death
        whenever he performs
                        above the heads
                                    of his audience   5
    the poet like an acrobat
                climbs on rime
                        to a high wire of his own making
    and balancing on eyebeams
                        above a sea of faces   10
            paces his way
                    to the other side of day
    performing entrechats
                    and sleight-of-foot tricks
    and other high theatrics   15
                    and all without mistaking
            any thing
                    for what it may not be

    For he's the super realist
                    who must perforce perceive   20
            taut truth
                    before the taking of each stance or step
    in his supposed advance
                    toward that still higher perch
    where Beauty stands and waits   25
                    with gravity
                        to start her death-defying leap

    And he
        a little charleychaplin man
                    who may or may not catch   30
            her fair eternal form
                        spreadeagled in the empty air
            of existence
</pre>

Lawrence Ferlinghetti (b. 1919)

---

*Whenever a title duplicates the first line of the poem or a substantial portion thereof, it is probable that the poet left the poem untitled and that the anthologist has substituted the first line or part of it as an editorial convenience. This is standard practice, and is true for this poem and for two of the four poems that follow in this chapter.

QUESTIONS

1. Vocabulary: *entrechats* (13). What meanings have "above the heads" (4), "sleight-of-foot tricks" (14), "high theatrics" (15), "with gravity" (26)?
2. The poet, it is said, "climbs on rime" (7). To what extent does this poem utilize rime and other sound correspondences? Point out examples.
3. What statement does the poem make about poetry, truth, and beauty?
4. What additional comments about poetry are implied by the figures of speech employed?
5. Does Ferlinghetti take poets and poetry seriously? Solemnly?

5. A BIRD CAME DOWN THE WALK

A bird came down the walk.
He did not know I saw.
He bit an angle-worm in halves
And ate the fellow, raw.

And then he drank a dew   5
From a convenient grass,
And then hopped sideways to the wall
To let a beetle pass.

He glanced with rapid eyes
That hurried all around;   10
They looked like frightened beads, I thought.
He stirred his velvet head

Like one in danger; cautious,
I offered him a crumb,
And he unrolled his feathers   15
And rowed him softer home

Than oars divide the ocean,
Too silver for a seam,
Or butterflies, off banks of noon,
Leap, plashless, as they swim.   20

Emily Dickinson (1830–1886)

QUESTIONS

1. The poem is based on a pair of contrasts: that between the observer (the human world) and the bird (the natural world); and that between the bird on the ground (1–14) and the bird in flight (15–20). Discuss the first contrast. What is the relationship between observer and bird? How do their "worlds" contrast?
2. How does the bird in the air differ from the bird on the ground? How do the sounds of the words in lines 15–20 reflect that difference?

3. Discuss the appropriateness of the word "rowed" (16). What is referred to in line 18? What image is suggested in lines 19–20, and how is *it* lightly reflected in the sounds of the words used?

6. THE TRIPLE FOOL

I am two fools, I know,
　For loving, and for saying so
　　In whining poetry.
But where's the wiseman that would not be I
　If she did not deny?   5
Then, as the earth's inward, narrow, crooked lanes
Do purge sea water's fretful salt away,
　I thought if I could draw my pains
Through rhyme's vexations, I should them allay.
Grief brought to numbers° cannot be so fierce,   verse   10
For he tames it that fetters it in verse.

　But when I have done so,
　　Some man, his art and voice to show,
　　　Doth set and sing my pain,
And by delighting many, frees again   15
　Grief, which verse did restrain.
To love and grief tribute of verse belongs,
But not of such which pleases when 'tis read;°   read aloud
　Both are increasèd by such songs,
For both their triumphs so are publishèd.   20
And I, which was two fools, do so grow three.
Who are a little wise, the best fools be.

John Donne (1572–1631)

QUESTIONS

1. Vocabulary: *allay* (9).
2. In line 2 does the poet refer to reciprocated love, unreciprocated love, or love in general? Justify your answer.
3. This chapter has been concerned with the value of poetry to the reader. This poem speaks of its value (or one of its values) to the writer. What is it? Discuss the appropriateness of the comparisons in lines 6–9 and 10–11.
4. What is the antecedent of "such" (18)? Of "both" (20)? What is the subject of "belongs" (17)?
5. Several of Donne's poems were set to music during his lifetime. What complaints does the speaker make against this practice?
6. Summarize the three reasons why the speaker considers himself a fool. How serious do you think he is in his self-condemnation?
7. In what respect does the poet/speaker consider himself "a little wise" (22) and therefore "the best" fool? Would he prefer to be otherwise?

7. THE RED WHEELBARROW

so much depends
upon

a red wheel
barrow

glazed with rain
water

beside the white
chickens.

William Carlos Williams (1883–1963)

QUESTIONS

1. The speaker asserts that "so much depends upon" the objects he refers to, leading the reader to ask "How much, and why?" This glimpse of a farm scene implies one kind of answer. What is the importance of wheelbarrow, rain, and chicken to a farmer? To all of us?
2. What further importance can be inferred from the references to color, shape, texture, and the juxtaposition of objects? Does the poem itself have a shape? What two ways of observing and valuing the world does the poem imply?

8. TERENCE, THIS IS STUPID STUFF

"Terence, this is stupid stuff:
You eat your victuals fast enough;
There can't be much amiss, 'tis clear,
To see the rate you drink your beer.
But oh, good Lord, the verse you make,   5
It gives a chap the belly-ache.
The cow, the old cow, she is dead;
It sleeps well the horned head:
We poor lads, 'tis our turn now
To hear such tunes as killed the cow.   10
Pretty friendship 'tis to rhyme
Your friends to death before their time
Moping melancholy mad:
Come, pipe a tune to dance to, lad."

Why, if 'tis dancing you would be,   15
There's brisker pipes than poetry.
Say, for what were hop-yards meant,
Or why was Burton built on Trent?

Oh many a peer of England brews
Livelier liquor than the Muse,   20
And malt does more than Milton can
To justify God's ways to man.
Ale, man, ale's the stuff to drink
For fellows whom it hurts to think:
Look into the pewter pot   25
To see the world as the world's not.
And faith, 'tis pleasant till 'tis past:
The mischief is that 'twill not last.
Oh I have been to Ludlow fair
And left my necktie God knows where,   30
And carried half-way home, or near,
Pints and quarts of Ludlow beer:
Then the world seemed none so bad,
And I myself a sterling lad;
And down in lovely muck I've lain,   35
Happy till I woke again.
Then I saw the morning sky:
Heigho, the tale was all a lie;
The world, it was the old world yet,
I was I, my things were wet,   40
And nothing now remained to do
But begin the game anew.

    Therefore, since the world has still
Much good, but much less good than ill,
And while the sun and moon endure   45
Luck's a chance, but trouble's sure,
I'd face it as a wise man would,
And train for ill and not for good.
'Tis true, the stuff I bring for sale
Is not so brisk a brew as ale: 50
Out of a stem that scored the hand
I wrung it in a weary land.
But take it: if the smack is sour,
The better for the embittered hour;
It should do good to heart and head   55
When your soul is in my soul's stead;
And I will friend you, if I may,
In the dark and cloudy day.

    There was a king reigned in the East:
There, when kings will sit to feast,   60
They get their fill before they think
With poisoned meat and poisoned drink.

He gathered all that springs to birth
From the many-venomed earth;
First a little, thence to more,   65
He sampled all her killing store;
And easy, smiling, seasoned sound,
Sate the king when healths went round.
They put arsenic in his meat
And stared aghast to watch him eat;   70
They poured strychnine in his cup
And shook to see him drink it up:
They shook, they stared as white's their shirt:
Them it was their poison hurt.
—I tell the tale that I heard told.   75
Mithridates, he died old.

A. E. Housman (1859–1936)

QUESTIONS

1. "Terence" (1) is Housman's poetic name for himself. Housman's poetry is
   largely pessimistic or sad; and this poem, placed near the end of his volume
   A Shropshire Lad, is his defense of the kind of poetry he wrote. Who is the
   speaker in the first fourteen lines? Who is the speaker in the rest of the
   poem? What is "the stuff I bring for sale" (49)?
2. "Hops" (17) and "malt" (21) are principal ingredients of beer and ale. Bur-
   ton-upon-Trent (18) is an English city famous for its breweries. Milton (21),
   in the invocation of his epic poem *Paradise Lost*, declares that his purpose is
   to "justify the ways of God to men." What, in Housman's eyes, is the effi-
   cacy of liquor in helping one live a difficult life?
3. What six lines of the poem most explicitly sum up the poet's philosophy?
   Most people like reading material that is cheerful and optimistic (on the
   argument that "there's enough suffering and unhappiness in the world already"). What for Housman is the value of pessimistic and tragic literature?
4. "Mithridates" (76) was a king of Pontus and a contemporary of Julius Cae-
   sar; his "tale" is told in Pliny's *Natural History*. What is the connection of
   this last verse paragraph with the rest of the poem?

Chapter two
Reading the Poem

The primary purpose of this book is to develop your ability to understand and appreciate poetry. Here are some preliminary suggestions:

1. Read a poem more than once. A good poem will no more yield its full meaning on a single reading than will a Beethoven symphony on a single hearing. Two readings may be necessary simply to let you get your bearings. And if the poem is a work of art, it will repay repeated and prolonged examination. One does not listen to a good piece of music once and forget it; one does not look at a good painting once and throw it away. A poem is not like a newspaper, to be hastily read and cast into the wastebasket. It is to be hung on the wall of one's mind.

2. Keep a dictionary by you and use it. It is futile to try to understand poetry without troubling to learn the meanings of the words of which it is composed. One might as well attempt to play tennis without a ball. One of your primary purposes while in college should be to build a good vocabulary, and the study of poetry gives you an excellent opportunity. A few other reference books will also be invaluable. Particularly desirable are a good book on mythology (your instructor can recommend one) and a Bible.

3. Read so as to hear the sounds of the words in your mind. Poetry is written to be heard: its meanings are conveyed through sound as well as through print. Every word is therefore important. The best way to read a poem is just the opposite of the best way to read a newspaper. One reads a newspaper as rapidly as possible; one should read a poem as

slowly as possible. When you cannot read a poem aloud, lip-read it: form the words with your tongue and mouth though you do not utter them. With ordinary reading material, lip-reading is a bad habit; with poetry it is a good habit.

4. Always pay careful attention to what the poem is saying. Though you should be conscious of the sounds of the poem, you should never be so exclusively conscious of them that you pay no attention to what the poem means. For some readers, reading a poem is like getting on board a rhythmical roller coaster. The car starts, and off they go, up and down, paying no attention to the landscape flashing past them, arriving at the end of the poem breathless, with no idea of what it has been about.* This is the wrong way to read a poem. One should make the utmost effort to follow the thought continuously and to grasp the full implications and suggestions. Because a poem says so much, several readings may be necessary, but on the very first reading you should determine the subjects of the verbs and the antecedents of the pronouns.

5. Practice reading poems aloud. When you find one you especially like, make friends listen to it. Try to read it to them in such a way that they will like it too. (a) Read it affectionately, but not affectedly. The two extremes oral readers often fall into are equally deadly. One is to read as if one were reading a tax report or a railroad timetable, unexpressively, in a monotone. The other is to elocute, with artificial flourishes and vocal histrionics. It is not necessary to put emotion into reading a poem. The emotion is already there. It only wants a fair chance to get out. It will express *itself* if the poem is read naturally and sensitively. (b) Of the two extremes, reading too fast offers greater danger than reading too slow. Read slowly enough that each word is clear and distinct and that the meaning has time to sink in. Remember that your friends do not have the advantage, as you do, of having the text before them. Your ordinary rate of reading will probably be too fast. (c) Read the poem so that the rhythmical pattern is felt but not exaggerated. Remember that poetry is written in sentences, just as prose is, and that punctuation is a signal as to how it should be read. Give all grammatical pauses their full due. Do not distort the natural pronunciation of words or a normal accentuation of the sentence to fit into what you have decided is its metrical pattern. One of the worst ways to read a poem is to read it ta-*dum* ta-*dum* ta-*dum* with an exagger-

---

*Some poems encourage this type of reading. When this is so, usually the poet has not made the best use of rhythm to support sense.

ated emphasis on every other syllable. On the other hand, it should not be read as if it were prose. An important test of your reading will be how you handle the end of a line when there is no punctuation there. A frequent mistake of the beginning reader is to treat each line as if it were a complete thought, whether grammatically complete or not, and to drop the voice at the end of it. A frequent mistake of the sophisticated reader is to take a running start upon approaching the end of a line and fly over it as if it were not there. The line is a rhythmical unit, and its end should be observed whether there is punctuation or not. If there is no punctuation, one observes it ordinarily by the slightest of pauses or by holding on to the last word in the line just a little longer than usual, without dropping one's voice. In line 12 of the following poem, you should hold on to the word "although" longer than if it occurred elsewhere in the line. But do not lower your voice on it: it is part of the clause that follows in the next stanza.

9. THE MAN HE KILLED

Had he and I but met
By some old ancient inn,
We should have sat us down to wet
Right many a nipperkin!°   half-pint cup

But ranged as infantry,   5
And staring face to face,
I shot at him as he at me,
And killed him in his place.

I shot him dead because—
Because he was my foe,   10
Just so: my foe of course he was;
That's clear enough; although

He thought he'd 'list, perhaps,
Off-hand-like—just as I—
Was out of work—had sold his traps—°   belongings   15
No other reason why.

Yes; quaint and curious war is!
You shoot a fellow down
You'd treat, if met where any bar is,
Or help to half-a-crown.   20

Thomas Hardy (1840–1928)

1. In informational prose the repetition of a word like "because" (9–10) would be an error. What purpose does the repetition serve here? Why does the speaker repeat to himself his "clear" reason for killing a man (10–11)? The word "although" (12) gets more emphasis than it ordinarily would because it comes not only at the end of a line but at the end of a stanza. What purpose does this emphasis serve? Can the redundancy of "old ancient" (2) be poetically justified?
2. Someone has defined poetry as "the expression of elevated thought in elevated language." Comment on the adequacy of this definition in the light of Hardy's poem.

To aid us in the understanding of a poem, we may ask ourselves a number of questions about it. One of the most important is *Who is the speaker and what is the occasion?* A cardinal error of some readers is to assume always that the speaker is the poet. A far safer course is to assume always that the speaker is someone other than the poet. For even when poets do speak directly and express their own thoughts and emotions, usually they do so as representative human beings rather than as individuals who live at particular addresses, dislike dill pickles, or favor blue sweaters. We must always be cautious about identifying anything in a poem with the biography of a poet. Like novelists and playwrights, they are fully justified in changing actual details of their own experience in order to make the experience of the poem more universal. We may well think of every poem, therefore, as being to some degree *dramatic*—that is, the utterance of a fictional character rather than of the person who wrote the poem. Many poems are expressly dramatic.

In "The Man He Killed" the speaker is a soldier; the occasion is his having been in battle and killed a man—obviously for the first time in his life. We can tell a good deal about him. He is not a career soldier: he enlisted only because he was out of work. He is a workingman: he speaks a simple and colloquial language ("nipperkin," "'list," "offhand-like," "traps"). He is a friendly, kindly sort who enjoys a neighborly drink of ale in a bar and will gladly lend a friend a half crown when he has it. He has known what it is to be poor. In any other circumstances he would have been horrified at taking a human life. He has been given pause as it is. He is trying to figure it out. But he is not a deep thinker and thinks he has supplied a reason when he has only supplied a name: "I killed the man . . . because he was my foe." The critical question, of course, is *Why was the man his "foe"?* Even the speaker is left unsatisfied by his answer, though he is not analytical enough to know what is wrong with it. Obviously this poem is expressly dramatic. We need know nothing about Thomas Hardy's life (he was never a soldier and never killed a man) to realize that the poem is dramatic. The internal evidence of the poem tells us so.

A second important question that we should ask ourselves upon reading any poem is *What is the central purpose of the poem?** The purpose may be to tell a story, to reveal human character, to impart a vivid impression of a scene, to express a mood or an emotion, or to convey vividly some idea or attitude. Whatever the purpose is, we must determine it for ourselves and define it mentally as precisely as possible. Only then can we fully understand the function and meaning of the various details in the poem by relating them to this central purpose. Only then can we begin to assess the value of the poem and determine whether it is a good one or a poor one. In "The Man He Killed" the central purpose is quite clear: it is to make us realize more keenly the irrationality of war. The puzzlement of the speaker may be our puzzlement. But even if we are able to give a more sophisticated answer than his as to why men kill each other, we ought still to have a greater awareness, after reading the poem, of the fundamental irrationality in war that makes men kill who have no grudge against each other and who might under different circumstances show each other considerable kindness.

10. IS MY TEAM PLOUGHING

> "Is my team ploughing,
>   That I was used to drive
> And hear the harness jingle
>   When I was man alive?"

---

*Our only reliable evidence of the poem's purpose, of course, is the poem itself. External evidence, when it exists, though often helpful, may also be misleading. Some critics have objected to the use of such terms as "purpose" and "intention" altogether; we cannot know, they maintain, what was *attempted* in the poem; we can know only what was *done*. Philosophically this position is impeccable. Yet it is possible to make inferences about purpose, and such inferences furnish a convenient and helpful way of talking about poetry.

Aye, the horses trample,   5
    The harness jingles now;
No change though you lie under
    The land you used to plough.

"Is football playing
    Along the river shore,   10
With lads to chase the leather,
    Now I stand up no more?"

Aye, the ball is flying,
    The lads play heart and soul;
The goal stands up, the keeper   15
    Stands up to keep the goal.

"Is my girl happy,
    That I thought hard to leave,
And has she tired of weeping
    As she lies down at eve?"   20

Aye, she lies down lightly,
    She lies not down to weep:
Your girl is well contented.
    Be still, my lad, and sleep.

"Is my friend hearty,   25
    Now I am thin and pine;
And has he found to sleep in
    A better bed than mine?"

Yes, lad, I lie easy,
    I lie as lads would choose;   30
I cheer a dead man's sweetheart,
    Never ask me whose.

A. E. Housman (1859–1936)

QUESTIONS

1. What is meant by "whose" in line 32?
2. Is Housman cynical in his observation of human nature and human life?
3. The word "sleep" in the concluding stanzas suggests three different meanings. What are they? How many meanings are suggested by the word "bed"?

Once we have answered the question *What is the central purpose of the poem?* we can consider another question, equally important to full understanding: *By what means is that purpose achieved?* It is important to distinguish means from ends. A student on an examination once used the poem "Is my team ploughing" as evidence that A. E. Housman believed in immortality, because in it a man speaks from the grave. This is as much a misconstruction as to say that Thomas Hardy in "The Man He Killed" joined the army because he was out of work. The purpose of Housman's poem is to communicate poignantly a certain truth about human life: life goes on after our deaths pretty much as it did before—our dying does not disturb the universe. This purpose is achieved by means of a fanciful dramatic framework in which a dead man converses with his still-living friend. The framework tells us nothing about whether Housman believed in immortality (as a matter of fact, he did not). It is simply an effective means by which we *can* learn how Housman felt a man's death affected the life he left behind. The question *By what means is the purpose of the poem achieved?* is partially answered by describing the poem's dramatic framework, if it has any. The complete answer requires an accounting of various resources of communication that we will discuss in the rest of this book.

The most important preliminary advice we can give for reading poetry is to maintain always, while reading it, the utmost mental alertness. The most harmful idea one can get about poetry is that its purpose is to soothe and relax and that the best place to read it is lying in a hammock with a cool drink beside one and low music in the background. You *can* read poetry lying in a hammock, but only if you refuse to put your mind in the same attitude as your body. Its purpose is not to soothe and relax but to arouse and awake, to shock us into life, to make us more alive. Poetry is not a substitute for a sedative.

An analogy can be drawn between reading poetry and playing tennis. Both offer great enjoyment if the game is played hard. Good tennis players must be constantly on the tips of their toes, concentrating on their opponent's every move. They must be ready for a drive to the right or left, a lob overhead, or a drop shot barely over the net. They must be ready for topspin or underspin, a ball that bounces crazily to the left or right. They must jump for the high ones and run for the far ones. And they will enjoy the game almost exactly in proportion to the effort they put into it. The same is true of reading poetry. Great enjoyment is there, but this enjoyment demands a mental effort equivalent to the physical effort one puts into tennis.

The reader of poetry has one advantage over the tennis player. Poets are not trying to win matches. They may expect the reader to stretch for their shots, but they *want* the reader to return them.

GENERAL QUESTIONS FOR ANALYSIS AND EVALUATION

Most of the poems in this book are accompanied by study questions that are by no means exhaustive. Following is a list of questions that you may apply to any poem. You may not be able to answer many of them until you have read further into the book.

1. Who is the speaker? What kind of person is the speaker?
2. Is there an identifiable audience for the speaker? What can we know about it (her, him, or them)?
3. What is the occasion?
4. What is the setting in time (hour, season, century, and so on)?
5. What is the setting in place (indoors or out, city or country, land or sea, region, country, hemisphere)?
6. What is the central purpose of the poem?
7. State the central idea or theme of the poem in a sentence.
8. What is the tone of the poem? How is it achieved?
9. a. Outline the poem so as to show its structure and development, or
   b. Summarize the events of the poem.
10. Paraphrase the poem.
11. Discuss the diction of the poem. Point out words that are particularly well chosen and explain why.
12. Discuss the imagery of the poem. What kinds of imagery are used? Is there a structure of imagery?
13. Point out examples of metaphor, simile, personification, and metonymy, and explain their appropriateness.
14. Point out and explain any symbols. If the poem is allegorical, explain the allegory.
15. Point out and explain examples of paradox, overstatement, understatement, and irony. What is their function?
16. Point out and explain any allusions. What is their function?
17. Point out significant examples of sound repetition and explain their function.
18. a. What is the meter of the poem?
    b. Copy the poem and mark its scansion.
19. Discuss the adaptation of sound to sense.
20. Describe the form or pattern of the poem.
21. Criticize and evaluate the poem.

*   *   *

11. MOWING

There was never a sound beside the wood but one,
And that was my long scythe whispering to the ground.
What was it it whispered? I knew not well myself;
Perhaps it was something about the heat of the sun,
Something, perhaps, about the lack of sound—   5
And that was why it whispered and did not speak.
It was no dream of the gift of idle hours,
Or easy gold at the hand of fay or elf:
Anything more than the truth would have seemed too weak
To the earnest love that laid the swale in rows,   10
Not without feeble-pointed spikes of flowers
(Pale orchises), and scared a bright green snake.
The fact is the sweetest dream that labor knows.
My long scythe whispered and left the hay to make.

Robert Frost (1874–1963)

QUESTIONS

1. Your instructor may occasionally ask you, as a test of your understanding of
a poem at its simplest level, or as a means of clearing up misunderstanding,
to paraphrase its content or part of its content. To **paraphrase** a poem means
to restate it in different language, so as to make its prose sense as plain as
possible. The paraphrase may be longer or shorter than the poem, but it
should contain as far as possible all the ideas in the poem in such a way as to
make them clear to a puzzled reader. Figurative language should be reduced
when possible to literal language; metaphors should be turned into similes.
Inverted syntax should be put into normal prose order. Though it is neither
necessary nor possible to avoid using any word occurring in the original, you
should in general use your own language. You should preserve, however, the
speaker's use of first or third person, and the tenses of the verbs.
The central idea, or **theme,** of "Mowing" is approximately this: Working
at a task one loves is its own best reward; or, The joy involved in work truly
done is sweeter than any dream. The poem may be paraphrased as follows:

The only sound in the field by the wood was made by my long scythe
as it cut through the tall grass. Its swishing sound made it seem as if it
were whispering to the earth beneath. What did it whisper? I couldn't tell.
Maybe, I imagined, it was whispering about the sun's warmth, or maybe
about the profound silence, and explaining that it whispered instead of
spoke because it didn't want to break the stillness. I am convinced that it
was *not* talking about the largess of leisure—of being idle and not having
to work. Nor was it speaking of the pleasure of finding a bag of money left
by a fairy or an elf. Such extravagant dreams, because they exceed the
truth, would have been a weak motivation as compared to the deep love I
felt as I cut the rank growth and left it in neat rows, also cutting the

intermingled spikes of wild orchises with their pale delicately pointed
flowers, and frightening a bright green snake. The joy of working at a task
one loves is the best reward that labor brings. My long scythe swished
through the grass and left it to dry into hay.

A paraphrase is useful only if you understand that it is the barest, most
inadequate approximation of what the poem really "says," and is no more
equivalent to the poem than a corpse is to a man. Once having made a
paraphrase, you should endeavor to see how far short of the poem it falls,
and why. In what respects does Frost's poem say more, and say it more
memorably, than the paraphrase? How, especially, is line 13 superior to its
paraphrase?
2. Since the scythe is not literally whispering, what can be deduced about the
speaker who hears its sound as a whisper? What quality of mind does he
reveal by imagining a whisper? By not knowing what is whispered? By
knowing what is *not* whispered? Of what significance is it that line 13 ends
with a period rather than a comma?
3. Why *might* a mower have the two dreams presented in lines 7–8? Why does
this mower reject them as "more than the truth"?
4. In the poem *fact*, *truth*, and *work* are set in opposition to *dream*, *fairy tale*,
and *idleness*. Since the speaker values the former series above the latter, how
are we to understand or interpret the apparent identification of the two sets
in line 13 (fact = dream)?
5. What do the orchises and snake (11–12) add to the poem?

12. BREAK OF DAY

'Tis true, 'tis day; what though it be?
Oh, wilt thou therefore rise from me?
Why should we rise because 'tis light?
Did we lie down because 'twas night?
Love which in spite of darkness brought us hither   5
Should, in despite of light, keep us together.

Light hath no tongue, but is all eye;
If it could speak as well as spy,
This were the worst that it could say:
That, being well, I fain would stay,   10
And that I loved my heart and honor so,
That I would not from him that had them go.

Must business thee from hence remove?
Oh, that's the worst disease of love;
The poor, the foul, the false, love can   15
Admit, but not the busied man.
He which hath business and makes love, doth do
Such wrong as when a married man doth woo.

John Donne (1572–1631)

1. Who is the speaker? Who is addressed? What is the situation? Can the speaker be identified with the poet?
2. Explain the comparison in line 7. To whom does "I" (10–12) refer? Is "love" (15) the subject or object of "can admit"?
3. Summarize the arguments used by the speaker to keep the person addressed from leaving. What is the speaker's scale of value?
4. Are the two persons married or unmarried? Justify your answer.

13. THERE'S BEEN A DEATH IN THE OPPOSITE HOUSE

There's been a death in the opposite house
As lately as today.
I know it by the numb look
Such houses have alway.

The neighbors rustle in and out,　　　　　　　　　　5
The doctor drives away.
A window opens like a pod,
Abrupt, mechanically;

Somebody flings a mattress out,—
The children hurry by;　　　　　　　　　　　　　　10
They wonder if it died on that,—
I used to when a boy.

The minister goes stiffly in
As if the house were his,
And he owned all the mourners now,　　　　　　　　15
And little boys besides;

And then the milliner, and the man
Of the appalling trade,
To take the measure of the house.
There'll be that dark parade　　　　　　　　　　　20

Of tassels and of coaches soon;
It's easy as a sign,—
The intuition of the news
In just a country town.

Emily Dickinson (1830–1886)

QUESTIONS

1. What can we know about the speaker in the poem?
2. By what signs does the speaker recognize that a death has occurred? Explain them stanza by stanza.
3. Comment on the words "appalling" (18) and "dark" (20).
4. What is the speaker's attitude toward death?

14. WHEN IN ROME

Mattie dear
the box is full
take
whatever you like
to eat   5
       (an egg
       or soup
       . . . there ain't no meat.)
there's endive there
and   10
cottage cheese
       (whew! if I had some
       black-eyed peas . . .)
there's sardines
on the shelves   15
and such
but
don't
get my anchovies
they cost   20
too much!
       (me get the
       anchovies indeed!
       what she think, she got—
       a bird to feed?)   25
there's plenty in there
to fill you up.
       (yes'm. just the
       sight's
       enough!   30

       Hope I lives till I get
       home
       I'm tired of eatin'
       what they eats in Rome . . .)

Mari Evans

1. Who are the two speakers? What is the situation? Why are the second speaker's words enclosed in parentheses?
2. What are the attitudes of the two speakers toward one another?
3. What implications have the title and the last two lines?

15. AND IF I DID WHAT THEN?

"And if I did what then?
Are you aggrieved therefore?
The sea hath fish for every man,
And what would you have more?"

Thus did my mistress once   5
Amaze my mind with doubt,
And popped a question for the nonce
To beat my brains about.

Whereto I thus replied,
"Each fisherman can wish   10
That all the sea at every tide
Were his alone to fish.

"And so did I—in vain;
But, since it may not be,
Let such fish there as find the gain   15
And leave the loss for me.

"And with such luck and loss
I will content myself
Till tides of turning time may toss
Such fishers on the shelf.   20

"And when they stick on sands,
That every man may see,
Then will I laugh and clap my hands
As they do now at me."

George Gascoigne (1525?–1577)

QUESTIONS

1. Is this literally a poem about fishing? If not, what does it mean by "fish" (3) and "the sea" (3, 11)? What does "fish" mean when used as a verb (12, 15)?
2. What has the speaker's mistress done? What had the speaker wished? What does he resolve to do? With what thought does he console himself?
3. Suppose that line 8 were rewritten "To stir my mind around." What would be lost? Can you find comparable effects elsewhere in the poem?

16. THE MILL

The miller's wife had waited long,
  The tea was cold, the fire was dead;
And there might yet be nothing wrong
  In how he went and what he said:
"There are no millers any more,"   5
  Was all that she had heard him say;
And he had lingered at the door
  So long that it seemed yesterday.

Sick with a fear that had no form
  She knew that she was there at last;   10
And in the mill there was a warm
  And mealy fragrance of the past.
What else there was would only seem
  To say again what he had meant;
And what was hanging from a beam   15
  Would not have heeded where she went.

And if she thought it followed her,
  She may have reasoned in the dark
That one way of the few there were
  Would hide her and would leave no mark: 20
Black water, smooth above the weir
  Like starry velvet in the night,
Though ruffled once, would soon appear
  The same as ever to the sight.

                    Edwin Arlington Robinson (1869–1935)

QUESTIONS

1. What is the meaning of the husband's remark in line 5? What has the husband's occupation been, and what historical developments would lead him to make that remark?
2. What does the miller's wife find in the mill in stanza 2? What does she do in stanza 3? Why?
3. Poets, especially modern poets, are often accused of being perversely obscure. Certainly this poem tells its story in a roundabout way—by hints and implications rather than by direct statements. Is there any justification for this "obscurity" or has the poet indeed been needlessly unclear?
4. What details of the poem especially bring it to life as experience?

17. MIRROR

I am silver and exact. I have no preconceptions.
Whatever I see I swallow immediately
Just as it is, unmisted by love or dislike.
I am not cruel, only truthful—
The eye of a little god, four-cornered.   5
Most of the time I meditate on the opposite wall.
It is pink, with speckles. I have looked at it so long
I think it is a part of my heart. But it flickers.
Faces and darkness separate us over and over.

Now I am a lake. A woman bends over me,   10
Searching my reaches for what she really is.
Then she turns to those liars, the candles or the moon.
I see her back, and reflect it faithfully.
She rewards me with tears and an agitation of hands.
I am important to her. She comes and goes.   15
Each morning it is her face that replaces the darkness.
In me she has drowned a young girl, and in me an old woman
Rises toward her day after day, like a terrible fish.

Sylvia Plath (1932–1963)

QUESTIONS

1. Who is the speaker? Distinguish means from ends.
2. In what ways is the mirror like and unlike a person (stanza 1)? In what ways
   is it like a lake (stanza 2)?
3. What is the meaning of the last two lines?

18. A STUDY OF READING HABITS

When getting my nose in a book
Cured most things short of school,
It was worth ruining my eyes
To know I could still keep cool,
And deal out the old right hook   5
To dirty dogs twice my size.

Later, with inch-thick specs,
Evil was just my lark:
Me and my cloak and fangs
Had ripping times in the dark.   10
The women I clubbed with sex!
I broke them up like meringues.

Don't read much now: the dude
Who lets the girl down before
The hero arrives, the chap   15
Who's yellow and keeps the store,
Seem far too familiar. Get stewed:
Books are a load of crap.

Philip Larkin (1922–1985)

QUESTIONS

1. The three stanzas delineate three stages in the speaker's life. Describe each.
2. What kind of person is the speaker? What kind of books does he read? May he be identified with the poet?
3. Contrast the advice given by the speaker in stanza 3 with the advice given by Terence in "Terence, this is stupid stuff " (No. 8). Are A. E. Housman and Philip Larkin at odds in their attitudes toward drinking and reading? Discuss.

EXERCISE

Here are three definitions of poetry, all framed by poets themselves. Which definition best fits the poems you have so far read? Discuss.

1. Poetry is Transfiguration, the transfiguration of the Actual or the Real into the Ideal, at a lofty elevation, through the medium of melodious or nobly sounding verse.   *Alfred Austin*

2. The art of poetry is simply the art of electrifying language with extraordinary meaning.   *Lascelles Abercrombie*

3. A poem consists of all the purest and most beautiful elements in the poet's nature, crystalized into the aptest and most exquisite language, and adorned with all the outer embellishment of musical cadence or dainty rhyme.
Grant Allen

Chapter three
Denotation and Connotation

.

A primary distinction between the practical use of language and the literary use is that in literature, especially in poetry, a *fuller* use is made of individual words. To understand this, we need to examine the composition of a word.

The average word has three component parts: sound, denotation, and connotation. It begins as a combination of tones and noises, uttered by the lips, tongue, and throat, for which the written word is a notation. But it differs from a musical tone or a noise in that it has a meaning attached to it. The basic part of this meaning is its **denotation** or denotations: that is, the dictionary meaning or meanings of the word. Beyond its denotations, a word may also have connotations. The **connotations** are what it suggests beyond what it expresses: its overtones of meaning. It acquires these connotations by its past history and associations, by the way and the circumstances in which it has been used. The word *home*, for instance, by denotation means only a place where one lives, but by connotation it suggests security, love, comfort, and family. The words *childlike* and *childish* both mean "characteristic of a child," but *childlike* suggests meekness, innocence, and wide-eyed wonder, while *childish* suggests pettiness, willfulness, and temper tantrums. If we name over a series of coins: *nickel, peso, lira, shilling, sen, doubloon*, the word *doubloon*, to four out of five readers, will immediately suggest pirates, though a dictionary definition includes nothing about pirates. Pirates are part of its connotation.

Connotation is very important in poetry, for it is one of the means by which the poet can concentrate or enrich meaning—say more in fewer words. Consider, for instance, the following short poem:

19. THERE IS NO FRIGATE LIKE A BOOK

There is no frigate like a book
    To take us lands away,
Nor any coursers like a page
    Of prancing poetry:
This traverse may the poorest take
    Without oppress of toll;
How frugal is the chariot
    That bears the human soul!

Emily Dickinson (1830–1886)

In this poem Emily Dickinson is considering the power of a book or of poetry to carry us away, to let us escape from our immediate surroundings into a world of the imagination. To do this she has compared literature to various means of transportation: a boat, a team of horses, a wheeled land vehicle. But she has been careful to choose kinds of transportation and names for them that have romantic connotations. "Frigate" suggests exploration and adventure; "coursers," beauty, spirit, and speed; "chariot," speed and the ability to go through the air as well as on land. (Compare "Swing Low, Sweet Chariot" and the myth of Phaëthon, who tried to drive the chariot of Apollo, and the famous painting of Aurora with her horses, once hung in almost every school.) How much of the meaning of the poem comes from this selection of vehicles and words is apparent if we try to substitute for them, say, *steamship*, *horses*, and *streetcar*.

QUESTIONS

1. What is lost if *miles* is substituted for "lands" (2) or *cheap* for "frugal" (7)?
2. How is "prancing" (4) peculiarly appropriate to poetry as well as to coursers? Could the poet have without loss compared a book to coursers and poetry to a frigate?
3. Is this account appropriate to all kinds of poetry or just to certain kinds? That is, was the poet thinking of poems like Wilfred Owen's "Dulce et Decorum Est" (No. 3) or of poems like Coleridge's "Kubla Khan" (No. 199) and Keats's "La Belle Dame sans Merci" (No. 217)?

Just as a word has a variety of connotations, so may it have more than one denotation. If we look up the word *spring* in the dictionary, for instance, we will find that it has between twenty-five and thirty distinguishable meanings: It may mean (1) a pounce or leap, (2) a season of the year, (3) a natural source of water, (4) a coiled elastic wire, and so forth. This variety of denotation, complicated by additional tones of connotation, makes language confusing and difficult to use. Any person using words must be careful to define precisely by context the meaning that is desired. But the difference between the writer using language to communicate information and the poet is this: the practical writer will always attempt to confine words to one meaning at a time; the poet will often take advantage of the fact that the word has more than one meaning by using it to mean more than one thing at the same time. Thus when Edith Sitwell in one of her poems writes, "This is the time of the wild spring and the mating of the tigers,"* she uses the word *spring* to denote both a season of the year and a sudden leap (and she uses *tigers* rather than *lambs* or *birds* because it has a connotation of fierceness and wildness that the other two lack).

20. WHEN MY LOVE SWEARS THAT SHE IS MADE OF TRUTH

When my love swears that she is made of truth,
I do believe her, though I know she lies,
That she might think me some untutored youth,
Unlearnèd in the world's false subtleties.
Thus vainly thinking that she thinks me young,   5
Although she knows my days are past the best,
Simply I credit her false-speaking tongue;
On both sides thus is simple truth supprest.
But wherefore says she not she is unjust?°   unfaithful
And wherefore say not I that I am old?   10
Oh, love's best habit is in seeming trust,
And age in love loves not to have years told:
Therefore I lie with her and she with me,
And in our faults by lies we flattered be.

William Shakespeare (1564–1616)

Collected Poems (New York: Vanguard, 1954), p. 392.

QUESTIONS

1. How old is the speaker in the poem? How old is his beloved? What is the nature of their relationship?
2. How is the contradiction in line 2 to be resolved? How is the one in lines 5–6 to be resolved? Who is lying to whom?
3. How do "simply" (7) and "simple" (8) differ in meaning? The words "vainly" (5), "habit" (11), "told" (12), and "lie" (13) all have double denotative meanings. What are they?
4. What is the tone of the poem—that is, the attitude of the speaker toward his situation? Should line 11 be taken as an expression of (a) wisdom, (b) conscious rationalization, or (c) self-deception? In answering these questions, consider both the situation and the connotations of all the important words beginning with "swears" (1) and ending with "flattered" (14).

A frequent misconception of poetic language is that poets seek always the most beautiful or noble-sounding words. What they really seek are the most *meaningful* words, and these vary from one context to another. Language has many levels and varieties, and poets may choose from them all. Their words may be grandiose or humble, fanciful or matter-of-fact, romantic or realistic, archaic or modern, technical or everyday, monosyllabic or polysyllabic. Usually a poem will be pitched pretty much in one key: the words in Emily Dickinson's "There is no frigate like a book" and those in Thomas Hardy's "The Man He Killed" (No. 9) are chosen from quite different areas of language, but both poets have chosen the words most meaningful for their own poetic context. Sometimes a poet may import a word from one level or area of language into a poem composed mostly of words from a different level or area. If this is done clumsily, the result will be incongruous and sloppy; if it is done skillfully, the result will be a shock of surprise and an increment of meaning for the reader. In fact, the many varieties of language open to poets provide their richest resource. Their task is one of constant exploration and discovery. They search always for the secret affinities of words that allow them to be brought together with soft explosions of meaning.

21. THE NAKED AND THE NUDE

For me, the naked and the nude
(By lexicographers construed
As synonyms that should express
The same deficiency of dress
Or shelter) stand as wide apart   5
As love from lies, or truth from art.

Lovers without reproach will gaze
On bodies naked and ablaze;
The Hippocratic eye will see
In nakedness, anatomy;   10
And naked shines the Goddess when
She mounts her lion among men.

The nude are bold, the nude are sly
To hold each treasonable eye.
While draping by a showman's trick   15
Their dishabille in rhetoric,
They grin a mock-religious grin
Of scorn at those of naked skin.

The naked, therefore, who compete
Against the nude may know defeat;   20
Yet when they both together tread
The briary pastures of the dead,
By Gorgons with long whips pursued,
How naked go the sometime nude!

Robert Graves (1895–1985)

QUESTIONS

1. Vocabulary: *lexicographers* (2), *construed* (2), *art* (6), *Hippocratic* (9), *dishabille* (16), *Gorgons* (23), *sometime* (24).
2. What kind of language is used in lines 2–5? Why? (For example, why is "deficiency" used in preference to *lack?* Purely because of meter?)
3. What is meant by "rhetoric" (16)? Why is the word "dishabille" used in this line instead of some less fancy word?
4. Explain why the poet chose his wording instead of the following alternatives: *brave* for "bold" (13), *clever* for "sly" (13), *clothing* for "draping" (15), *smile* for "grin" (17).
5. What, for the poet, is the difference in connotation between "naked" and "nude"? Try to explain reasons for the difference. If your own sense of the two words differs from that of Graves, state the difference and give reasons to support your sense of them.
6. Explain the reversal in the last line.

The person using language to convey information is largely indifferent to the sound of the words and is hampered by their connotations and multiple denotations. He tries to confine each word to a single exact meaning. He uses, one might say, a fraction of the word and throws the rest away. The poet, on the other hand, uses as much of the word as possible. He is interested in connotation and uses it to enrich and convey meaning. And he may use more than one denotation.

The purest form of practical language is scientific language. Scientists need a precise language to convey information precisely. The existence of multiple denotations and various overtones of meaning hinders them in accomplishing their purpose. Their ideal language would be a language with a one-to-one correspondence between word and meaning; that is, every word would have one meaning only, and for every meaning there would be only one word. Since ordinary language does not fulfill these conditions, scientists have invented languages that do. A statement in one of these languages may look like this:

$$SO_2 + H_2O = H_2SO_3$$

In such a statement the symbols are entirely unambiguous; they have been stripped of all connotation and of all denotations but one. The word *sulfurous*, if it occurred in poetry, might have all kinds of connotations: fire, smoke, brimstone, hell, damnation. But H_2SO_3 means one thing and one thing only: sulfurous acid.

The ambiguity and multiplicity of meanings possessed by words are an obstacle to the scientist but a resource to the poet. Where the scientist wants singleness of meaning, the poet wants richness of meaning. Where the scientist requires and has invented a strictly one-dimensional language in which every word is confined to one denotation, the poet needs a multidimensional language, and creates it partly by using a multidimensional vocabulary, in which the dimensions of connotation and sound are added to the dimension of denotation.

The poet, we may say, plays on a many-stringed instrument, and sounds more than one note at a time.

The first problem in reading poetry, therefore, or in reading any kind of literature, is to develop a sense of language, a feeling for words. One needs to become acquainted with their shape, their color, and their flavor. There are two ways of doing this: extensive use of the dictionary and extensive reading.

EXERCISES

1. Which word in each group has the most "romantic" connotations? (a) horse, steed, nag; (b) king, ruler, tyrant, autocrat; (c) Chicago, Pittsburgh, Samarkand, Birmingham.
2. Which word in each group is the most emotionally connotative? (a) female parent, mother, dam; (b) offspring, children, progeny; (c) brother, sibling.
3. Which word in each group has the most favorable connotation? (a) skinny, thin, slender; (b) prosperous, wealthy, moneyed, opulent; (c) brainy, intelligent, smart.

4. Which of the following should you be less offended at being accused of? (a) having acted foolishly, (b) having acted like a fool.
5. In any competent piece of writing, the possibly multiple denotations and connotations of the words used are controlled by context. The context screens out irrelevant meanings while allowing the relevant meanings to pass through. What denotation has the word *fast* in the following contexts? (a) a fast runner, (b) a fast color.
6. In the following examples the denotation of the word *white* remains the same, but the connotations differ. Explain. (a) The young princess had blue eyes, golden hair, and a breast as white as snow. (b) Confronted with the evidence, the false princess turned as white as a sheet.

*   *   *

22. RICHARD CORY

Whenever Richard Cory went down town,
We people on the pavement looked at him:
He was a gentleman from sole to crown,
Clean favored, and imperially slim.

And he was always quietly arrayed,   5
And he was always human when he talked;
But still he fluttered pulses when he said,
"Good-morning," and he glittered when he walked.

And he was rich—yes, richer than a king—
And admirably schooled in every grace: 10
In fine, we thought that he was everything
To make us wish that we were in his place.

So on we worked, and waited for the light,
And went without the meat, and cursed the bread;
And Richard Cory, one calm summer night,   15
Went home and put a bullet through his head.

Edwin Arlington Robinson (1869–1935)

QUESTIONS

1. In how many senses is Richard Cory a gentleman?
2. The word "crown" (3), meaning the top of the head, is familiar to you from "Jack and Jill," but why does Robinson use the unusual phrase "from sole to crown" instead of the common *from head to foot* or *from top to toe*?
3. List the words that express or suggest the idea of aristocracy or royalty.
4. Try to explain why the poet chose his wording rather than the following alternatives: *sidewalk* for "pavement" (2), *good-looking* for "Clean favored"

(4), *thin* for "slim" (4), *dressed* for "arrayed" (5), *courteous* for "human" (6), *wonderfully* for "admirably" (10), *trained* for "schooled" (10), *manners* for "every grace" (10), *in short* for "in fine" (11). What other examples of effective diction do you find in the poem?

5. Why is "Richard Cory" a good name for the character in this poem?
6. This poem is a good example of how ironic contrast (see Chapter 7) generates meaning. The poem makes no direct statement about life; it simply relates an incident. What larger meanings about life does it suggest?
7. A leading American critic has said of this poem: "In 'Richard Cory' . . . we have a superficially neat portrait of the elegant man of mystery; the poem builds up deliberately to a very cheap surprise ending; but all surprise endings are cheap in poetry, if not indeed, elsewhere, for poetry is written to be read not once but many times."* Do you agree with this evaluation? Discuss.

23. NAMING OF PARTS

To-day we have naming of parts. Yesterday,
We had daily cleaning. And to-morrow morning,
We shall have what to do after firing. But to-day,
To-day we have naming of parts. Japonica
Glistens like coral in all of the neighboring gardens,   5
    And to-day we have naming of parts.

This is the lower sling swivel. And this
Is the upper sling swivel, whose use you will see,
When you are given your slings. And this is the piling swivel,
Which in your case you have not got. The branches   10
Hold in the gardens their silent, eloquent gestures,
    Which in our case we have not got.

This is the safety-catch, which is always released
With an easy flick of the thumb. And please do not let me
See anyone using his finger. You can do it quite easy   15
If you have any strength in your thumb. The blossoms
Are fragile and motionless, never letting anyone see
    Any of them using their finger.

And this you can see is the bolt. The purpose of this
Is to open the breech, as you see. We can slide it   20
Rapidly backwards and forwards: we call this
Easing the spring. And rapidly backwards and forwards
The early bees are assaulting and fumbling the flowers:
    They call it easing the Spring.

*Yvor Winters, *Edwin Arlington Robinson* (Norfolk, Conn.: New Directions, 1946), p. 52.

They call it easing the Spring: it is perfectly easy   25
If you have any strength in your thumb: like the bolt,
And the breech, and the cocking-piece, and the point of balance,
Which in our case we have not got; and the almond-blossom
Silent in all of the gardens and the bees going backwards and forwards,
    For to-day we have naming of parts.   30

Henry Reed (b. 1914)

QUESTIONS

1. Who is the speaker (or who are the speakers) in the poem, and what is the situation?
2. What basic contrasts are represented by the trainees and by the gardens?
3. What is it that the trainees "have not got" (28)? How many meanings have the phrases "easing the Spring" (22) and "point of balance" (27)?
4. What differences in language and rhythm do you find between the lines concerning "naming of parts" and those describing the gardens?
5. Does the repetition of certain phrases throughout the poem have any special function or is it done only to create a kind of refrain?
6. What statement does the poem make about war as it affects men and their lives?

24. PORTRAIT D'UNE FEMME

Your mind and you are our Sargasso Sea,
London has swept about you this score years
And bright ships left you this or that in fee:
Ideas, old gossip, oddments of all things,
Strange spars of knowledge and dimmed wares of price.   5
Great minds have sought you—lacking someone else.
You have been second always. Tragical?
No. You preferred it to the usual thing:
One dull man, dulling and uxorious,
One average mind—with one thought less, each year.   10
Oh, you are patient, I have seen you sit
Hours, where something might have floated up.
And now you pay one. Yes, you richly pay.
You are a person of some interest, one comes to you
And takes strange gain away: 15
Trophies fished up; some curious suggestion;
Fact that leads nowhere; and a tale for two,
Pregnant with mandrakes, or with something else
That might prove useful and yet never proves,

That never fits a corner or shows use,   20
Or finds its hour upon the loom of days:
The tarnished, gaudy, wonderful old work;
Idols and ambergris and rare inlays.
These are your riches, your great store; and yet
For all this sea-hoard of deciduous things,   25
Strange woods half sodden, and new brighter stuff:
In the slow float of differing light and deep,
No! there is nothing! In the whole and all,
Nothing that's quite your own.
                                        Yet this is you.   30

Ezra Pound (1885–1972)

QUESTIONS

1. Vocabulary: *in fee* (3), *uxorious* (9), *mandrakes* (18), *ambergris* (23), *deciduous* (25).
2. The Sargasso Sea, an area of still water in the North Atlantic, is legendarily a place where ships have become entangled in seaweed and where the ocean floor is littered with sunken vessels and their scattered cargoes. What kind of woman is Pound describing? In what ways is her mind like the Sargasso Sea?
3. Pound seeks to create an impression of the rich and strange, as opposed to the dull and average. How does he do it?
4. Comment on the phrases "in fee" (3), "of price" (5), "richly pay" (13), "of some interest" (14), "strange gain" (15), "your riches" (24), "your great store" (24), "this sea-hoard" (25). What do they have in common? What is their effect?
5. Comment on the phrase "pregnant with mandrakes" (18). Why do these two words go well together?
6. Pound might have called his poem "Portrait of a Woman" or "Portrait of a Lady." Which would have been more accurate? What advantages does the French title have over either?

25. CROSS

My old man's a white old man
And my old mother's black.
If ever I cursed my white old man
I take my curses back.

If ever I cursed my black old mother   5
And wished she were in hell,
I'm sorry for that evil wish
And now I wish her well.

My old man died in a fine big house.
My ma died in a shack.   10
I wonder where I'm gonna die,
Being neither white nor black?

Langston Hughes (1902–1967)

QUESTIONS

1. What different denotations does the title have? Explain.
2. The language in this poem, such as "old man" (1, 3, 9), "ma" (10), and
   "gonna" (11), is plain, and even colloquial. Is it appropriate to the subject?
   Why?

26. THE WORLD IS TOO MUCH WITH US

The world is too much with us; late and soon,
Getting and spending, we lay waste our powers:
Little we see in nature that is ours;
We have given our hearts away, a sordid boon!
This sea that bares her bosom to the moon,   5
The winds that will be howling at all hours,
And are up-gathered now like sleeping flowers,
For this, for everything, we are out of tune;
It moves us not.—Great God! I'd rather be
A pagan suckled in a creed outworn;   10
So might I, standing on this pleasant lea,
Have glimpses that would make me less forlorn;
Have sight of Proteus rising from the sea;
Or hear old Triton blow his wreathèd horn.

William Wordsworth (1770–1850)

QUESTIONS

1. Vocabulary: *boon* (4), *Proteus* (13), *Triton* (14). What two relevant denotations has "wreathèd" (14)?
2. Try to explain why the poet chose his wording rather than the following
   alternatives: *earth* for "world" (1), *selling and buying* for "getting and spending" (2), *exposes* for "bares" (5), *stomach* for "bosom" (5), *dozing* for "sleeping" (7), *posies* for "flowers" (7), *nourished* for "suckled" (10), *visions* for
   "glimpses" (12), *sound* for "blow" (14).
3. Should "Great God!" (9) be considered as a vocative (term of address) or an
   expletive (exclamation)? Or something of both?
4. State the theme (central idea) of the poem in a sentence.

27. A HYMN TO GOD THE FATHER

Wilt thou forgive that sin where I begun,
　　Which is my sin though it were done before?
Wilt thou forgive those sins through which I run,°　　　　ran
　　And do them still, though still I do deplore?
　　　　When thou hast done, thou hast not done,　　　　5
　　　　　　For I have more.

Wilt thou forgive that sin by which I won
　　Others to sin, and made my sin their door?
Wilt thou forgive that sin which I did shun
　　A year or two, but wallowed in a score?　　　　10
　　　　When thou hast done, thou hast not done,
　　　　　　For I have more.

I have a sin of fear, that when I have spun
　　My last thread, I shall perish on the shore;
Swear by thyself that at my death thy Sun　　　　15
　　Shall shine as it shines now, and heretofore;
　　　　And having done that, thou hast done.
　　　　　　I have no more.

John Donne (1572–1631)

QUESTIONS

1. In 1601, John Donne at 29 secretly married Anne More, aged 17, infuriating her upper-class father, who had him imprisoned for three days. Because of the marriage, Donne lost his job as private secretary to an important official at court, and probably ruined his chances for the career at court that he wanted. It was, however, a true love match. In 1615 Donne entered the church. In 1617 his wife, then 33, died after bearing him twelve children. In 1621 he was appointed Dean of St. Paul's Cathedral in London and quickly won a large reputation for his eloquent sermons. His religious poems differ markedly in tone from the often cynical, sometimes erotic poems of his youth. The foregoing poem was written during a severe illness in 1623. Is this information of any value to a reader of the poem?
2. What sin is referred to in lines 1–2? What is meant by "when I have spun / My last thread" (13–14)? By "I shall perish on the shore" (14)?
3. What three puns give structure and meaning to the poem? Explain the relevance of each.

28. BASE DETAILS

If I were fierce, and bald, and short of breath,
    I'd live with scarlet Majors at the Base,
And speed glum heroes up the line to death.
    You'd see me with my puffy petulant face,
Guzzling and gulping in the best hotel,   5
    Reading the Roll of Honor. "Poor young chap,"
I'd say—"I used to know his father well;
    Yes, we've lost heavily in this last scrap."
And when the war is done and youth stone dead,
    I'd toddle safely home and die—in bed.   10

Siegfried Sassoon (1886–1967)

QUESTIONS

1. Vocabulary: *petulant* (4).
2. In what two ways may the title be interpreted? (Both words have two pertinent denotative meanings.) What applications has "scarlet" (2)? What is the force of "fierce" (1)? Try to explain why the poet chose his wording rather than the following alternatives: *fleshy* for "puffy" (4), *eating and drinking* for "guzzling and gulping" (5), *battle* for "scrap" (8), *totter* for "toddle" (10).
3. Who evidently is the speaker? (The poet, a British captain in World War I, was decorated for bravery on the battlefield.) Does he mean what he says? What is the purpose of the poem?

EXERCISES

1. Robert Frost has said that "Poetry is what evaporates from all translations." Why might this be true? How much of a word can be translated?
2. Ezra Pound has defined great literature as being "simply language charged with meaning to the utmost possible degree." Would this be a good definition of poetry? The word "charged" is roughly equivalent to *filled*. Why is "charged" a better word in Pound's definition?

Chapter four

Imagery

Experience comes to us largely through the senses. My experience of a spring day, for instance, may consist partly of certain emotions I feel and partly of certain thoughts I think, but most of it will be a cluster of sense impressions. It will consist of *seeing* blue sky and white clouds, budding leaves and daffodils; of *hearing* robins and bluebirds singing in the early morning; of *smelling* damp earth and blossoming hyacinths; and of *feeling* a fresh wind against my cheek. A poet seeking to express the experience of a spring day must therefore provide a selection of sense impressions. So Gerard Manley Hopkins (No. 37) gives us "racing lambs" and "glassy peartree leaves and blooms," "thrush's eggs" looking like "little low heavens," the thrush itself singing through the "echoing timber," and "the descending blue" of the sky "all in a rush with richness." Had he not done so, he would probably have failed to evoke the emotions that accompanied his sensations. The poet's language, therefore, must be more *sensuous* than ordinary language. It must be more full of imagery.

Imagery may be defined as the representation through language of sense experience. Poetry appeals directly to our senses, of course, through its music and rhythms, which we actually hear when it is read aloud. But indirectly it appeals to our senses through imagery, the representation to the imagination of sense experience. The word *image* perhaps most often suggests a mental picture, something seen in the mind's eye—and *visual* imagery is the kind of imagery that occurs most frequently in poetry. But an image may also represent a sound (*auditory* *imagery); * a smell *(olfactory imagery); * a taste *(gustatory imagery); * touch, such as hardness, softness, wetness, or heat and cold *(tactile imagery); * an internal sensation, such as hunger, thirst, fatigue, or nausea *(organic imagery); * or movement or tension in the muscles or joints *(kinesthetic imagery). * If we wished to be scientific, we could extend this list further, for psychologists no longer confine themselves to five or even six senses, but for purposes of discussing poetry the preceding classification should ordinarily be sufficient.

29. MEETING AT NIGHT

The gray sea and the long black land;
And the yellow half-moon large and low;
And the startled little waves that leap
In fiery ringlets from their sleep,
As I gain the cove with pushing prow,   5
And quench its speed i' the slushy sand.

Then a mile of warm sea-scented beach;
Three fields to cross till a farm appears;
A tap at the pane, the quick sharp scratch
And blue spurt of a lighted match,   10
And a voice less loud, through its joys and fears,
Than the two hearts beating each to each!

Robert Browning (1812–1889)

"Meeting at Night" is a poem about love. It makes, one might say, a number of statements about love: being in love is a sweet and exciting experience; when one is in love everything seems beautiful, and the most trivial things become significant; when one is in love one's sweetheart seems the most important object in the world. But the poet actually *tells* us none of these things directly. He does not even use the word *love* in his poem. His business is to communicate experience, not information. He does this largely in two ways. First, he presents us with a specific situation, in which a lover goes to meet his sweetheart. Second, he describes the lover's journey so vividly in terms of sense impressions that the reader virtually sees and hears what the lover saw and heard and shares his anticipation and excitement.

Every line in the poem contains some image, some appeal to the senses: the gray sea, the long black land, the yellow half-moon, the startled little waves with their fiery ringlets, the blue spurt of the lighted match—all appeal to our sense of sight and convey not only shape but also color and motion. The warm sea-scented beach appeals to the senses of both smell and touch. The pushing prow of the boat on the slushy sand, the tap at the pane, the quick scratch of the match, the low speech of the lovers, and the sound of their hearts beating—all appeal to the sense of hearing.

30. PARTING AT MORNING

Round the cape of a sudden came the sea,
And the sun looked over the mountain's rim:
And straight was a path of gold for him,
And the need of a world of men for me.

Robert Browning (1812–1889)

QUESTIONS

1. This poem is a sequel to "Meeting at Night." "Him" (3) refers to the sun. Does the last line mean that the lover needs the world of men or that the world of men needs the lover? Or both?
2. Does the sea *actually* come suddenly around the cape or *appear* to? Why does Browning mention the *effect* before its *cause* (the sun looking over the mountain's rim)?
3. Do these poems, taken together, suggest any larger truths about love? Browning, in answer to a question, said that the second part is the man's confession of "how fleeting is the belief (implied in the first part) that such raptures are self-sufficient and enduring—as for the time they appear."

The sharpness and vividness of any image will ordinarily depend on how specific it is and on the poet's use of effective detail. The word *hummingbird*, for instance, conveys a more definite image than does *bird*, and *ruby-throated hummingbird* is sharper and more specific still. For a vivid representation, however, it is not necessary that something be completely described. One or two especially sharp and representative details will ordinarily serve, allowing the reader's imagination to fill in the rest. Tennyson in "The Eagle" (No. 1) gives only one detail about the eagle itself—that he clasps the crag with "crooked hands"—but this detail is an effective and memorable one. Robinson tells us that Richard Cory (No. 22) was "clean favored," "slim," and "quietly arrayed," but the detail that really brings Cory before us is that he "glittered when he walked." Browning, in "Meeting at Night," calls up a whole scene with "A tap at the pane, the quick sharp scratch / And blue spurt of a lighted match."

Since imagery is a peculiarly effective way of evoking vivid experience, and since it may be used to convey emotion and suggest ideas as well as to cause a mental reproduction of sensations, it is an invaluable resource of the poet. In general, the poet will seek concrete or image-bearing words in preference to abstract or non-image-bearing words. We cannot evaluate a poem, however, by the amount or quality of its imagery alone. Sense impression is only one of the elements of experience. Poetry may attain its ends by other means. We should never judge any single element of a poem except in reference to the total intention of that poem.

* * *

31. A LATE AUBADE

You could be sitting now in a carrel
Turning some liver-spotted page,
Or rising in an elevator-cage
Toward Ladies' Apparel.

You could be planting a raucous bed   5
Of salvia, in rubber gloves,
Or lunching through a screed of someone's loves
With pitying head,

Or making some unhappy setter
Heel, or listening to a bleak   10
Lecture on Schoenberg's serial technique.
Isn't this better?

Think of all the time you are not
Wasting, and would not care to waste,
Such things, thank God, not being to your taste.   15
Think what a lot

Of time, by woman's reckoning,
You've saved, and so may spend on this,
You who had rather lie in bed and kiss
Than anything.   20

It's almost noon, you say? If so,
Time flies, and I need not rehearse
The rosebuds-theme of centuries of verse.
If you *must* go,

Wait for a while, then slip downstairs   25
And bring us up some chilled white wine,
And some blue cheese, and crackers, and some fine
Ruddy-skinned pears.

Richard Wilbur (b. 1921)

QUESTIONS

1. Vocabulary: *Aubade* (see Glossary), *carrel* (1), *raucous* (5), *screed* (7), *Schoenberg* (11).
2. Who is the speaker? What is the situation? What plea is the speaker making?
3. As lines 22–23 suggest, this poem treats an age-old theme of poetry. What is it? In what respects is this an original treatment of it? Though line 23 is general in reference, it alludes specifically to a famous poem by Robert Herrick (No. 59). In what respects are these two poems similar? In what respects are they different?
4. What clues are there in the poem as to the characters and personalities of the two people involved?
5. How does the last stanza provide a fitting conclusion to the poem?

32. AFTER APPLE-PICKING

My long two-pointed ladder's sticking through a tree
Toward heaven still,
And there's a barrel that I didn't fill
Beside it, and there may be two or three
Apples I didn't pick upon some bough.   5
But I am done with apple-picking now.
Essence of winter sleep is on the night,
The scent of apples: I am drowsing off.
I cannot rub the strangeness from my sight
I got from looking through a pane of glass   10
I skimmed this morning from the drinking trough
And held against the world of hoary grass.
It melted, and I let it fall and break.
But I was well
Upon my way to sleep before it fell,   15
And I could tell
What form my dreaming was about to take.
Magnified apples appear and disappear,
Stem end and blossom end,

And every fleck of russet showing clear.   20
My instep arch not only keeps the ache,
It keeps the pressure of a ladder-round.
I feel the ladder sway as the boughs bend.
And I keep hearing from the cellar bin
The rumbling sound   25
Of load on load of apples coming in.
For I have had too much
Of apple-picking: I am overtired
Of the great harvest I myself desired.
There were ten thousand thousand fruit to touch,   30
Cherish in hand, lift down, and not let fall.
For all
That struck the earth,
No matter if not bruised or spiked with stubble,
Went surely to the cider-apple heap   35
As of no worth.
One can see what will trouble
This sleep of mine, whatever sleep it is.
Were he not gone,
The woodchuck could say whether it's like his   40
Long sleep, as I describe its coming on,
Or just some human sleep.

Robert Frost (1874–1963)

QUESTIONS

1. How does the poet convey so vividly the experience of "apple-picking"?
   Point out effective examples of each kind of imagery used.
2. How does the speaker regard his work? Has he done it well or poorly? Does
   he find it enjoyable or tedious? Is he dissatisfied with its results?
3. The speaker predicts what he will dream about in his sleep. Why does he
   shift to the present tense (18) when he begins describing a dream he has not
   yet had? How sharply are real experience and dream experience differentiated in the poem?
4. The poem uses the word "sleep" six times. Does it, through repetition,
   come to suggest a meaning beyond the purely literal? If so, what attitude
   does the speaker take toward this second signification? Does he fear it? Does
   he look forward to it? What does he expect of it?
5. If sleep is symbolic (both literal and metaphorical), other details may also
   take on additional meaning. If so, how would you interpret (a) the ladder,
   (b) the season of the year, (c) the harvesting, (d) the "pane of glass" (10)?
   What meanings has the word "Essence" (7)?
6. How does the woodchuck's sleep differ from "just some human sleep"?

33. A NARROW FELLOW IN THE GRASS

A narrow fellow in the grass
Occasionally rides;
You may have met him. Did you not,
His notice sudden is:

The grass divides as with a comb,   5
A spotted shaft is seen,
And then it closes at your feet
And opens further on.

He likes a boggy acre,
A floor too cool for corn,   10
Yet when a boy, and barefoot,
I more than once at noon

Have passed, I thought, a whip-lash
Unbraiding in the sun,
When, stooping to secure it,   15
It wrinkled, and was gone.

Several of nature's people
I know, and they know me;
I feel for them a transport
Of cordiality;   20

But never met this fellow,
Attended or alone,
Without a tighter breathing
And zero at the bone.

Emily Dickinson (1830–1886)

QUESTIONS

1. The subject of this poem is never named. What is it? How does the imagery identify it?
2. The last two lines might be paraphrased as "without being frightened." Why is Dickinson's wording more effective?
3. Who is the speaker?

34. LIVING IN SIN

She had thought the studio would keep itself;
no dust upon the furniture of love.
Half heresy, to wish the taps less vocal,
the panes relieved of grime. A plate of pears,
a piano with a Persian shawl, a cat   5
stalking the picturesque amusing mouse
had risen at his urging.
Not that at five each separate stair would writhe
under the milkman's tramp; that morning light
so coldly would delineate the scraps   10
of last night's cheese and three sepulchral bottles;
that on the kitchen shelf among the saucers
a pair of beetle-eyes would fix her own—
envoy from some village in the moldings . . .
Meanwhile, he, with a yawn,   15
sounded a dozen notes upon the keyboard,
declared it out of tune, shrugged at the mirror,
rubbed at his beard, went out for cigarettes;
while she, jeered by the minor demons,
pulled back the sheets and made the bed and found   20
a towel to dust the table-top,
and let the coffee-pot boil over on the stove.
By evening she was back in love again,
though not so wholly but throughout the night
she woke sometimes to feel the daylight coming   25
like a relentless milkman up the stairs.

Adrienne Rich (b. 1929)

QUESTIONS

1. Explain the grammatical structure and meaning of the sentence in lines 4–7.
   What are its subject and verb? To whom or what does "his" (7) refer? What
   kind of life do its images conjure up?
2. On what central contrast is the poem based? What is its central mood or
   emotion?
3. Discuss the various kinds of imagery used and their function in conveying
   the experience of the poem.

35. THOSE WINTER SUNDAYS

Sundays too my father got up early
and put his clothes on in the blueblack cold,
then with cracked hands that ached
from labor in the weekday weather made
banked fires blaze. No one ever thanked him.   5

I'd wake and hear the cold splintering, breaking.
When the rooms were warm, he'd call,
and slowly I would rise and dress,
fearing the chronic angers of that house,

Speaking indifferently to him,   10
who had driven out the cold
and polished my good shoes as well.
What did I know, what did I know
of love's austere and lonely offices?

Robert Hayden (1913–1980)

QUESTIONS

1. Vocabulary: *offices* (14).
2. What kind of imagery is central to the poem? How is this imagery related to the emotional concerns of the poem?
3. How do the subsidiary images relate to the central images?
4. From what point in time does the speaker view the subject matter of the poem? What has happened to him in the interval?

36. THE DARKLING THRUSH

I leant upon a coppice gate
    When Frost was specter-gray,
And Winter's dregs made desolate
    The weakening eye of day.
The tangled bine-stems scored the sky   5
    Like strings of broken lyres,
And all mankind that haunted nigh
    Had sought their household fires.

The land's sharp features seemed to be
    The Century's corpse outleant,   10
His crypt the cloudy canopy,
    The wind his death-lament.
The ancient pulse of germ and birth
    Was shrunken hard and dry,
And every spirit upon earth   15
    Seemed fervorless as I.

At once a voice arose among
    The bleak twigs overhead
In a full-hearted evensong
    Of joy illimited;   20
An aged thrush, frail, gaunt, and small,
    In blast-beruffled plume,
Had chosen thus to fling his soul
    Upon the growing gloom.

So little cause for carolings   25
    Of such ecstatic sound
Was written on terrestrial things
    Afar or nigh around,
That I could think there trembled through
    His happy good-night air   30
Some blessed Hope, whereof he knew
    And I was unaware.

31 December 1900

Thomas Hardy (1840–1928)

QUESTIONS

1. Vocabulary: *coppice* (1).
2. What three periods of time simultaneously end in the poem? What is the emotional effect of these terminations?
3. Two emotional states are contrasted in the poem. Pick out the words that contribute to each. How many of these words belong to images?
4. The image in lines 5–6 is visual. What additional values does it have?
5. Define as precisely as possible the change, if any, produced by the thrush's song in the outlook of the speaker. Does the bird know of a hope unknown to the speaker? Does the speaker think it does? Why does the bird sing? Is this an optimistic poem?

37. SPRING

Nothing is so beautiful as spring—
   When weeds, in wheels, shoot long and lovely and lush;
   Thrush's eggs look little low heavens, and thrush
Through the echoing timber does so rinse and wring
The ear, it strikes like lightnings to hear him sing;   5
   The glassy peartree leaves and blooms, they brush
   The descending blue; that blue is all in a rush
With richness; the racing lambs too have fair their fling.

What is all this juice and all this joy?
   A strain of the earth's sweet being in the beginning   10
In Eden garden.—Have, get, before it cloy,

   Before it cloud, Christ, lord, and sour with sinning,
Innocent mind and Mayday in girl and boy,
   Most, O maid's child, thy choice and worthy the winning.

Gerard Manley Hopkins (1844–1889)

QUESTIONS

1. The first line makes an abstract statement. How is this statement brought to carry conviction?
2. The sky is described as being "all in a rush / With richness" (7–8). In what other respects is the poem "rich"?
3. The author was a Catholic priest as well as a poet. To what two things does he compare the spring in lines 9–14? In what ways are the comparisons appropriate?

38. TO AUTUMN

Season of mists and mellow fruitfulness,
   Close bosom-friend of the maturing sun;
Conspiring with him how to load and bless
   With fruit the vines that round the thatch-eaves run;
To bend with apples the mossed cottage-trees,   5
   And fill all fruit with ripeness to the core;
     To swell the gourd, and plump the hazel shells
With a sweet kernel; to set budding more,
   And still more, later flowers for the bees,
   Until they think warm days will never cease,   10
     For summer has o'er-brimmed their clammy cells.

Who hath not seen thee oft amid thy store?
  Sometimes whoever seeks abroad may find
Thee sitting careless on a granary floor,
  Thy hair soft-lifted by the winnowing wind;   15
Or on a half-reaped furrow sound asleep,
  Drowsed with the fume of poppies, while thy hook
    Spares the next swath and all its twinèd flowers:
And sometimes like a gleaner thou dost keep
  Steady thy laden head across a brook;   20
  Or by a cider-press, with patient look,
    Thou watchest the last oozings hours by hours.

Where are the songs of spring? Ay, where are they?
  Think not of them, thou hast thy music too,—
While barred clouds bloom the soft-dying day,   25
  And touch the stubble-plains with rosy hue;
Then in a wailful choir the small gnats mourn
  Among the river sallows, borne aloft
    Or sinking as the light wind lives or dies;
And full-grown lambs loud bleat from hilly bourn;   30
  Hedge-crickets sing; and now with treble soft
The red-breast whistles from a garden-croft;
  And gathering swallows twitter in the skies.

                              John Keats (1795–1821)

QUESTIONS

1. Vocabulary: *hook* (17), *barred* (25), *sallows* (28), *bourn* (30), *croft* (32).
2. How many kinds of imagery do you find in the poem? Give examples of each.
3. Are the images arranged haphazardly or are they carefully organized? In answering this question, consider: (a) With what aspect of autumn is each stanza particularly concerned? (b) What kind of imagery is dominant in each stanza? (c) What time of the season is presented in each stanza? (d) Is there any progression in time of day?
4. What is autumn personified as in stanza 2? Is there any suggestion of personification in the other two stanzas?
5. Although the poem is primarily descriptive, what attitude toward transience and passing beauty is implicit in it?

Chapter five

Figurative Language 1
Metaphor, Personification, Metonymy

Poetry provides the one permissible way
of saying one thing and meaning another.
ROBERT FROST

Let us assume that your brother has just come in out of a rainstorm and you say to him, "Well, you're a pretty sight! Got slightly wet, didn't you?" And he replies, "Wet? I'm drowned! It's raining cats and dogs, and my raincoat's like a sieve!"

You and your brother probably understand each other well enough; yet if you examine this conversation literally, that is to say unimaginatively, you will find that you have been speaking nonsense. Actually you have been speaking figuratively. You have been saying less than what you mean, or more than what you mean, or the opposite of what you mean, or something other than what you mean. You did not mean that your brother was a pretty sight but that he was a wretched sight. You did not mean that he got slightly wet but that he got very wet. Your brother did not mean that he got drowned but that he got drenched. It was not raining cats and dogs; it was raining water. And your brother's raincoat is so unlike a sieve that not even a child would confuse them.

If you are familiar with Molière's play *Le Bourgeois Gentilhomme*, you will remember how delighted M. Jourdain was to discover that he had been speaking prose all his life. Many people might be equally surprised to learn that they have been speaking a kind of subpoetry all their lives. The difference between their figures of speech and the poet's is that theirs are probably worn and trite, the poet's fresh and original.

On first examination, it might seem absurd to say one thing and mean another. But we all do it—and with good reason. We do it because we can say what we want to say more vividly and forcefully by figures than we can by saying it directly. And we can say more by figurative statement than we can by literal statement. Figures of speech offer another way of adding extra dimensions to language.

Broadly defined, a **figure of speech** is any way of saying something other than the ordinary way, and some rhetoricians have classified as many as 250 separate figures. For our purposes, however, a figure of speech is more narrowly definable as a way of saying one thing and meaning another, and we need to be concerned with no more than a dozen. **Figurative language**—language using figures of speech—is language that cannot be taken literally (or should not be taken literally only).

Metaphor and **simile** are both used as a means of comparing things that are essentially unlike. The only distinction between them is that in simile the comparison is *expressed* by the use of some word or phrase, such as *like, as, than, similar to, resembles,* or *seems;* in metaphor the comparison is *implied*—that is, the figurative term is *substituted for* or *identified with* the literal term.

39. THE GUITARIST TUNES UP

With what attentive courtesy he bent
Over his instrument;
Not as a lordly conqueror who could
Command both wire and wood,
But as a man with a loved woman might,
Inquiring with delight
What slight essential things she had to say
Before they started, he and she, to play.

Frances Cornford (1886–1960)

QUESTION

Explore the comparison. Does it principally illuminate the guitarist or the lovers or both? What one word brings its two terms together?

40. THE HOUND

Life the hound
Equivocal
Comes at a bound
Either to rend me
Or to befriend me.　　　　　　　　5
I cannot tell
The hound's intent
Till he has sprung
At my bare hand
With teeth or tongue.　　　　　　　10
Meanwhile I stand
And wait the event.

Robert Francis (b. 1901)

QUESTION

What does "equivocal" (2) mean? Show how this is the key word in the poem. What is the effect of placing it on a line by itself?

Metaphors may take one of four forms, depending on whether the literal and figurative terms are respectively *named* or *implied*. In the first form of metaphor, as in simile, both the literal and figurative terms are named. In Francis's poem, for example, the literal term is "life" and the figurative term is "hound." In the second form, the literal term is *named* and the figurative term is *implied*.

41. BEREFT

Where had I heard this wind before
Change like this to a deeper roar?
What would it take my standing there for,
Holding open a restive door,
Looking downhill to a frothy shore?　　　5
Summer was past and day was past.
Somber clouds in the west were massed.
Out in the porch's sagging floor
Leaves got up in a coil and hissed,
Blindly struck at my knee and missed.　　10

Something sinister in the tone
Told me my secret must be known:
Word I was in the house alone
Somehow must have gotten abroad,
Word I was in my life alone,   15
Word I had no one left but God.

                                      Robert Frost (1874–1963)

QUESTIONS

1. Describe the situation precisely. What time of day and year is it? Where is the speaker? What is happening to the weather?
2. To what are the leaves in lines 9–10 compared?
3. The word "hissed" (9) is onomatopoetic (see Glossary of Poetic Terms). How is its effect reinforced in the lines following?
4. Though lines 9–10 present the clearest example of the second form of metaphor, there are others. To what is the wind ("it") compared in line 3? Why is the door (4) "restive" and what does this do (figuratively) to the door? To what is the speaker's "life" compared (15)?
5. What is the tone of the poem? How reassuring is the last line?

In the third form of metaphor, the literal term is *implied* and the figurative term is *named*. In the fourth form, both the literal *and* figurative terms are *implied*. The following poem exemplifies both types:

42. IT SIFTS FROM LEADEN SIEVES

It sifts from leaden sieves,
It powders all the wood.
It fills with alabaster wool
The wrinkles of the road.

It makes an even face   5
Of mountain and of plain—
Unbroken forehead from the east
Unto the east again.

It reaches to the fence,
It wraps it rail by rail   10
Till it is lost in fleeces;
It deals celestial veil

To stump and stack and stem—
A summer's empty room—
Acres of joints where harvests were,   15
Recordless,° but for them.   °unrecorded

It ruffles wrists of posts
As ankles of a queen,
Then stills its artisans like ghosts,
Denying they have been.   20

Emily Dickinson (1830–1886)

QUESTIONS

1. This poem consists essentially of a series of metaphors having the same
   literal term identified only as "It." What is "It"?
2. In several of these metaphors the figurative term is named—"alabaster
   wool" (3), "fleeces" (11), "celestial veil" (12). In two of them, however, the
   figurative term as well as the literal term is left unnamed. To what is "It"
   compared in lines 1–2? In lines 17–18?
3. Comment on the additional metaphorical expressions or complications contained in "leaden sieves" (1), "alabaster wool" (3), "even face" (5), "unbroken forehead" (7), "a summer's empty room" (14), "artisans" (19).

Metaphors of the fourth form, as one might guess, are comparatively
rare. An extended example, however, is provided by Dickinson's "I
like to see it lap the miles" (No. 148).

   Personification consists in giving the attributes of a human being to
an animal, an object, or a concept. It is really a subtype of metaphor, an
implied comparison in which the figurative term of the comparison is
always a human being. When Sylvia Plath makes a mirror speak and
think (No. 17), she is personifying an object. When Keats describes
autumn as a harvester "sitting careless on a granary floor" or "on a
half-reaped furrow sound asleep"(No. 38), he is personifying a concept.
Personifications differ in the degree to which they ask the reader actually to visualize the literal term in human form. In Keats's comparison
we are asked to make a complete identification of autumn with a human
being. In Sylvia Plath's, though the mirror speaks and thinks, we continue to visualize it as a mirror; similarly, in Frost's "Bereft" (No. 41),
the "restive" door remains in appearance a door tugged by the wind. In
Browning's reference to "the startled little waves" (No. 29), a personification is barely suggested; we would make a mistake if we tried to

visualize the waves in human form or even, really, to think of them as having human emotions.*

Closely related to personification is **apostrophe**, which consists in addressing someone absent or dead or something nonhuman as if that person or thing were present and alive and could reply to what is being said. The speaker in A. E. Housman's "To an Athlete Dying Young" (No. 214) apostrophizes a dead runner. William Blake apostrophizes a tiger throughout his famous poem (No. 197) but does not otherwise personify it. Keats apostrophizes as well as personifies autumn (No. 38). Personification and apostrophe are both ways of giving life and immediacy to one's language, but since neither requires great imaginative power on the part of the poet—apostrophe especially does not—they may degenerate into mere mannerisms and are to be found as often in bad and mediocre poetry as in good. We need to distinguish between their effective use and their merely conventional use.

43. THE QUIP

The merry world did on a day
With his train-bands and mates agree
To meet together, where I lay,
And all in sport to jeer at me.

First, Beauty crept into a rose,   5
Which when I pluckt not, Sir, said she,
Tell me, I pray, Whose hands are those?
But thou shalt answer, Lord, for me.

Then Money came, and chinking still,
What tune is this, poor man? said he;   10
I heard in Music you had skill.
But thou shalt answer, Lord, for me.

---

*The various figures of speech blend into each other, and it is sometimes difficult to classify a specific example as definitely metaphor or symbol, symbolism or allegory, understatement or irony, irony or paradox. Often a given example may exemplify two or more figures at once. In "The Guitarist Tunes Up" (No. 39), "wire and wood" are metonymies (see page 65) for a guitar and are personified as subjects, slaves, or soldiers who could be commanded by a lordly conquerer. In "A bird came down the walk" (No. 5), when the bird glances around with eyes that look "like frightened beads," the beads function as part of a simile and are personified as something that can be "frightened." The important consideration in reading poetry is not that we classify figures definitively but that we construe them correctly.

Then came brave Glory puffing by
In silks that whistled, who but he?
He scarce allowed me half an eye. 15
But thou shalt answer, Lord, for me.

Then came quick Wit and Conversation,
And he would needs a comfort be,
And, to be short, made an Oration.
But thou shalt answer, Lord, for me. 20

Yet when the hour of thy design
To answer these fine things shall come,
Speak not at large, say, I am thine:
And then they have their answer home.

George Herbert (1593–1633)

QUESTIONS

1. "Train-bands" (1) are trained bands of citizen-soldiers. What is the speaker's attitude toward the "merry world" (1)? What connotations does "merry world" have in this context? Is it a personification? A metonymy? Literal?
2. How many personifications are there in this poem? How are they brought alive rather than left as empty abstractions? Explain the appropriateness of each one's taunt.
3. Do they come together merely to mock the speaker, or is there a possible deeper motive? How does the speaker respond to their taunts?
4. What are the antecedents of the two pronouns in line 23?
5. George Herbert, son of a nobleman, was educated at Cambridge and appointed Public Orator while there. A witty conversationalist, he had a sensitive love for beauty and a deep love of music. He sang, and accompanied himself on the lute. A favorite of King James I, he aspired to a position at court but was thwarted by the death of the king. At 32 he entered the Church, and at 36 was made rector of a rural parish, where he made himself beloved by his religious devotion and his concern for his parishioners. His poems, unpublished till after his death, are all religious in nature. Is this information of any relevance to the reading of this poem? How?

44. THE DARK HILLS

Dark hills at evening in the west,
Where sunset hovers like a sound
Of golden horns that sang to rest
Old bones of warriors underground,

Far now from all the bannered ways
Where flash the legions of the sun,
You fade—as if the last of days
Were fading, and all wars were done.

Edwin Arlington Robinson (1869–1935)

QUESTIONS

1. This poem consists of one sentence. What is its subject? What is its verb? What is the antecedent of the pronoun "You" (7)?
2. Is the poem primarily narrative, descriptive, or philosophical? What one word in the poem names what it is literally about?
3. Point out and explain the figures of speech in the poem. What are "the bannered ways" and "the legions of the sun"? From what realm of human activity does the figurative language come? What idea about human life arises from its imagery and its figurative design?
4. What does the use of apostrophe do for the poem?

Synecdoche (the use of the part for the whole) and **metonymy** (the use of something closely related for the thing actually meant) are alike in that both substitute some significant detail or aspect of an experience for the experience itself. Thus, when Pound's speaker in "Portrait d'une Femme" (No. 24) says "Great minds have sought you," he is using synecdoche, because what he means is "men with great minds." Robert Graves uses synecdoche when he refers to a doctor as a "Hippocratic eye" (No. 21). Housman's Terence (No. 8) uses synecdoche when he declares that "Malt does more than Milton can / To justify God's ways to man," for "malt" means beer or ale, of which malt is an essential ingredient. On the other hand, when Terence advises "fellows whom it hurts to think" to "Look into the pewter pot / To see the world as the world's not," he is using metonymy, for by "pewter pot" he means the ale that's *in* the pot, not the pot itself, and by "world" he means human life and the conditions under which it is lived. Robert Frost uses metonymy in "Out, Out—" (No. 84) when he describes an injured boy holding up his cut hand "as if to keep / the life from spilling," for literally he means to keep the blood from spilling. In each case, however, there is a gain in vividness, meaning, or compactness. Pound's "minds" says in one word what otherwise would have taken many, and that one word largely indicates what the poem is about. Housman's "malt" not only serves as a substitute for beer *and* ale, but also introduces, by its similarities in sound to "Milton," the statement in the following line of Milton's purpose in *Paradise Lost*, which is a central issue in Housman's poem as well. Frost tells us both that the boy's hand is bleeding and that his life is in danger.

Many synecdoches and metonymies, of course, like many metaphors, have become so much a part of the language that they no longer strike us as figurative; such is the case with *redhead* for a red-haired person, *hands* for manual workers, *highbrow* for a sophisticate, *tongues* for languages, and a boiling *kettle* for the water *in* the kettle. Such figures are often referred to as *dead metaphors* (where the word *metaphor* is itself a metonymy for all figurative speech). Synecdoche and metonymy are so much alike that it is hardly worthwhile to distinguish between them, and the latter term is increasingly coming to be used for both. In this book metonymy will be used for both figures—that is, for any figure in which a part or something closely related is substituted for the thing literally meant.

45. A HUMMINGBIRD

A route of evanescence
With a revolving wheel;
A resonance of emerald,
A rush of cochineal;
And every blossom on the bush
Adjusts its tumbled head,—
The mail from Tunis, probably,
An easy morning's ride.

Emily Dickinson (1830–1886)

QUESTIONS

1. Vocabulary: *evanescence* (1), *cochineal* (4). Tunis (7), on the north coast of Africa, is literally quite distant from Amherst, Massachusetts, where the poet lived, but as a symbol for remoteness it gets its main force from Shakespeare's *Tempest* (II, i, 246–49), where the next heir to the throne of Naples is described as "She that is Queen of Tunis; she that dwells / Ten leagues beyond man's life; she that from Naples / Can have no note, unless the sun were post— / The man i' th' moon's too slow."
2. "A Hummingbird" is one of the very few of her poems for which Dickinson provided a title. Do you think she was right to do so? In framing your reasons, compare this poem with "It sifts from leaden sieves" (No. 42) and "I like to see it lap the miles" (No. 148), for which she did *not* provide titles.

3. Identify and explain three metonymies and a metaphor in lines 1–4.
4. Account fully for the vividness of the poem.

We said at the beginning of this chapter that figurative language often provides a more effective means of saying what we mean than does direct statement. What are some of the reasons for that effectiveness?

First, figurative language affords us imaginative pleasure. Imagination might be described in one sense as that faculty or ability of the mind that proceeds by sudden leaps from one point to another, that goes up a stair by leaping in one jump from the bottom to the top rather than by climbing up one step at a time.* The mind takes delight in these sudden leaps, in seeing likenesses between unlike things. We have probably all taken pleasure in staring into a fire and seeing castles and cities and armies in it, or in looking into the clouds and shaping them into animals or faces, or in seeing a man in the moon. We name our plants and flowers after fancied resemblances: jack-in-the-pulpit, babies'-breath, Queen Anne's lace. Figures of speech are therefore satisfying in themselves, providing us with a source of pleasure in the exercise of the imagination.

Second, figures of speech are a way of bringing additional imagery into verse, of making the abstract concrete, of making poetry more sensuous. When Lawrence Ferlinghetti, writing of truth and beauty (No. 4), metaphorically pictures "taut truth" as a high-wire and personifies Beauty as a female aerialist about to make a death-defying leap into the poet's arms, he gives vivid visual embodiment to what had previously been only abstract concepts. When Emily Dickinson compares poetry to prancing coursers (No. 19), she objectifies imaginative and rhythmical qualities by presenting them in visual terms. When Robert Browning compares the crisping waves to "fiery ringlets" (No. 29), he starts with one image and transforms it into three. Figurative language is a way of multiplying the sense appeal of poetry.

Third, figures of speech are a way of adding emotional intensity to otherwise merely informative statements and of conveying attitudes along with information. If we say, "So-and-so is a rat" or "My feet are killing me," our meaning is as much emotional as informative. When Thomas Hardy compares "tangled bine-stems" to "strings of broken

---

*It is also the faculty of mind that is able to "picture" or "image" absent objects as if they were present. It was with imagination in this sense that we were concerned in the chapter on imagery.

lyres" (No. 36), he not only draws an exact visual comparison but also conjures up a feeling of despondency through the suggestion of discarded instruments no longer capable of making music. When Wilfred Owen compares a soldier caught in a gas attack to a man drowning under a green sea (No. 3), he conveys a feeling of despair and suffocation as well as a visual image.

Fourth, figures of speech are a means of concentration, a way of saying much in brief compass. Like words, they may be multidimensional. Consider, for instance, the merits of comparing life to a candle, as Shakespeare does in a passage from *Macbeth* (No. 85). Life is like a candle in that it begins and ends in darkness; in that while it burns, it gives off light and energy, is active and colorful; in that it gradually consumes itself, gets shorter and shorter; in that it can be snuffed out at any moment; in that it is brief at best, burning only for a short duration. Possibly your imagination can suggest other similarities. But at any rate, Macbeth's compact metaphorical description of life as a "brief candle" suggests certain truths about life that would require dozens of words to state in literal language. At the same time it makes the abstract concrete, provides imaginative pleasure, and adds a degree of emotional intensity.

Obviously, if we are to read poetry well, we must be able to interpret figurative language. Every use of figurative language involves a risk of misinterpretation, though the risk is well worth taking. For the person who can translate the figure, the dividends are immense. Fortunately all people have imagination to some degree, and imagination can be cultivated. By practice one's ability to interpret figures of speech can be increased.

EXERCISE

Identify each of the following quotations as literal or figurative. If figurative, explain what is being compared to what and explain the appropriateness of the comparison. EXAMPLE: "Talent is a cistern; genius is a fountain." ANSWER: Metaphor. Talent = cistern; genius = fountain. Talent exists in finite supply; it can be used up. Genius is inexhaustible, ever renewing.

1. O tenderly the haughty day
   Fills his blue urn with fire.   *Ralph Waldo Emerson*

2. It is with words as with sunbeams—the more
   they are condensed, the deeper they burn.   *Robert Southey*

3. Joy and Temperance and Repose
   Slam the door on the doctor's nose.   *Anonymous*

4. The pen is mightier than the sword.   *Edward Bulwer-Lytton*

5. The strongest oaths are straw
   To the fire i' the blood.   *William Shakespeare*

6. The Cambridge ladies . . . live in furnished souls.   *e. e. cummings*

7. Dorothy's eyes, with their long brown lashes,
   looked very much like her mother's.   *Laetitia Johnson*

8. The tawny-hided desert crouches watching her.   *Francis Thompson*

9. Let us eat and drink, for tomorrow we shall die.   *Isaiah 22:13*

10. Let us eat and drink, for tomorrow we may die.

    Common misquotation of the above

*   *   *

46. THERE IS A GARDEN IN HER FACE

There is a garden in her face
Where roses and white lilies grow;
A heavenly paradise is that place,
Wherein all pleasant fruits do flow.
There cherries grow which none can buy   5
Till "Cherry-ripe" themselves do cry.

Those cherries fairly do enclose
Of orient pearl a double row,
Which when her lovely laughter shows,
They look like rosebuds filled with snow,   10
Yet them nor peer nor prince can buy
Till "Cherry-ripe" themselves do cry.

Her eyes like angels watch them still;
Her brows like bended bows do stand,
Threatening with piercing frowns to kill   15
All that attempt with eye or hand
Those sacred cherries to come nigh
Till "Cherry-ripe" themselves do cry.

Thomas Campion (1567–1620)

QUESTIONS

1. Vocabulary: *orient* (8). "Cherry-ripe" is the cry of a street vendor selling ripe cherries.
2. The poem contains an extended metaphor in which a lady's face is compared to a garden. What literal terms may be supplied for "roses and white lilies"

(2), "pleasant fruits" (4), "cherries" (5), "rosebuds" (10), "snow" (10)? Is this any garden or a particular garden? What one metaphor does not belong to the garden comparison? In the third stanza the lady's eyes are compared to guardian angels. Name *two* metaphorical equivalents for her brows. What is the figurative term for her "frowns" (15)?
3. The refrains may be interpreted as containing three fourth-form metaphors. To what is kissing compared? To what is an invitation or consent to be kissed compared? To what *two* things are the lady's lips compared?
4. For what two qualities is the lady praised?

47. THE SILKEN TENT

She is as in a field a silken tent
At midday when a sunny summer breeze
Has dried the dew and all its ropes relent,
So that in guys it gently sways at ease,
And its supporting central cedar pole,   5
That is its pinnacle to heavenward
And signifies the sureness of the soul,
Seems to owe naught to any single cord,
But strictly held by none, is loosely bound
By countless silken ties of love and thought   10
To everything on earth the compass round,
And only by one's going slightly taut
In the capriciousness of summer air
Is of the slightest bondage made aware.

Robert Frost (1874–1963)

QUESTIONS

1. A poet may use a variety of metaphors and similes in developing his subject or may, as Frost does here, develop a single figure at length (this poem is an excellent example of **extended** or **sustained simile**). What are the advantages of each type of development?
2. Explore the similarities between the two things compared in this poem.

48. METAPHORS

I'm a riddle in nine syllables,
An elephant, a ponderous house,
A melon strolling on two tendrils,
O red fruit, ivory, fine timbers!

This loaf's big with its yeasty rising.   5
Money's new-minted in this fat purse.
I'm a means, a stage, a cow in calf.
I've eaten a bag of green apples,
Boarded the train there's no getting off.

Sylvia Plath (1932-1963)

QUESTIONS

1. Like its first metaphor, this poem is a riddle to be solved by identifying the literal terms of its metaphors. After you have identified the speaker ("riddle," "elephant," "house," "melon," "stage," "cow"), identify the literal meanings of the related metaphors ("syllables," "tendrils," "fruit," "ivory," "timbers," "loaf," "yeasty rising," "money," "purse," "train"). How is line 8 to be interpreted?
2. How does the form of the poem relate to its content?

49. TOADS

Why should I let the toad *work*
    Squat on my life?
Can't I use my wit as a pitchfork
    And drive the brute off?

Six days of the week it soils   5
    With its sickening poison—
Just for paying a few bills!
    That's out of proportion.

Lots of folk live on their wits:
    Lecturers, lispers,   10
Losels,° loblolly-men,° louts—   scoundrels; bumpkins
    They don't end as paupers;

Lots of folk live up lanes
    With fires in a bucket,
Eat windfalls and tinned sardines—   15
    They seem to like it.

Their nippers° have got bare feet,   children
    Their unspeakable wives
Are skinny as whippets—and yet
    No one actually *starves*.   20

Ah, were I courageous enough
To shout *Stuff your pension!*
But I know, all too well, that's the stuff
That dreams are made on;

For something sufficiently toad-like   25
Squats in me, too;
Its hunkers° are heavy as hard luck,   haunches
And cold as snow,

And will never allow me to blarney
My way to getting   30
The fame and the girl and the money
All at one sitting.

I don't say, one bodies the other
One's spiritual truth;
But I do say it's hard to lose either,   35
When you have both.

Philip Larkin (1922–1985)

QUESTIONS

1. How many "toads" are described in the poem? Where is each located? How
   are they described? What are the antecedents of the pronouns "one" and
   "the other / one" (33–34) respectively?
2. What characteristics in common have the people mentioned in lines 9–12?
   Those mentioned in 13–20?
3. Explain the pun in lines 22–23, and the literary allusion it leads into. (If you
   don't recognize the allusion, check Shakespeare's *Tempest*, Act IV, scene 1,
   lines 156–58.)
4. The first "toad" is explicitly identified as "work" (1). The literal term
   for the second "toad" is not named. Why not? What do you take it
   to be?
5. What kind of person is the speaker? What are his attitudes toward
   work?

50. A VALEDICTION: FORBIDDING MOURNING

As virtuous men pass mildly away,
    And whisper to their souls to go,
While some of their sad friends do say,
    The breath goes now, and some say, no:

So let us melt, and make no noise, 5
    No tear-floods, nor sigh-tempests move;
'Twere profanation of our joys
    To tell the laity our love.

Moving of th' earth brings harms and fears,
    Men reckon what it did and meant, 10
But trepidation of the spheres,
    Though greater far, is innocent.

Dull sublunary lovers' love
    (Whose soul is sense) cannot admit
Absence, because it doth remove 15
    Those things which elemented it.

But we by a love so much refined,
    That ourselves know not what it is,
Inter-assurèd of the mind,
    Care less, eyes, lips, and hands to miss. 20

Our two souls therefore, which are one,
    Though I must go, endure not yet
A breach, but an expansion,
    Like gold to airy thinness beat.

If they be two, they are two so 25
    As stiff twin compasses are two;
Thy soul the fixed foot, makes no show
    To move, but doth, if th' other do.

And though it in the center sit,
    Yet when the other far doth roam, 30
It leans, and hearkens after it,
    And grows erect, as that comes home.

Such wilt thou be to me, who must
    Like th' other foot, obliquely run;
Thy firmness makes my circle just, 35
    And makes me end, where I begun.

John Donne (1572–1631)

QUESTIONS

1. Vocabulary: *valediction* (title), *mourning* (title), *profanation* (7), *laity* (8), *trepidation* (11), *innocent* (12), *sublunary* (13), *elemented* (16). Line 11 is a reference to the spheres of the Ptolemaic cosmology, whose movements caused

no such disturbance as does a movement of the earth—that is, an earthquake.
2. Is the speaker in the poem about to die? Or about to leave on a journey? (The answer may be found in a careful analysis of the simile in the last three stanzas.)
3. The poem is organized around a contrast of two kinds of lovers: the "laity" (8) and, as their implied opposite, the "priesthood." Are these terms literal or metaphorical? What is the essential difference between their two kinds of love? How, according to the speaker, does their behavior differ when they must separate from each other? What is the motivation of the speaker in this "valediction"?
4. Find and explain three similes and one metaphor used to describe the parting of true lovers. The figure in the last three stanzas is one of the most famous in English literature. Demonstrate its appropriateness by obtaining a drawing compass or by using two pencils to imitate the two legs.
5. What kind of language is used in the poem? Is the language consonant with the figures of speech?

51. TO HIS COY MISTRESS

Had we but world enough, and time,
This coyness, lady, were no crime.
We would sit down, and think which way
To walk, and pass our long love's day.
Thou by the Indian Ganges' side   5
Shouldst rubies find; I by the tide
Of Humber would complain. I would
Love you ten years before the Flood,
And you should, if you please, refuse
Till the conversion of the Jews.   10
My vegetable love should grow
Vaster than empires, and more slow;
An hundred years should go to praise
Thine eyes, and on thy forehead gaze;
Two hundred to adore each breast,   15
But thirty thousand to the rest;
An age at least to every part,
And the last age should show your heart.
For, lady, you deserve this state,
Nor would I love at lower rate.   20
But at my back I always hear
Time's wingèd chariot hurrying near;

And yonder all before us lie
Deserts of vast eternity.
Thy beauty shall no more be found,   25
Nor, in thy marble vault, shall sound
My echoing song; then worms shall try
That long-preserved virginity,
And your quaint honor turn to dust,
And into ashes all my lust: 30
The grave's a fine and private place,
But none, I think, do there embrace.
    Now therefore, while the youthful hue
Sits on thy skin like morning dew,
And while thy willing soul transpires   35
At every pore with instant fires,
Now let us sport us while we may,
And now, like amorous birds of prey,
Rather at once our time devour
Than languish in his slow-chapped power.   40
Let us roll all our strength and all
Our sweetness up into one ball,
And tear our pleasures with rough strife
Thorough° the iron gates of life.   through
Thus, though we cannot make our sun   45
Stand still, yet we will make him run.

Andrew Marvell (1621–1678)

QUESTIONS

1. Vocabulary: *coy* (title), *Humber* (7), *transpires* (35). "Mistress" (title) has the now archaic meaning of *sweetheart;* "slow-chapped" (40) derives from *chap*, meaning *jaw*.
2. What is the speaker urging his sweetheart to do? Why is she being "coy"?
3. Outline the speaker's argument in three sentences that begin with the words *If, But,* and *Therefore*. Is the argument valid?
4. Explain the appropriateness of "vegetable love" (11). What simile in the third section contrasts with it and how? What image in the third section contrasts with the distance between the Ganges and the Humber? Of what would the speaker be "complaining" by the Humber (7)?
5. Explain the figures in lines 22, 24, and 40 and their implications.
6. Explain the last two lines. For what is "sun" a metonymy?
7. Is this poem principally about love or about time? If the latter, what might making love represent? What philosophy is the poet advancing here?

52. TO SLEEP

O soft embalmer of the still midnight,
    Shutting, with careful fingers and benign,
Our gloom-pleased eyes, embowered from the light,
    Enshaded in forgetfulness divine:
O soothest Sleep! if so it please thee, close,   5
    In midst of this thine hymn, my willing eyes,
Or wait the Amen, ere thy poppy throws
    Around my bed its lulling charities.
Then save me, or the passed day will shine
    Upon my pillow, breeding many woes: 10
Save me from curious conscience, that still hoards
    Its strength for darkness, burrowing like the mole;
Turn the key deftly in the oiled wards,
    And seal the hushed casket of my soul.

John Keats (1795–1821)

QUESTIONS

1. Vocabulary: *soothest* (5), *curious* (11), *wards* (13).
2. "Sleep" is not only apostrophized and personified but personified as a particular kind of person. What kind? What extended metaphor does this lead into? What activity is going on during the course of the poem?
3. Poppies are a source of opium. In the poem is "poppy" (7) literal or figurative? Explain. What are the "lulling charities" (8)? Explain the figurative language in lines 9–10.

53. LOVELIEST OF TREES

Loveliest of trees, the cherry now
Is hung with bloom along the bough,
And stands about the woodland ride
Wearing white for Eastertide.

Now, of my threescore years and ten,   5
Twenty will not come again,
And take from seventy springs a score,
It only leaves me fifty more.

And since to look at things in bloom
Fifty springs are little room,   10
About the woodlands I will go
To see the cherry hung with snow.

A. E. Housman (1859–1936)

QUESTIONS

1. Very briefly, this poem presents a philosophy of life. In a sentence, what is it?
2. How old is the speaker? Why does he assume that his life will be seventy years in length? What is surprising about the words "only" (8) and "little" (10)?
3. A good deal of ink has been spilt over whether "snow" (12) is literal or figurative. What do you say? Justify your answer.

54. DREAM DEFERRED

What happens to a dream deferred?

Does it dry up
like a raisin in the sun?
Or fester like a sore—
And then run?   5
Does it stink like rotten meat?
Or crust and sugar over—
like a syrupy sweet?

Maybe it just sags
like a heavy load.   10

Or does it explode?

Langston Hughes (1902–1967)

QUESTIONS

1. Of the six images, five are similes. Which is a metaphor? Comment on its position and its effectiveness.
2. Since the dream could be any dream, the poem is general in its implication. What happens to your understanding of it on learning that its author was a black American?

Chapter six

Figurative Language 2
Symbol, Allegory

55. THE ROAD NOT TAKEN

Two roads diverged in a yellow wood,
And sorry I could not travel both
And be one traveler, long I stood
And looked down one as far as I could
To where it bent in the undergrowth;   5

Then took the other, as just as fair,
And having perhaps the better claim,
Because it was grassy and wanted wear;
Though as for that the passing there
Had worn them really about the same,   10

And both that morning equally lay
In leaves no step had trodden black.
Oh, I kept the first for another day!
Yet knowing how way leads on to way,
I doubted if I should ever come back.   15

I shall be telling this with a sigh
Somewhere ages and ages hence:
Two roads diverged in a wood, and I—
I took the one less traveled by,
And that has made all the difference.   20

Robert Frost (1874–1963)

1. Does the speaker feel that he has made the wrong choice in taking the road "less traveled by"? If not, why will he sigh? What does he regret?
2. Why will the choice between two roads that seem very much alike make such a big difference many years later?

A **symbol** may be roughly defined as something that means *more* than what it is. "The Road Not Taken," for instance, concerns a choice made between two roads by a person out walking in the woods. He would like to explore both roads. He tells himself that he will explore one and then come back and explore the other, but he knows that he will probably be unable to do so. By the last stanza, however, we realize that the poem is about something more than the choice of paths in a wood, for such a choice would be relatively unimportant, while this choice, the speaker believes, is one that will make a great difference in his life and is one that he will remember with a sigh "ages and ages hence." We must interpret his choice of a road as a symbol for any choice in life between alternatives that appear almost equally attractive but will result through the years in a large difference in the kind of experience one knows.

Image, metaphor, and symbol shade into each other and are sometimes difficult to distinguish. In general, however, an image means only what it is; the figurative term in a metaphor means something other than what it is; and a symbol means what it is and something more, too. A symbol, that is, functions literally and figuratively at the same time.* If I say that a shaggy brown dog was rubbing its back against a white picket fence, I am talking about nothing but a dog (and a picket fence) and am therefore presenting an image. If I say, "Some dirty dog stole my wallet at the party," I am not talking about a dog at all and am therefore using a metaphor. But if I say, "You can't teach an old dog new tricks," I am talking not only about dogs but about living creatures of any species and am therefore speaking symbolically. Images, of course, do not cease to be images when they become incorporated in metaphors or symbols. If we are discussing the sensuous qualities of "The Road Not Taken" we should refer to the two leaf-strewn roads in

---

*This account does not hold for nonliterary symbols such as the letters of the alphabet and algebraic signs (the symbol ∞ for infinity or = for equals). Here, the symbol is meaningless except as it stands for something else, and the connection between the sign and what it stands for is purely arbitrary.

the yellow wood as an image; if we are discussing the significance of the poem, we talk about them as symbols.

The symbol is the richest and at the same time the most difficult of the poetic figures. Both its richness and its difficulty result from its imprecision. Although the poet may pin down the meaning of a symbol to something fairly definite and precise, more often the symbol is so general in its meaning that it can suggest a great variety of specific meanings. It is like an opal that flashes out different colors when slowly turned in the light. The choice in "The Road Not Taken," for instance, concerns some choice in life, but what choice? Was it a choice of profession? A choice of residence? A choice of mate? It might be any, all, or none of these. We cannot determine what particular choice the poet had in mind, if any, and it is not important that we do so. It is enough if we see in the poem an expression of regret that the possibilities of life experience are so sharply limited. The speaker in the poem would have liked to explore both roads, but he could explore only one. The person with a craving for life, whether satisfied or dissatisfied with the choices he has made, will always long for the realms of experience that had to be passed by. Because the symbol is a rich one, the poem suggests other meanings too. It affirms a belief in the possibility of choice and says something about the nature of choice—how each choice narrows the range of possible future choices, so that we make our lives as we go, both freely choosing and being determined by past choices. Though not a philosophical poem, it obliquely comments on the issue of free will and determinism and indicates the poet's own position. It can do all these things, concretely and compactly, by its use of an effective symbol.

Symbols vary in the degree of identification and definition given them by their authors. In this poem Frost forces us to interpret the choice of roads symbolically by the degree of importance he gives it in the last stanza. Sometimes poets are much more specific in identifying their symbols. Sometimes they do not identify them at all. Consider, for instance, the next two poems.

56. AT CAPE BOJEADOR

Walking the beach at daybreak I came on a violet sea urchin
geometrically perfect in its delicate design;
and I thought of a certain woman whom I know and admire,
as fragile as that urchin, as flawless in color and line.

Going back the next morning I saw it there again,   5
crushed in a foot-print, thin bone mixed with sand.
And I grieved for it and for women, millions of eggshell women,
and time in his heedless stroll over brow and breast and hand.

Dorothy Lee Richardson (b. 1900)

In the first stanza of this poem the speaker is reminded, by a violet sea urchin found on the beach, of an admired female friend. In the fourth line she identifies the qualities that the sea urchin and her friend have in common. Clearly, all the elements necessary for a symbol are here—both the symbolic object (the sea urchin) and the symbolic referent (the remembered woman). In the second stanza the speaker returns to the beach the next day and finds the sea urchin crushed. If the poem ended with line 6 we would know, without further explanation, that the sea urchin was a symbol for the woman and its destruction a symbol for her destruction. The poet enlarges the meaning of the symbol in the last two lines, however, making its destruction symbolic of the destruction of all delicate, fragile women. She also names the destructive agent: time.

QUESTIONS

1. Robert Frost compares a beautiful and admired woman to a silken tent (No. 47). Richardson compares a beautiful and admired woman to a violet sea urchin. Why is Frost's comparison a simile and Richardson's symbolic? What additional comparison involving women does Richardson make? What figure of speech is it?
2. What word in Richardson's first stanza anticipates the action of the second? What words in the poem serve to personify time? Why is the detail of "thin bone mixed with sand" (6) especially effective?
3. The woman in Frost's poem is praised principally for inward qualities ("silken ties of love and thought"), though physical beauty is also strongly implied. Would it be fair to say that Richardson's concentrates on external rather than internal beauty? Why, or why not?

57. THE SICK ROSE

O Rose, thou art sick!
The invisible worm
That flies in the night,
In the howling storm,

Has found out thy bed
Of crimson joy,
And his dark secret love
Does thy life destroy.

William Blake (1757–1827)

QUESTIONS

1. What figures of speech do you find in the poem in addition to symbol? How do they contribute to its force or meaning?
2. Several symbolic interpretations of this poem are given below. Do you think of others?
3. Should symbolic meanings be sought for the night and the storm? If so, what meanings would you suggest?

In "At Cape Bojeador" the symbolic meaning of the crushed sea urchin is identified and named. In "The Sick Rose," however, no meanings are explicitly indicated for the rose and the worm. Indeed, we are not *compelled* to assign them specific meanings. The poem is validly read as being about a rose that has been attacked on a stormy night by a cankerworm.

The organization of "The Sick Rose" is so rich, however, and its language so powerful that the rose and the worm refuse to remain *merely* a flower and an insect. The rose, apostrophized and personified in the first line, has traditionally been a symbol of feminine beauty and of love, as well as of sensual pleasures. "Bed" can refer to a woman's bed as well as to a flower bed. "Crimson joy" suggests the intense pleasure of passionate lovemaking as well as the brilliant beauty of a red flower. The "dark secret love" of the "invisible worm" is more strongly suggestive of a concealed or illicit love affair than of the feeding of a cankerworm on a plant, though it fits that too. For all these reasons the rose almost immediately suggests a woman and the worm her secret lover—and the poem suggests the corruption of innocent but physical love by concealment and deceit. But the possibilities do not stop there. The worm is a common symbol or metonymy for death; and for readers steeped in Milton (as Blake was) it recalls the "undying worm" of *Paradise Lost,* Milton's metaphor for the snake (or Satan in the form of a snake) that tempted Eve. Meanings multiply also for the reader who is familiar with Blake's other writings. Thus "The Sick Rose" has been variously interpreted as referring to the destruction of joyous physical love by jealousy, deceit, concealment, or the possessive instinct; of innocence by experience; of humanity by Satan; of imagination and joy by analytic reason; of life by death. We cannot say what specifically the poet had in mind, nor do we need to. A symbol defines an *area* of meaning, and any interpretation which falls within that area is permissible. In Blake's poem the rose stands for something beautiful, or desirable, or good. The worm stands for some corrupting agent. Within these limits, the meaning is largely "open." And because the meaning is open, the reader is justified in bringing personal experience to its interpretation. Blake's poem, for instance, might remind someone of a gifted friend whose promise has been destroyed by drug addiction.

Between the extremes represented by "At Cape Bojeador" and "The Sick Rose" a poem may exercise all degrees of control over the range and meaning of its symbolism. Consider another example.

58. YOU, ANDREW MARVELL

And here face down beneath the sun
And here upon earth's noonward height
To feel the always coming on
The always rising of the night:

To feel creep up the curving east   5
The earthly chill of dusk and slow
Upon those under lands the vast
And ever-climbing shadow grow

And strange at Ecbatan the trees
Take leaf by leaf the evening strange   10
The flooding dark about their knees
The mountains over Persia change

And now at Kermanshah the gate
Dark empty and the withered grass
And through the twilight now the late   15
Few travelers in the westward pass

And Baghdad darken and the bridge
Across the silent river gone
And through Arabia the edge
Of evening widen and steal on   20

And deepen on Palmyra's street
The wheel rut in the ruined stone
And Lebanon fade out and Crete
High through the clouds and overblown

And over Sicily the air   25
Still flashing with the landward gulls
And loom and slowly disappear
The sails above the shadowy hulls

And Spain go under and the shore
Of Africa the gilded sand   30
And evening vanish and no more
The low pale light across that land

Nor now the long light on the sea:
And here face downward in the sun
To feel how swift how secretly   35
The shadow of the night comes on . . .

Archibald MacLeish (1892–1982)

QUESTIONS

1. We ordinarily speak of *nightfall*. Why does MacLeish speak of the "rising" of the night? What implicit metaphorical comparison is suggested by phrases like "rising of the night" (4), "the flooding dark" (11), "the bridge / Across the silent river gone" (17–18), "deepen on Palmyra's street" (21), "Spain go under" (29), and so on?
2. Does the comparative lack of punctuation serve any function? What is the effect of the repetition of "and" throughout the poem?
3. Ecbatan was founded in 700 B.C. and is associated in history with Cyrus the Great, founder of the Persian Empire, and with Alexander the Great. Kermanshah was another ancient city of Persia. Where are Baghdad, Palmyra, Lebanon, Crete?

   On the literal level, "You, Andrew Marvell" is about the coming on of night. The speaker, lying at noon full length in the sun somewhere in the United States,* pictures in his mind the earth's shadow, halfway around the world, moving silently westward over Persia, Syria, Crete, Sicily, Spain, Africa, and finally the Atlantic—approaching swiftly, in fact, the place where he himself lies. But the title of the poem tells us that, though particularly concerned with the passage of a day, it is more generally concerned with the swift passage of time; for the title is an allusion to a famous poem on this subject by Andrew Marvell ("To His Coy Mistress," No. 51) and especially to two lines of that poem:

*MacLeish has identified the fixed location of the poem as Illinois on the shore of Lake Michigan.

But at my back I always hear
Time's wingèd chariot hurrying near.

Once we are aware of this larger concern of the poem, two symbolic levels of interpretation open to us. Marvell's poem is primarily concerned with the swift passing of man's life; and the word *night*, we know, from our experience with other literature, is a natural and traditional metaphor or symbol for death. The speaker, then, is thinking not only about the passing of a day but about the passing of his life. He is at present "upon earth's noonward height"—in the full flush of manhood—but he is acutely conscious of the declining years ahead and of "how swift how secretly" his death comes on.

If we are to account fully for all the data of the poem, however, a third level of interpretation is necessary. What has dictated the poet's choice of geographical references? The places named, of course, progress from east to west; but they have a further linking characteristic. Ecbatan, Kermanshah, Baghdad, and Palmyra are all ancient or ruined cities, the relics of past empires and crumbled civilizations. Lebanon, Crete, Sicily, Spain, and North Africa are places where civilization once flourished more vigorously than it does at present. On a third level, then, the poet is concerned, not with the passage of a day nor with the passage of a lifetime, but with the passage of historical epochs. The poet's own country—the United States— now shines "upon earth's noonward height" as a favored nation in the sun of history, but its civilization, too, will pass.

Meanings ray out from a symbol, like the corona around the sun or like connotations around a richly suggestive word. But the very fact that a symbol may be so rich in meanings requires that we use the greatest tact in its interpretation. Although Blake's "The Sick Rose" might, because of personal association, remind us of a friend destroyed by drug addiction, it would be unwise to say that Blake uses the rose to symbolize a gifted person succumbing to drug addiction, for this interpretation is private, idiosyncratic, and narrow. The poem allows it, but does not itself suggest it.

Moreover, we should never assume that because the meaning of a symbol is more or less open, we may make it mean anything we choose. We would be wrong, for instance, in interpreting the choice in "The Road Not Taken" as some choice between good and evil, for the poem tells us that the two roads are much alike and that both lie "in leaves no step had trodden black." Whatever the choice is, it is a choice between two goods. Whatever our interpretation of a symbolic poem, it must be tied firmly to the facts of the poem. We must not let loose of the string and let our imaginations go ballooning up among the clouds. Because the symbol is capable of adding so many dimensions to a poem, it is a peculiarly effective resource of the poet, but it is also peculiarly susceptible of misinterpretation by the incautious reader.

Accurate interpretation of the symbol requires delicacy, tact, and good sense. The reader must maintain balance while walking a tightrope between too little and too much—between underinterpretation and overinterpretation. If the reader falls off, however, it is much more desirable to fall off on the side of too little. Someone who reads "The Road Not Taken" as being only about a choice between two roads in a wood has at least understood part of the experience that the poem communicates, but the reader who reads into it anything imaginable might as well discard the poem and simply daydream.

Above all, we should avoid the disease of seeing symbols everywhere, like a man with hallucinations, whether there are symbols there or not. It is better to miss a symbol now and then than to walk constantly among shadows and mirages.

59. TO THE VIRGINS, TO MAKE MUCH OF TIME

Gather ye rosebuds while ye may,
    Old Time is still a-flying;
And this same flower that smiles today
    Tomorrow will be dying.

The glorious lamp of heaven, the Sun,   5
    The higher he's a-getting,
The sooner will his race be run,
    And nearer he's to setting.

That age is best which is the first,
    When youth and blood are warmer;   10
But being spent, the worse, and worst
    Times still succeed the former.

Then be not coy, but use your time;
    And while ye may, go marry;
For having lost but once your prime,   15
    You may forever tarry.

Robert Herrick (1591–1674)

1. The first two stanzas might be interpreted literally if the third and fourth stanzas did not force us to interpret them symbolically. What do the rose-buds symbolize (stanza 1)? What does the course of a day symbolize (stanza 2)? Does the poet narrow the meaning of the rosebud symbol in the last stanza or merely name *one* of its specific meanings?
2. How does the title help us interpret the meaning of the symbol? Why did Herrick use "virgins" instead of *maidens?*
3. Why is such haste necessary in gathering the rosebuds? True, the blossoms die quickly, but they are replaced by others. Who *really* is dying?
4. What are the "worse, and worst" times (11)? Why?
5. Why did the poet use his wording rather than the following alternatives: *blooms* for "smiles" (3), *course* for "race" (7), *used* for "spent" (11), *spend* for "use" (13)?

Allegory is a narrative or description that has a second meaning beneath the surface. Although the surface story or description may have its own interest, the author's major interest is in the ulterior meaning. When Pharaoh in the Bible, for instance, has a dream in which seven fat kine are devoured by seven lean kine, the story does not really become significant until Joseph interprets its allegorical meaning: that Egypt is to enjoy seven years of fruitfulness and prosperity followed by seven years of famine. Allegory has been defined sometimes as an extended metaphor and sometimes as a series of related symbols. But it is usually distinguishable from both of these. It is unlike extended metaphor in that it involves a *system* of related comparisons rather than one compari-son drawn out. It differs from symbolism in that it puts less emphasis on the images for their own sake and more on their ulterior meanings. Also, these meanings are more fixed. In allegory there is usually a one-to-one correspondence between the details and a single set of ulterior meanings. In complex allegories the details may have more than one meaning, but these meanings tend to be definite. Meanings do not ray out from allegory as they do from a symbol.

Allegory is less popular in modern literature than it was in medieval and Renaissance writing, and it is much less often found in short poems than in long narrative works such as *The Faerie Queene, Everyman,* and *Pilgrim's Progress.* It has sometimes, especially with political allegory, been used to disguise meaning rather than reveal it (or, rather, to dis-guise it from some people while revealing it to others). Though less rich than the symbol, allegory is an effective way of making the abstract concrete and has occasionally been used effectively even in fairly short poems.

60. REDEMPTION

Having been tenant long to a rich Lord,
Not thriving, I resolvèd to be bold,
And make a suit unto him, to afford
A new small-rented lease and cancel the old.
In heaven at his manor I him sought: 5
They told me there that he was lately gone
About some land which he had dearly bought
Long since on earth, to take possessiön.
I straight returned, and knowing his great birth,
Sought him accordingly in great resorts;   10
In cities, theaters, gardens, parks, and courts:
At length I heard a ragged noise and mirth
Of thieves and murderers; there I him espied,
Who straight, "Your suit is granted," said, and died.

George Herbert (1593–1633)

QUESTIONS

1. Vocabulary: *suit* (3, 14), *afford* (3), *dearly* (7).
2. On the surface this poem tells about a business negotiation between a tenant landholder and his landlord. What clues indicate that the poem really concerns something deeper?
3. Who is the "rich Lord"? Who is the tenant? What is the old lease? What is the new one? Where does the tenant find his Lord? What is the significance of his suit being granted just as the landlord dies?
4. What are the implications of the landlord's having gone to take possession of some land which he "had dearly bought / Long since on earth"? In what senses (on both levels of meaning) is the landlord of "great birth"? What is "a ragged noise and mirth / Of thieves and murderers"?

*   *   *

61. FIRE AND ICE

Some say the world will end in fire,
Some say in ice.
From what I've tasted of desire
I hold with those who favor fire.

But if it had to perish twice,
I think I know enough of hate
To say that for destruction ice
Is also great
And would suffice.

Robert Frost (1874–1963)

QUESTIONS

1. Who are "Some"? To what two theories do lines 1–2 refer?
2. What do "fire" and "ice" respectively symbolize? What two meanings has "the world"?
3. The poem ends with an *understatement* (see Chapter 7). How does it affect the tone of the poem?

62. THE DEAD

These hearts were woven of human joys and cares,
    Washed marvelously with sorrow, swift to mirth.
The years had given them kindness. Dawn was theirs,
    And sunset, and the colors of the earth.
These had seen movement, and heard music; known   5
    Slumber and waking; loved; gone proudly friended;
Felt the quick stir of wonder; sat alone;
    Touched flowers and furs and cheeks. All this is ended.

There are waters blown by changing winds to laughter
And lit by the rich skies, all day. And after,   10
    Frost, with a gesture, stays the winds that dance
And wandering loveliness. He leaves a white
    Unbroken glory, a gathered radiance,
A width, a shining peace, under the night.

Rupert Brooke (1887–1915)

QUESTIONS

1. This poem, the fourth in a group of five sonnets collectively entitled *1914*, was written a few months after the outbreak of World War I and the voluntary enlistment of its author in the British navy. To whom do the pronouns "These" (1, 5), "them" (3)," and "theirs" (3) refer? What, according to the poet, was the quality of their lives?
2. What is the literal term in the metaphor of which "laughter" (9) is the figurative term? With what word in the first eight lines is it kin?

\t *happens* in the last six lines? What is the literal term for which the
\te / Unbroken glory," "gathered radiance," "width," and "shining
peace" are metonymies? How are the last six lines related to the first eight?
Why does the poet substitute these metonymies for the literal term? Of what
is "night" (14) a symbol?

63. ULYSSES

It little profits that an idle king,
By this still hearth, among these barren crags,
Matched with an agèd wife, I mete and dole
Unequal laws unto a savage race,
That hoard, and sleep, and feed, and know not me.   5
I cannot rest from travel; I will drink
Life to the lees. All times I have enjoyed
Greatly, have suffered greatly, both with those
That loved me, and alone; on shore, and when
Through scudding drifts the rainy Hyades   10
Vext the dim sea. I am become a name;
For always roaming with a hungry heart
Much have I seen and known,—cities of men,
And manners, climates, councils, governments,
Myself not least, but honored of them all;   15
And drunk delight of battle with my peers,
Far on the ringing plains of windy Troy.
I am a part of all that I have met;
Yet all experience is an arch wherethrough
Gleams that untraveled world, whose margin fades   20
For ever and for ever when I move.
How dull it is to pause, to make an end,
To rust unburnished, not to shine in use!
As though to breathe were life! Life piled on life
Were all too little, and of one to me   25
Little remains; but every hour is saved
From that eternal silence, something more,
A bringer of new things; and vile it were
For some three suns to store and hoard myself,
And this grey spirit yearning in desire   30
To follow knowledge like a sinking star,
Beyond the utmost bound of human thought.

This is my son, mine own Telemachus,
To whom I leave the scepter and the isle—
Well-loved of me, discerning to fulfil   35
This labor, by slow prudence to make mild

A rugged people, and through soft degrees
Subdue them to the useful and the good.
Most blameless is he, centered in the sphere
Of common duties, decent not to fail   40
In offices of tenderness, and pay
Meet adoration to my household gods,
When I am gone. He works his work, I mine.

There lies the port; the vessel puffs her sail:
There gloom the dark, broad seas. My mariners,   45
Souls that have toiled, and wrought, and thought with me—
That ever with a frolic welcome took
The thunder and the sunshine, and opposed
Free hearts, free foreheads—you and I are old;
Old age hath yet his honor and his toil.   50
Death closes all; but something ere the end,
Some work of noble note, may yet be done,
Not unbecoming men that strove with Gods.
The lights begin to twinkle from the rocks;
The long day wanes; the slow moon climbs; the deep   55
Moans round with many voices. Come, my friends,
'Tis not too late to seek a newer world.
Push off, and sitting well in order smite
The sounding furrows; for my purpose holds
To sail beyond the sunset, and the baths   60
Of all the western stars, until I die.
It may be that the gulfs will wash us down;
It may be we shall touch the Happy Isles,
And see the great Achilles, whom we knew.
Though much is taken, much abides; and though   65
We are not now that strength which in old days
Moved earth and heaven, that which we are, we are:
One equal temper of heroic hearts,
Made weak by time and fate, but strong in will
To strive, to seek, to find, and not to yield.   70

Alfred, Lord Tennyson (1809–1892)

QUESTIONS

1. Vocabulary: *lees* (7), *Hyades* (10), *meet* (42).
2. Ulysses, king of Ithaca, is a legendary Greek hero, a major figure in Homer's
   Iliad, the hero of Homer's *Odyssey,* and a minor figure in Dante's *Divine
   Comedy.* After ten years at the siege of Troy, Ulysses set sail for home but,
   having incurred the wrath of the god of the sea, he was subjected to storms

and vicissitudes and was forced to wander for another ten years, having many adventures and seeing most of the Mediterranean world before again reaching Ithaca, his wife, and his son. Once back home, according to Dante, he still wished to travel and "to follow virtue and knowledge." In Tennyson's poem, Ulysses is represented as about to set sail on a final voyage from which he will not return. Locate Ithaca on a map. Where exactly, in geographical terms, does Ulysses intend to sail (59–64)? (The Happy Isles were the Elysian fields, or Greek paradise; Achilles was another Greek prince, the hero of the *Iliad*, who was killed at the siege of Troy.)

3. Ulysses's speech is divided into three sections. What is the topic or purpose of each section? To whom, specifically, is the third section addressed? To whom, would you infer, are sections 1 and 2 addressed? Where do you visualize Ulysses as standing during his speech?

4. Characterize Ulysses. What kind of person is he as Tennyson represents him?

5. What does Ulysses symbolize? What way of life is being recommended? Find as many evidences as you can that Ulysses's desire for travel represents something more than mere wanderlust and wish for adventure.

6. Give two symbolic implications of the westward direction of Ulysses's journey.

7. Interpret lines 18–21 and 26–29. What is symbolized by "the thunder and the sunshine" (48)? What do the two metonymies in line 49 stand for? What metaphor is implied in line 23?

64. CURIOSITY

may have killed the cat; more likely
the cat was just unlucky, or else curious
to see what death was like, having no cause
to go on licking paws, or fathering
litter on litter of kittens, predictably.   5

Nevertheless, to be curious
is dangerous enough. To distrust
what is always said, what seems,
to ask odd questions, interfere in dreams,
leave home, smell rats, have hunches   10
do not endear cats to those doggy circles
where well-smelt baskets, suitable wives, good lunches
are the order of things, and where prevails
much wagging of incurious heads and tails.

Face it. Curiosity   15
will not cause us to die—
only lack of it will.
Never to want to see
the other side of the hill

or that improbable country   20
where living is an idyll
(although a probable hell)
would kill us all.
Only the curious
have, if they live, a tale   25
worth telling at all.

Dogs say cats love too much, are irresponsible,
are changeable, marry too many wives,
desert their children, chill all dinner tables
with tales of their nine lives.   30
Well, they are lucky. Let them be
nine-lived and contradictory,
curious enough to change, prepared to pay
the cat price, which is to die
and die again and again,   35
each time with no less pain.
A cat minority of one
is all that can be counted on
to tell the truth. And what cats have to tell
on each return from hell   40
is this: that dying is what the living do,
that dying is what the loving do,
and that dead dogs are those who do not know
that dying is what, to live, each has to do.

Alastair Reid (b. 1926)

QUESTIONS

1. On the surface this poem is a dissertation on cats. What deeper comments
   does it make? Of what are cats and dogs, in this poem, symbols?
2. In what different senses are the words "death," "die," and "dying" here
   used?
3. Compare and contrast this poem in meaning and manner with "Ulysses."

65. LOVE SONG: I AND THOU

Nothing is plumb, level or square:
    the studs are bowed, the joists
are shaky by nature, no piece fits
    any other piece without a gap
or pinch, and bent nails   5
    dance all over the surfacing

like maggots. By Christ
   I am no carpenter. I built
the roof for myself, the walls
   for myself, the floors   10
for myself, and got
   hung up in it myself. I
danced with a purple thumb
   at this house-warming, drunk
with my prime whiskey: rage.   15
   Oh I spat rage's nails
into the frame-up of my work:
   it held. It settled plumb,
level, solid, square and true
   for that one great moment. Then   20
it screamed and went on through,
   skewing as wrong the other way.
God damned it. This is hell,
   but I planned it, I sawed it,
I nailed it, and I   25
   will live in it until it kills me.
I can nail my left palm
   to the left-hand cross-piece but
I can't do everything myself.
   I need a hand to nail the right,   30
a help, a love, a you, a wife.

Alan Dugan (b. 1923)

QUESTIONS

1. What clues are there that this house is not literal? What does it stand for?
2. Why does the speaker swear "By Christ" rather than *By God* (7)? Where else in the poem is Christ alluded to? What parallels and differences does the speaker see between himself and Christ?
3. "God damned it" (23) at first sounds like another curse, but the past tense makes its meaning more precise. What are the implications of lines 24–26? What implications are added in the phrase "by nature" (3)? What meanings has "prime" (15)?
4. What is the meaning of the last three lines? (Note: *I and Thou* is the title of a very influential book by the Jewish theologian Martin Buber. Briefly, it argues that, though suffering is inescapable, human life becomes meaningful as man forms "I–Thou" relationships, as opposed to "I–It" relationships— that is, as one becomes deeply involved with and committed to other human beings in relationships of love and concern.)

66. HYMN TO GOD MY GOD, IN MY SICKNESS

Since I am coming to that holy room
  Where, with thy choir of saints for evermore,
I shall be made thy music, as I come
  I tune the instrument here at the door,
  And what I must do then, think now before.   5

Whilst my physicians by their love are grown
  Cosmographers, and I their map, who lie
Flat on this bed, that by them may be shown
  That this is my southwest discovery,
  Per fretum febris,° by these straits to die,   through the 10
                                                      raging of fever
I joy that in these straits I see my west;
  For though those currents yield return to none,
What shall my west hurt me? As west and east
  In all flat maps (and I am one) are one,
  So death doth touch the resurrectiön.   15

Is the Pacific Sea my home? Or are
  The eastern riches? Is Jerusalem?
Anyan° and Magellan and Gibraltar,   Bering Strait
  All straits, and none but straits, are ways to them,
  Whether where Japhet dwelt, or Cham, or Shem.   20

We think that Paradise and Calvary,
  Christ's cross and Adam's tree, stood in one place;
Look, Lord, and find both Adams met in me;
  As the first Adam's sweat surrounds my face,
  May the last Adam's blood my soul embrace.   25

So, in his purple wrapped receive me, Lord;
  By these his thorns give me his other crown;
And as to others' souls I preached thy word,
  Be this my text, my sermon to mine own:
  Therefore that he may raise, the Lord throws down.   30

John Donne (1572–1631)

QUESTIONS

1. Vocabulary: *cosmographers* (7).
2. For the last ten years of his life John Donne was Dean of St. Paul's Cathedral in London, and he is famous for his sermons (see lines 28–30) as well

as his poems. According to his earliest biographer (though some scholars disagree), this poem was written eight days before Donne's death. What are "that holy room" (1) and "the instrument" (4)? What is the speaker doing in stanza 1?

3. During Donne's lifetime such explorers as Henry Hudson and Martin Frobisher sought for a Northwest Passage to the East Indies to match Magellan's discovery in 1520 of a southwest passage through the straits that bear his name. Why is "southwest" more appropriate to the speaker's condition than "northwest"? In what ways is his raging fever like a strait? What different meanings of the word "straits" (10) are operative here? What do the straits symbolize?

4. In what ways does the speaker's body resemble a map?

5. Although the map is metaphorical, its parts are symbolic. What does the west symbolize? The east? The fact that west and east are one?

6. What meanings has the word "return" (12)? (Compare line 17.)

7. Japheth, Cham (or Ham), and Shem (20)—the sons of Noah—are in Christian legend the ancestors of the three races of man, roughly identifiable with the populations of Europe, Africa, and Asia. What must one go through, according to the speaker, to reach any place more important? In what ways are the Pacific Ocean, the East Indies, and Jerusalem (16–17) each a fitting symbol for the speaker's own destination?

8. The locations of the garden of Eden and of Calvary (21) were identical according to early Christian scholars. How does this tie in with the poem's geographical symbolism? What connection is there between Adam's "sweat" (24) and Christ's "blood" (25)? Because Adam is said in the Bible to prefigure Christ (Romans 5:12–21), Christ is sometimes called the second Adam. How do the two Adams meet in the speaker? What do blood and sweat (together and separately) symbolize?

9. For what are "eastern riches" (17), "his purple" (26), and "his thorns" (27) respectively metonymies? What do "purple" and "thorns" symbolize? What is Christ's "other crown" (27)?

10. With what earlier paradoxes (see Chapter 7) in the poem does the paradox in the final line (very roughly paraphrased from Psalms 146:8) tie in? What, according to Donne, is the explanation and meaning of human suffering?

67. UPHILL

Does the road wind uphill all the way?
 Yes, to the very end.
Will the day's journey take the whole long day?
 From morn to night, my friend.

But is there for the night a resting-place? 5
 A roof for when the slow dark hours begin.
May not the darkness hide it from my face?
 You cannot miss that inn.

Shall I meet other wayfarers at night?
    Those who have gone before.   10
Then must I knock, or call when just in sight?
    They will not keep you standing at that door.

Shall I find comfort, travel-sore and weak?
    Of labor you shall find the sum.
Will there be beds for me and all who seek?   15
    Yea, beds for all who come.

Christina Rossetti (1830–1894)

QUESTIONS

1. How many speakers has this poem? Who are they? Why did the poet not use quotation marks to indicate the change from one speaker to another?
2. What are the key symbols in the poem? What clues prompt the reader to interpret them symbolically? What do they symbolize?

68. DUST OF SNOW

The way a crow
Shook down on me
The dust of snow
From a hemlock tree

Has given my heart   5
A change of mood
And saved some part
Of a day I had rued.

Robert Frost (1874–1963)

69. SOFT SNOW

I walked abroad in a snowy day;
I asked the soft snow with me to play;
She played and she melted in all her prime,
And the winter called it a dreadful crime.

William Blake (1757–1827)

QUESTION

In what respects are the two preceding poems alike? In what respects are they essentially different?

Chapter seven

Figurative Language 3
Paradox, Overstatement, Understatement, Irony

Aesop tells the tale of a traveler who sought refuge with a Satyr on a bitter winter night. On entering the Satyr's lodging, he blew on his fingers, and was asked by the Satyr why he did it. "To warm them up," he explained. Later, on being served a piping hot bowl of porridge, he blew also on it, and again was asked why he did it. "To cool it off," he explained. The Satyr thereupon thrust him out of doors, for he would have nothing to do with a man who could blow hot and cold with the same breath.

A **paradox** is an apparent contradiction that is nevertheless somehow true. It may be either a situation or a statement. Aesop's tale of the traveler illustrates a paradoxical situation. As a figure of speech, paradox is a statement. When Alexander Pope wrote that a literary critic of his time would "damn with faint praise," he was using a verbal paradox, for how can a man damn by praising?

When we understand all the conditions and circumstances involved in a paradox, we find that what at first seemed impossible is actually entirely plausible and not strange at all. The paradox of the cold hands and hot porridge is not strange to anyone who knows that a stream of air directed upon an object of different temperature will tend to bring that object closer to its own temperature. And Pope's paradox is not strange when we realize that *damn* is being used figuratively, and that Pope means only that a too reserved praise may damage an author with the public almost as much as adverse criticism. In a paradoxical statement the contradiction usually stems from one of the words being used figuratively or in more than one sense.

The value of paradox is its shock value. Its seeming impossibility startles the reader into attention and, by the fact of its apparent absurdity, underscores the truth of what is being said.

70. MY LIFE CLOSED TWICE

My life closed twice before its close;
It yet remains to see
If Immortality unveil
A third event to me,

So huge, so hopeless to conceive,⠀⠀⠀⠀⠀⠀⠀⠀⠀5
As these that twice befell.
Parting is all we know of heaven,
And all we need of hell.

Emily Dickinson (1830–1886)

QUESTIONS

1. Do lines 2–6 mean: (a) I do not know yet whether there is a life after death—a continued existence in heaven and hell or (b) I do not know yet whether my entry into heaven or hell—whichever place I go—will be as "huge" an event as two events that have already happened to me during my life? Or both?
2. The poem sets forth two or possibly three paradoxes: (a) that the speaker's life closed twice before its close; (b) (if we accept the second alternative above) that death and entry into immortality may possibly be "lesser" events than two not extraordinary occurrences that happened during the speaker's lifetime; (c) that parting from a loved one is *both* heaven and hell. Resolve (that is, explain) each of these paradoxes.

Overstatement, understatement, and verbal irony form a continuous series, for they consist, respectively, of saying more, saying less, and saying the opposite of what one really means.

Overstatement, or *hyperbole,* is simply exaggeration, but exaggeration in the service of truth. It is not the same as a fish story. If you say, "I'm starved!" or "You could have knocked me over with a feather!" or "I'll die if I don't pass this course!" you do not expect to be believed; you are merely adding emphasis to what you really mean. (And if you say, "There were literally millions of people at the beach!" you are merely piling one overstatement on top of another, for you really mean that "There were figuratively millions of people at the beach," or, literally, "The beach was very crowded.") Like all figures of speech, overstatement may be used with a variety of effects. It may be humorous or grave, fanciful or restrained, convincing or unconvincing. When Tennyson says of his eagle (No. 1) that it is "*Close* to the sun in lonely lands," he says what appears to be literally true, though we know from our study of astronomy that it is not. When Wordsworth reports of his daffodils in "I wandered lonely as a cloud" (No. 260) that they "stretched *in never-ending line*" along the margin of a bay, he too reports faithfully a visual appearance. When Frost says, at the conclusion of "The Road Not Taken" (No. 55),

> I shall be telling this with a sigh
> Somewhere *ages and ages hence,*

we are scarcely aware of the overstatement, so quietly is the assertion made. Unskillfully used, however, overstatement may seem strained and ridiculous, leading us to react as Gertrude does to the player-queen's speeches in *Hamlet:* "The lady doth protest too much."

It is paradoxical that one can emphasize a truth either by overstating it or by understating it. **Understatement,** or saying less than one means, may exist in what one says or merely in how one says it. If, for instance, upon sitting down to a loaded dinner plate, you say, "This looks like a nice snack," you are actually stating less than the truth; but if you say, with Artemus Ward, that a man who holds his hand for half an hour in a lighted fire will experience "a sensation of excessive and disagreeable warmth," you are stating what is literally true but with a good deal less force than the situation might seem to warrant.

71. THE SUN RISING

Busy old fool, unruly sun,
  Why dost thou thus
Through windows and through curtains call on us?
Must to thy motions lovers' seasons run?
  Saucy pedantic wretch, go chide   5
  Late schoolboys and sour prentices,
  Go tell court-huntsmen that the king will ride,
  Call country ants to harvest offices;
Love, all alike, no season knows, nor clime,
Nor hours, days, months, which are the rags of time.   10

Thy beams so reverend and strong
Why shouldst thou think?
I could eclipse and cloud them with a wink,
But that I would not lose her sight so long;
If her eyes have not blinded thine, 15
Look, and tomorrow late tell me
Whether both th' Indias of spice and mine
Be where thou left'st them, or lie here with me.
Ask for those kings whom thou saw'st yesterday,
And thou shalt hear, "All here in one bed lay." 20

She's all states, and all princes I;
Nothing else is.
Princes do but play us; compared to this,
All honor's mimic, all wealth alchemy.
Thou, sun, art half as happy as we, 25
In that the world's contracted thus;
Thine age asks ease, and since thy duties be
To warm the world, that's done in warming us.
Shine here to us, and thou art everywhere;
This bed thy center is, these walls thy sphere. 30

John Donne (1572–1631)

QUESTIONS

1. Vocabulary: *offices* (8), *alchemy* (24).
2. As precisely as possible, identify the time and the locale. What three "persons" does the poem involve?
3. What is the speaker's attitude toward the sun in stanzas 1 and 2? How and why does it change in stanza 3?
4. Does the speaker understate or overstate the actual qualities of the sun? Point out specific examples. Identify the overstatements in lines 9–10, 13, 15, 16–20, 21–24, 29–30. What do these overstatements achieve?
5. Line 17 introduces a geographical image referring to the East and West Indies, sources respectively of spices and gold. What relationship between the lovers and the rest of the world is expressed in lines 15–22?
6. Who is actually the intended listener for this extended apostrophe? What is the speaker's purpose?

72. INCIDENT

Once riding in old Baltimore
Heart-filled, head-filled with glee,
I saw a Baltimorean
Keep looking straight at me.

Now I was eight and very small,   5
And he was no whit bigger,
And so I smiled, but he poked out
His tongue, and called me, "Nigger."

I saw the whole of Baltimore
From May until December;   10
Of all the things that happened there
That's all that I remember.

Countee Cullen (1903–1946)

QUESTION

What accounts for the effectiveness of the last stanza? Comment on the title. Is it in key with the meaning of the poem?

Like paradox, *irony* has meanings that extend beyond its use merely as a figure of speech.

Verbal irony, saying the opposite of what one means, is often confused with sarcasm and with satire, and for that reason it may be well to look at the meanings of all three terms. Sarcasm and satire both imply ridicule, one on the colloquial level, the other on the literary level. **Sarcasm** is simply bitter or cutting speech, intended to wound the feelings (it comes from a Greek word meaning to tear flesh). **Satire** is a more formal term, usually applied to written literature rather than to speech and ordinarily implying a higher motive: it is ridicule (either bitter or gentle) of human folly or vice, with the purpose of bringing about reform or at least of keeping other people from falling into similar folly or vice. Irony, on the other hand, is a literary device or figure that may be used in the service of sarcasm or ridicule or may not. It is popularly confused with sarcasm and satire because it is so often used as their tool; but irony may be used without either sarcastic or satirical intent, and sarcasm and satire may exist (though they do not usually) without irony. If, for instance, one of the members of your class raises his hand on the discussion of this point and says, "I don't understand," and your instructor replies, with a tone of heavy disgust in his voice, "Well, I wouldn't expect *you* to," he is being sarcastic but not ironic; he means exactly what he says. But if, after you have done particularly well on an examination, your instructor brings your test papers into the classroom saying, "Here's some *bad* news for you: you all got A's and B's!" he is being ironic but not sarcastic. Sarcasm, we may say, is cruel, as a bully is cruel: it intends to give hurt. Satire is both cruel and kind, as a surgeon is cruel and kind: it gives hurt in the interest of the patient or of society. Irony is neither cruel nor kind: it is simply a device, like a surgeon's scalpel, for performing any operation more skillfully.

Though verbal irony always implies the opposite of what is said, it has many gradations, and only in its simplest forms does it mean *only* the opposite of what is said. In more complex forms it means both what is said and the opposite of what is said, at once, though in different ways and with different degrees of emphasis. When Terence's critic, in "Terence, this is stupid stuff" (No. 8) says, "*Pretty* friendship 'tis to rhyme / Your friends to death before their time" (11–12), we may substitute the literal *sorry* for the ironic "pretty" with little or no loss of meaning. When Terence speaks in reply, however, of the pleasure of drunkenness—"And down in *lovely* muck I've lain, / Happy till I woke again" (35–36)—we cannot substitute *loathsome* for "lovely" without considerable loss of meaning, for, while muck is actually extremely unpleasant to lie in, it may *seem* lovely to an intoxicated person. Thus two meanings—one the opposite of the other—operate at once.

Like all figures of speech, verbal irony runs the danger of being misunderstood. With irony the risks are perhaps greater than with other figures, for if metaphor is misunderstood, the result may be simply bewilderment; but if irony is misunderstood, the reader goes away with exactly the opposite idea from what the user meant to convey. The results of misunderstanding if, for instance, you ironically called someone a villain, might be calamitous. For this reason the user of irony must be very skillful in its use, conveying by an altered tone, or by a wink of the eye or pen, that irony is intended; and the reader of literature must be always alert to recognize the subtle signs of irony.

No matter how broad or obvious the irony, there will always be in any large audience, a number who will misunderstand. The humorist Artemus Ward used to protect himself against these people by writing at the bottom of his newspaper column, "This is writ ironical." But irony is most delightful and most effective when it is subtlest. It sets up a special understanding between writer and reader that may add either grace or force. If irony is too obvious, it sometimes seems merely crude. But if effectively used, it, like all figurative language, is capable of adding extra dimensions to meaning.

73. ON A CERTAIN LADY AT COURT

I know the thing that's most uncommon—
    Envy, be silent, and attend!—
I know a reasonable woman,
    Handsome and witty, yet a friend.

Not warped by passion, awed by rumor,   5
Not grave through pride, or gay through folly,
An equal mixture of good humor,
And sensible soft melancholy.

"Has she no faults then," Envy says, "Sir?"
Yes, she has one, I must aver;   10
When all the world conspires to praise her,
The woman's deaf, and does not hear.

Alexander Pope (1688–1744)

QUESTIONS

1. Vocabulary: *attend* (2), *melancholy* (8), *conspires* (11).
2. Which line of the poem is ironic? To what purpose is irony put?
3. What other lines in the poem are figurative? Explain.

The term *irony* always implies some sort of discrepancy or incongruity. In verbal irony the discrepancy is between what is said and what is meant. In other forms the discrepancy may be between appearance and reality or between expectation and fulfillment. These other forms of irony are, on the whole, more important resources for the poet than is verbal irony. Two types are especially important.

In **dramatic irony*** the discrepancy is not between what the speaker says and what the speaker means but between what the speaker says and what the author means. The speaker's words may be perfectly straightforward, but the author, by putting these words in a particular speaker's mouth, may be indicating to the reader ideas or attitudes quite opposed to those the speaker is voicing. This form of irony is more complex than verbal irony and demands a more complex response from the reader. It may be used not only to convey attitudes but also to

---

*The term *dramatic irony*, which stems from Greek tragedy, often connotes something more specific and perhaps a little different from what I am developing here. It is used of a speech or an action in a story which has much greater significance to the audience than to the character who speaks or performs it, because of possession by the audience of knowledge the character does not have, as when the enemies of Ulysses, in the *Odyssey*, wish good luck and success to a man who the reader knows is Ulysses himself in disguise, or as when Oedipus, in the play by Sophocles, bends every effort to discover the murderer of Laius so that he may avenge the death, not knowing, as the audience does, that Laius is the man whom he himself once slew. I have appropriated the term for a perhaps slightly different situation, because no other suitable term exists. Both uses have the common characteristic—that the author conveys to the reader something different, or at least something more, than the character himself intends or understands.

illuminate character, for the author who uses it is indirectly commenting not only upon the value of the ideas uttered but also upon the nature of the person who utters them. Such comment may be harsh, gently mocking, or sympathetic.

74. THE CHIMNEY SWEEPER

When my mother died I was very young,
And my father sold me while yet my tongue
Could scarcely cry "'weep! 'weep! 'weep! 'weep!"
So your chimneys I sweep, and in soot I sleep.

There's little Tom Dacre, who cried when his head, 5
That curled like a lamb's back, was shaved; so I said,
"Hush, Tom! never mind it, for, when your head's bare,
You know that the soot cannot spoil your white hair."

And so he was quiet, and that very night,
As Tom was asleeping, he had such a sight! 10
That thousands of sweepers, Dick, Joe, Ned, and Jack,
Were all of them locked up in coffins of black.

And by came an Angel who had a bright key,
And he opened the coffins and set them all free;
Then down a green plain leaping, laughing, they run, 15
And wash in a river, and shine in the sun.

Then naked and white, all their bags left behind,
They rise upon clouds and sport in the wind;
And the Angel told Tom, if he'd be a good boy,
He'd have God for his father, and never want joy. 20

And so Tom awoke, and we rose in the dark,
And got with our bags and our brushes to work.
Though the morning was cold, Tom was happy and warm;
So if all do their duty they need not fear harm.

William Blake (1757–1827)

QUESTIONS

1. In the eighteenth century small boys, sometimes no more than four or five years old, were employed to climb up the narrow chimney flues and clean them, collecting the soot in bags. Such boys, sometimes sold to the master sweepers by their parents, were miserably treated by their masters and often suffered disease and physical deformity. Characterize the boy who speaks in

this poem. How do his and the poet's attitudes toward his lot in life differ? How, especially, are the meanings of the poet and the speaker different in lines 3, 7–8, and 24?

2. The dream in lines 11–20, besides being a happy dream, is capable of allegorical interpretations. Point out possible significances of the sweepers' being "locked up in coffins of black" and the Angel's releasing them with a bright key to play upon green plains.

A third type of irony, **irony of situation,** occurs when a discrepancy exists between the actual circumstances and those that would seem appropriate or between what one anticipates and what actually comes to pass. If a man and his second wife, on the first night of their honeymoon, are accidentally seated at the theater next to the man's first wife, we should call the situation ironic. When, in O. Henry's famous short story "The Gift of the Magi" a poor young husband pawns his most prized possession, a gold watch, in order to buy his wife a set of combs for her hair for Christmas, and his wife sells her most prized possession, her long brown hair, in order to buy a fob for her husband's watch, we call the situation ironic. When King Midas, in the famous fable, is granted his fondest wish, that anything he touch turn to gold, and then finds that he cannot eat because even his food turns to gold, we call the situation ironic. When Coleridge's Ancient Mariner finds himself in the middle of the ocean with "Water, water, everywhere" but not a "drop to drink," we call the situation ironic. In each case the circumstances are not what would seem appropriate or what we would expect.

Dramatic irony and irony of situation are powerful devices for poetry, for, like symbol, they enable it to suggest meanings without stating them—to communicate a great deal more than is said. We have seen one effective use of irony of situation in "Richard Cory" (No. 22). Another is in "Ozymandias," which follows.

Irony and paradox may be trivial or powerful devices, depending on their use. At their worst they may degenerate into mere mannerism and mental habit. At their best they may greatly extend the dimensions of meaning in a work of literature. Because irony and paradox demand an exercise of critical intelligence, they are particularly valuable as safeguards against sentimentality.

75. OZYMANDIAS

I met a traveler from an antique land
Who said: Two vast and trunkless legs of stone
Stand in the desert . . . Near them, on the sand,
Half sunk, a shattered visage lies, whose frown,

And wrinkled lip, and sneer of cold command,   5
Tell that its sculptor well those passions read
Which yet survive, stamped on these lifeless things,
The hand that mocked them, and the heart that fed;
And on the pedestal these words appear:
"My name is Ozymandias, king of kings;   10
Look on my works, ye Mighty, and despair!"
Nothing beside remains. Round the decay
Of that colossal wreck, boundless and bare
The lone and level sands stretch far away.

Percy Bysshe Shelley (1792–1822)

QUESTIONS

1. "Survive" (7) is a transitive verb with "hand" and "heart" as direct objects. Whose hand? Whose heart? What figure of speech is exemplified in "hand" and "heart"?
2. Characterize Ozymandias.
3. Ozymandias was an ancient Egyptian tyrant. This poem was first published in 1817. Of what is Ozymandias a *symbol?* What contemporary reference might the poem have had in Shelley's time?
4. What is the theme of the poem and how is it "stated"?

EXERCISE

Identify each of the following quotations as literal or figurative. If figurative, identify the figure as paradox, overstatement, understatement, or irony— and explain the use to which it is put (emotional emphasis, humor, satire, etc.).

1. Poetry is a language that tells us, through a more or less emotional reaction, something that cannot be said.   *Edwin Arlington Robinson*

2. Have not the Indians been kindly and justly treated? Have not the temporal things, the vain baubles and filthy lucre of this world, which were too apt to engage their worldly and selfish thoughts, been benevolently taken from them? And have they not instead thereof, been taught to set their affections on things above?   *Washington Irving*

3. A man who could make so vile a pun would not scruple to pick a pocket.   *John Dennis*

4. Last week I saw a woman flayed, and you will hardly believe how much it altered her person for the worse.   *Jonathan Swift*

5. . . . Where ignorance is bliss,
'Tis folly to be wise.   *Thomas Gray*

6. All night I made my bed to swim; with my tears I dissolved my couch.   *Psalms 6:6*

7. Believe him, he has known the world too long,
   And seen the death of much immortal song.   *Alexander Pope*

8. Give me my Romeo: and, when he shall die,
   Take him and cut him out in little stars,
   And he will make the face of heaven so fine
   That all the world will be in love with night,
   And pay no worship to the garish sun.   *Juliet, in Shakespeare*

9. Immortality will come to such as are fit for it; and he who would be a great
   soul in the future must be a great soul now.   *Ralph Waldo Emerson*

10. Whoe'er their crimes for interest only quit,
    Sin on in virtue, and good deeds *commit.*   *Edward Young*

*   *   *

76. BATTER MY HEART, THREE-PERSONED GOD

Batter my heart, three-personed God; for you
As yet but knock, breathe, shine, and seek to mend;
That I may rise and stand, o'erthrow me, and bend
Your force to break, blow, burn, and make me new.
I, like an usurped town, to another due,   5
Labor to admit you, but oh, to no end;
Reason, your viceroy in me, me should defend,
But is captived, and proves weak or untrue.
Yet dearly I love you and would be lovèd fain,°   gladly
But am betrothed unto your enemy;   10
Divorce me, untie or break that knot again,
Take me to you, imprison me, for I,
Except° you enthrall me, never shall be free,   unless
Nor ever chaste, except you ravish me.

John Donne (1572–1631)

QUESTIONS

1. In this sonnet (one in a group called "Holy Sonnets") the speaker addresses
   God in a series of metaphors and paradoxes. What is the paradox in the first
   quatrain? To what is the "three-personed God" metaphorically compared?
   To what is the speaker compared? Can the first three verbs of the parallel
   lines 2 and 4 be taken as addressed to specific "persons" of the Trinity
   (Father, Son, Holy Spirit)? If so, to which are "knock" and "break" addressed? "breathe" and "blow"? "shine" and "burn"? (What concealed
   pun helps in the attribution of the last pair? What etymological pun in the
   attribution of the second?)

2. To what does the speaker compare himself in the second quatrain? To what is God compared? Who is the usurper? What role does Reason play in this political metaphor, and why is it a weak one?

3. To what does the speaker compare himself in the sestet (lines 9–14)? To what does he compare God? Who is the "enemy" (10)? Resolve the paradox in lines 12–13 by explaining the double meaning of "enthrall." Resolve the paradox in line 14 by explaining the double meaning of "ravish."

77. LOVE POEM

My clumsiest dear, whose hands shipwreck vases,
At whose quick touch all glasses chip and ring,
Whose palms are bulls in china, burs in linen,
And have no cunning with any soft thing

Except all ill-at-ease fidgeting people: 5
The refugee uncertain at the door
You make at home; deftly you steady
The drunk clambering on his undulant floor.

Unpredictable dear, the taxi drivers' terror,
Shrinking from far headlights pale as a dime   10
Yet leaping before red apoplectic streetcars—
Misfit in any space. And never on time.

A wrench in clocks and the solar system. Only
With words and people and love you move at ease.
In traffic of wit expertly manoeuvre   15
And keep us, all devotion, at your knees.

Forgetting your coffee spreading on our flannel,
Your lipstick grinning on our coat,
So gayly in love's unbreakable heaven
Our souls on glory of spilt bourbon float.   20

Be with me, darling, early and late. Smash glasses—
I will study wry music for your sake.
For should your hands drop white and empty
All the toys of the world would break.

John Frederick Nims (b. 1913)

QUESTIONS

1. Overstatement is the traditional language of love poetry. Point out examples here. How does this poem differ from traditional love poems?

2. What is the meaning of the last two lines?

78. ON TREASON

Treason doth never prosper: what's the reason?
For if it prosper, none dare call it treason.

Sir John Harington (1561?–1612)

QUESTION

This two-line epigram is divided by its punctuation into four parts. Which of the four displays verbal irony?

79. FORMAL APPLICATION

"The poets apparently want to rejoin the human race." TIME

I shall begin by learning to throw
the knife, first at trees, until it sticks
in the trunk and quivers every time;

next from a chair, using only wrist
and fingers, at a thing on the ground,   5
a fresh ant hill or a fallen leaf;

then at a moving object, perhaps
a pieplate swinging on twine, until
I pot it at least twice in three tries.

Meanwhile, I shall be teaching the birds   10
that the skinny fellow in sneakers
is a source of suet and bread crumbs,

first putting them on a shingle nailed
to a pine tree, next scattering them
on the needles, closer and closer   15

to my seat, until the proper bird,
a towhee, I think, in black and rust
and gray, takes tossed crumbs six feet away.

Finally, I shall coordinate
conditioned reflex and functional   20
form and qualify as Modern Man.

You see the splash of blood and feathers
and the blade pinning it to the tree?
It's called an "Audubon Crucifix."

The phrase has pleasing (even pious)   25
connotations, like *Arbeit Macht Frei,*
"Molotov Cocktail," and *Enola Gay.*

Donald W. Baker (b. 1923)

QUESTIONS

1. This poem has an epigraph: a quotation following the title which relates to the theme of the poem or provides the stimulus which gave rise to its writing. How is this poem related to its epigraph? Who is the speaker?
2. What meanings has the title?
3. *Arbeit Macht Frei* (26) ("Labor liberates") was a slogan of the German Nazi Party, inscribed (among other places) at entrances to labor camps. "Molotov Cocktail" (27), a homemade hand grenade named after Stalin's foreign minister, was widely used during the Spanish Civil War and World War II. *Enola Gay* (27) was the American plane that dropped the first atom bomb on Hiroshima. In what ways are the connotations of these phrases—and of "Audubon Crucifix" (24)—"pleasing" (25)?
4. What different kinds of irony operate in this poem? Discuss.

80. THE UNKNOWN CITIZEN

(To JS/07/M/378 This Marble Monument Is Erected by the State)

He was found by the Bureau of Statistics to be
One against whom there was no official complaint,
And all the reports on his conduct agree
That, in the modern sense of an old-fashioned word, he was a saint,
For in everything he did he served the Greater Community.   5
Except for the War till the day he retired
He worked in a factory and never got fired,
But satisfied his employers, Fudge Motors Inc.
Yet he wasn't a scab or odd in his views,
For his Union reports that he paid his dues   10
(Our report on his Union shows it was sound),
And our Social Psychology workers found
That he was popular with his mates and liked a drink.
The Press are convinced that he bought a paper every day
And that his reactions to advertisements were normal in every way. 15
Policies taken out in his name prove that he was fully insured,
And his Health-card shows he was once in hospital but left it cured.
Both Producers Research and High-Grade Living declare
He was fully sensible to the advantages of the Installment Plan
And had everything necessary to the Modern Man,   20
A phonograph, a radio, a car and a frigidaire.

Our researchers into Public Opinion are content
That he held the proper opinions for the time of year;
When there was peace, he was for peace; when there was war, he went.
He was married and added five children to the population,   25
Which our Eugenist says was the right number for a parent of
his generation,
And our teachers report that he never interfered with their education.
Was he free? Was he happy? The question is absurd:
Had anything been wrong, we should certainly have heard.

W. H. Auden (1907–1973)

QUESTIONS

1. Vocabulary: *scab* (9), *Eugenist* (26).
2. Explain the allusion and the irony in the title. Why was the citizen "unknown"?
3. This obituary of an unknown state "hero" was apparently prepared by a functionary of the state. Give an account of the citizen's life and character from Auden's own point of view.
4. What trends in modern life and social organization does the poem satirize?

81. DEPARTMENTAL

An ant on the tablecloth
Ran into a dormant moth
Of many times his size.
He showed not the least surprise.
His business wasn't with such.   5
He gave it scarcely a touch,
And was off on his duty run.
Yet if he encountered one
Of the hive's enquiry squad
Whose work is to find out God   10
And the nature of time and space,
He would put him onto the case.
Ants are a curious race;
One crossing with hurried tread
The body of one of their dead   15
Isn't given a moment's arrest—
Seems not even impressed.
But he no doubt reports to any
With whom he crosses antennae,
And they no doubt report   20
To the higher up at court.
Then word goes forth in Formic:

"Death's come to Jerry McCormic,
Our selfless forager Jerry.
Will the special Janizary   25
Whose office it is to bury
The dead of the commissary
Go bring him home to his people.
Lay him in state on a sepal.
Wrap him for shroud in a petal.   30
Embalm him with ichor of nettle.
This is the word of your Queen."
And presently on the scene
Appears a solemn mortician;
And taking formal position   35
With feelers calmly atwiddle,
Seizes the dead by the middle,
And heaving him high in air,
Carries him out of there.
No one stands round to stare.   40
It is nobody else's affair.

It couldn't be called ungentle.
But how thoroughly departmental.

Robert Frost (1874–1963)

QUESTIONS

1. Vocabulary: *dormant* (2), *Formic* (22), *Janizary* (25), *commissary* (27), *sepal* (29), *ichor* (31).
2. The poem is ostensibly about ants. Is it ultimately about ants? Give reasons to support your view that it is or is not.
3. What is the author's attitude toward the "departmental" organization of ant society? How is it indicated? Could this poem be described as "gently satiric"? If so, in what sense?
4. Compare and contrast this poem with "The Unknown Citizen" in content and manner.

82. MR. Z

Taught early that his mother's skin was the sign of error,
He dressed and spoke the perfect part of honor;
Won scholarships, attended the best schools,
Disclaimed kinship with jazz and spirituals;
Chose prudent, raceless views of each situation,   5
Or when he could not cleanly skirt dissension,
Faced up to the dilemma, firmly seized
Whatever ground was Anglo-Saxonized.

In diet, too, his practice was exemplary:
Of pork in its profane forms he was wary;   10
Expert in vintage wines, sauces and salads,
His palate shrank from cornbread, yams and collards.

He was as careful whom he chose to kiss:
His bride had somewhere lost her Jewishness,
But kept her blue eyes; an Episcopalian   15
Prelate proclaimed them matched chameleon.
Choosing the right addresses, here, abroad,
They shunned those places where they might be barred;
Even less anxious to be asked to dine
Where hosts catered to kosher accent or exotic skin.   20

And so he climbed, unclogged by ethnic weights,
An airborne plant, flourishing without roots.
Not one false note was struck—until he died:
His subtly grieving widow could have flayed
The obit writers, ringing crude changes on a clumsy phrase: 25
"One of the most distinguished members of his race."

M. Carl Holman (b. 1919)

QUESTIONS

1. Vocabulary: *profane* (10), *kosher* (20), *exotic* (20), *ethnic* (21), *obit* (25).
2. Explain Mr. Z's motivation and the strategies he used to achieve his goal.
3. What is the author's attitude toward Mr. Z? Is he satirizing him or the society that produced him? Why does he not give Mr. Z a name?
4. What judgments on Mr. Z are implied by the metaphors in lines 16 and 22? Explain them.
5. What kind of irony is operating in the last line? As you reread the poem, where else do you detect ironic overtones?
6. What is Mr. Z's color?

83. MY LAST DUCHESS

FERRARA

That's my last duchess painted on the wall,
Looking as if she were alive. I call
That piece a wonder, now; Fra Pandolf's hands
Worked busily a day, and there she stands.
Will't please you sit and look at her? I said   5
"Fra Pandolf" by design, for never read
Strangers like you that pictured countenance,

The depth and passion of its earnest glance,
But to myself they turned (since none puts by
The curtain I have drawn for you, but I)   10
And seemed as they would ask me, if they durst,
How such a glance came there; so, not the first
Are you to turn and ask thus. Sir, 'twas not
Her husband's presence only, called that spot
Of joy into the Duchess' cheek; perhaps   15
Fra Pandolf chanced to say, "Her mantle laps
Over my lady's wrist too much," or, "Paint
Must never hope to reproduce the faint
Half-flush that dies along her throat." Such stuff
Was courtesy, she thought, and cause enough   20
For calling up that spot of joy. She had
A heart—how shall I say?—too soon made glad,
Too easily impressed; she liked whate'er
She looked on, and her looks went everywhere.
Sir, 'twas all one! My favor at her breast,   25
The dropping of the daylight in the West,
The bough of cherries some officious fool
Broke in the orchard for her, the white mule
She rode with round the terrace—all and each
Would draw from her alike the approving speech,   30
Or blush, at least. She thanked men—good! but thanked
Somehow—I know not how—as if she ranked
My gift of a nine-hundred-years-old name
With anybody's gift. Who'd stoop to blame
This sort of trifling? Even had you skill   35
In speech—which I have not—to make your will
Quite clear to such an one, and say, "Just this
Or that in you disgusts me; here you miss,
Or there exceed the mark"—and if she let
Herself be lessoned so, nor plainly set   40
Her wits to yours, forsooth, and made excuse—
E'en then would be some stooping; and I choose
Never to stoop. Oh, sir, she smiled, no doubt,
Whene'er I passed her; but who passed without
Much the same smile? This grew; I gave commands;   45
Then all smiles stopped together. There she stands
As if alive. Will 't please you rise? We'll meet
The company below, then. I repeat,
The Count your master's known munificence
Is ample warrant that no just pretense   50
Of mine for dowry will be disallowed;
Though his fair daughter's self, as I avowed

At starting, is my object. Nay, we'll go
Together down, sir. Notice Neptune, though,
Taming a sea-horse, thought a rarity, 55
Which Claus of Innsbruck cast in bronze for me!

Robert Browning (1812–1889)

QUESTIONS

1. Vocabulary: *officious* (27), *munificence* (49).
2. Ferrara is in Italy. The time is during the Renaissance, probably the sixteenth century. To whom is the Duke speaking? What is the occasion? Are the Duke's remarks about his last Duchess a digression, or do they have some relation to the business at hand?
3. Characterize the Duke as fully as you can. How does your characterization differ from the Duke's opinion of himself? What kind of irony is this?
4. Why was the Duke dissatisfied with his last Duchess? Was it sexual jealousy? What opinion do you get of the Duchess's personality, and how does it differ from the Duke's opinion?
5. What characteristics of the Italian Renaissance appear in the poem (marriage customs, social classes, art)? What is the Duke's attitude toward art? Is it insincere?
6. What happened to the Duchess? Should we have been told?

EXERCISE

Follow the instructions for the exercise on page 107, of which this is a continuation.

11. No doubt but ye are the people, and wisdom shall die with you.
    Book of Job, 12:1

12. One soul was ours, one mind, one heart devoted,
    That, wisely doting, asked not why it doted. *Hartley Coleridge*

13. Cowards die many times before their deaths;
    The valiant never die but once. *William Shakespeare*

14. . . . all men would be cowards if they durst.
    John Wilmot, Earl of Rochester

15. Christians have burnt each other, quite persuaded
    That all the Apostles would have done as they did. *Lord Byron*

16. There lives more faith in honest doubt,
    Believe me, than in half the creeds. *Alfred, Lord Tennyson*

Chapter eight
Allusion

The famous English diplomat and letter writer Lord Chesterfield was once invited to a great dinner given by the Spanish ambassador. At the conclusion of the meal the host rose and proposed a toast to his master, the king of Spain, whom he compared to the sun. The French ambassador followed with a health to the king of France, whom he likened to the moon. It was then Lord Chesterfield's turn. "Your excellencies have taken from me," he said, "all the greatest luminaries of heaven, and the stars are too small for me to make a comparison of my royal master; I therefore beg leave to give your excellencies—Joshua!"*

For a reader familiar with the Bible—that is, for one who recognizes the Biblical allusion—Lord Chesterfield's story will come as a stunning revelation of his wit. For an **allusion**—a reference to something in history or previous literature—is, like a richly connotative word or a symbol, a means of suggesting far more than it says. The one word "Joshua," in the context of Chesterfield's toast, calls up in the reader's mind the whole Biblical story of how the Israelite captain stopped the sun and the moon in order that the Israelites might finish a battle and conquer their enemies before nightfall.† The force of the toast lies in its extreme economy; it says so much in so little, and it exercises the mind of the reader to make the connection for himself.

---

*Samuel Shellabarger, *Lord Chesterfield and His World* (Boston: Little, Brown, 1951), p. 132.

†Joshua 10:12–14.

The effect of Chesterfield's allusion is chiefly humorous or witty, but allusions may also have a powerful emotional effect. The essayist William Hazlitt writes of addressing a fashionable audience about the lexicographer Samuel Johnson. Speaking of Johnson's great heart and of his charity to the unfortunate, Hazlitt recounted how, finding a drunken prostitute lying in Fleet Street late at night, Johnson carried her on his broad back to the address she managed to give him. The audience, unable to face the picture of the famous dictionary-maker doing such a thing, broke out in titters and expostulations. Whereupon Hazlitt simply said: "I remind you, ladies and gentlemen, of the parable of the Good Samaritan." The audience was promptly silenced.*

Allusions are a means of reinforcing the emotion or the ideas of one's own work with the emotion or ideas of another work or occasion. Because they are capable of saying so much in so little, they are extremely useful to the poet.

84. "OUT, OUT—"

The buzz-saw snarled and rattled in the yard
And made dust and dropped stove-length sticks of wood,
Sweet-scented stuff when the breeze drew across it.
And from there those that lifted eyes could count
Five mountain ranges one behind the other   5
Under the sunset far into Vermont.
And the saw snarled and rattled, snarled and rattled,
As it ran light, or had to bear a load.
And nothing happened: day was all but done.
Call it a day, I wish they might have said   10
To please the boy by giving him the half hour
That a boy counts so much when saved from work.
His sister stood beside them in her apron
To tell them "Supper." At the word, the saw,
As if to prove saws knew what supper meant,   15
Leaped out at the boy's hand, or seemed to leap—
He must have given the hand. However it was,
Neither refused the meeting. But the hand!
The boy's first outcry was a rueful laugh,
As he swung toward them holding up the hand   20
Half in appeal, but half as if to keep
The life from spilling. Then the boy saw all—
Since he was old enough to know, big boy

* Jacques Barzun, *Teacher in America* (Boston: Little, Brown, 1945), p. 160.

Doing a man's work, though a child at heart—
He saw all spoiled. "Don't let him cut my hand off—   25
The doctor, when he comes. Don't let him, sister!"
So. But the hand was gone already.
The doctor put him in the dark of ether.
He lay and puffed his lips out with his breath.
And then—the watcher at his pulse took fright.   30
No one believed. They listened at his heart.
Little—less—nothing!—and that ended it.
No more to build on there. And they, since they
Were not the one dead, turned to their affairs.

Robert Frost (1874–1963)

QUESTIONS

1. How does this poem differ from a newspaper account that might have dealt with the same incident?
2. To whom does "they" (33) refer? The boy's family? The doctor and medical attendants? Casual onlookers? Need we assume that all these people— whoever they are—turned immediately "to their affairs"? Does the ending of this poem seem to you callous or merely realistic? Would a more tearful and sentimental ending have made the poem better or worse?
3. What figure of speech is used in lines 21–22?

Allusions vary widely in the burden put on them by the poet to convey his meaning. Lord Chesterfield risked his whole meaning on his hearers' recognizing his allusion. Robert Frost in "Out, Out—" makes his meaning entirely clear even for the reader who does not recognize the allusion contained in his title. His theme is the uncertainty and unpredictability of life, which may be accidentally ended at any moment, and the tragic waste of human potentiality which takes place when such premature deaths occur. A boy who is already "doing a man's work" and gives every promise of having a useful life ahead of him is suddenly wiped out. There seems no rational explanation for either the accident or the death. The only comment to be made is, "No more to build on there."

Frost's title, however, is an allusion to one of the most famous passages in all English literature, and it offers a good illustration of how a poet may use allusion not only to reinforce emotion but also to help define his theme. The passage is that in *Macbeth* in which Macbeth has just been informed of his wife's death. A good many readers will recall the key phrase, "Out, out, brief candle!" with its underscoring of the tragic brevity and uncertainty of life that can be snuffed out at any moment. For some readers, however, the allusion will summon up the whole passage in Act V, scene 5, in which this phrase occurs. Macbeth's words are:

85.
         She should have died hereafter;
         There would have been a time for such a word.
         To-morrow, and to-morrow, and to-morrow
         Creeps in this petty pace from day to day
         To the last syllable of recorded time;   5
         And all our yesterdays have lighted fools
         The way to dusty death. Out, out, brief candle!
         Life's but a walking shadow, a poor player,
         That struts and frets his hour upon the stage
         And then is heard no more. It is a tale   10
         Told by an idiot, full of sound and fury,
         Signifying nothing.

Macbeth's first words underscore the theme of premature death. The boy also "should have died hereafter." The rest of the passage, with its marvelous evocation of the vanity and meaninglessness of life, expresses neither Shakespeare's philosophy nor, ultimately, Frost's, but it is Macbeth's philosophy at the time of his bereavement, and it is likely to express the feelings of us all when such tragic accidents occur. Life does indeed seem cruel and meaningless, a tale told by an idiot, signifying nothing, when human life and potentiality are thus without explanation so suddenly ended.

Allusions vary widely in the number of readers to whom they will be familiar. The poet, in using an allusion as in using a figure of speech, is always in danger of not being understood. In appealing powerfully to one reader, he may lose another reader altogether. But the poet must assume a certain fund of common experience with his readers. He could not even write about the ocean unless he could assume that his readers had seen the ocean or pictures of it. In the same way he will assume a certain common fund of literary experience, most frequently of classical mythology, Shakespeare, and the Bible. He is often justified in expecting a rather wide range of literary experience in his readers, for the people who read poetry for pleasure are generally people of good minds and good education who have read widely. But, obviously, beginning readers will not have this range, just as they will not know the meanings of as many words as will more mature readers. Students should therefore be prepared to look up certain allusions, just as they should be eager to look up in their dictionaries the meanings of unfamiliar words. They will find that every increase in knowledge broadens their base for understanding both literature and life.

86. IN JUST-

in Just-
spring   when the world is mud-
luscious the little
lame balloonman

whistles   far   and wee   5

and eddieandbill come
running from marbles and
piracies and it's
spring

when the world is puddle-wonderful   10

the queer
old balloonman whistles
far   and   wee
and bettyandisbel come dancing

from hop-scotch and jump-rope and   15

it's
spring
and
    the

        goat-footed   20

balloonMan   whistles
far
and
wee

e. e. cummings (1894–1962)

QUESTION

Why is the balloonman called "goat-footed"? How does the identification made by this mythological allusion enrich the meaning of the poem?

87. ON HIS BLINDNESS

When I consider how my light is spent
  Ere half my days in this dark world and wide,
  And that one talent which is death to hide
  Lodged with me useless, though my soul more bent
To serve therewith my Maker, and present   5
  My true account, lest he returning chide,
  "Doth God exact day-labor, light denied?"
  I fondly ask. But Patience, to prevent
That murmur, soon replies, "God doth not need
  Either man's work or his own gifts. Who best   10
  Bear his mild yoke, they serve him best. His state
Is kingly: thousands at his bidding speed,
  And post o'er land and ocean without rest;
  They also serve who only stand and wait."

John Milton (1608–1674)

QUESTIONS

1. Vocabulary: *spent* (1), *fondly* (8), *prevent* (8), *post* (13).
2. What two meanings has "talent" (3)? What is Milton's "one talent"?
3. The poem is unified and expanded in its dimensions by a Biblical allusion that Milton's original readers would have recognized immediately. What is it? If you do not know, look up Matthew 25:14–30. In what ways is the situation in the poem similar to that in the parable? In what ways is it different?
4. What is the point of the poem?

88. HERO AND LEANDER

Both robbed of air, we both lie in one ground,
Both whom one fire had burnt, one water drowned.

John Donne (1572–1631)

QUESTIONS

1. After looking up the story of Hero and Leander (if necessary), explain each of the four parts into which this epigram is divided by its punctuation. Which parts are literal? Which are metaphorical?
2. The subject of the poem is taken from Greek legend; its structure is based on Greek science. Explain.

89. LAST STAND

When the alarm came
He saddled up his fence,
Took the bit in his teeth
And mounted.
Closing his eyes
He put his ear to the ground
And waited, trembling, for the sound
Of the approaching windmills.

Keith Jennison (b. 1911)

QUESTIONS

1. This poem is full of trite phrases, either used entire or alluded to. Identify them. Do they add up to a trite poem? Explain.
2. Is the image created by these trite metaphors visually consistent? Poetically valid? Explain.
3. Behind two of the trite phrases are respectively a historical allusion and a literary allusion. How does the subject of the poem resemble and how does it differ from the subject of the literary allusion? Are these allusions used directly or ironically?

90. MINIVER CHEEVY

Miniver Cheevy, child of scorn,
    Grew lean while he assailed the seasons;
He wept that he was ever born,
    And he had reasons.

Miniver loved the days of old   5
    When swords were bright and steeds were prancing;
The vision of a warrior bold
    Would set him dancing.

Miniver sighed for what was not,
    And dreamed, and rested from his labors;   10
He dreamed of Thebes and Camelot,
    And Priam's neighbors.

Miniver mourned the ripe renown
    That made so many a name so fragrant;
He mourned Romance, now on the town,   15
    And Art, a vagrant.

Miniver loved the Medici,
   Albeit he had never seen one;
He would have sinned incessantly
   Could he have been one.   20

Miniver cursed the commonplace
   And eyed a khaki suit with loathing;
He missed the medieval grace
   Of iron clothing.

Miniver scorned the gold he sought,   25
   But sore annoyed was he without it;
Miniver thought, and thought, and thought,
   And thought about it.

Miniver Cheevy, born too late,
   Scratched his head and kept on thinking;   30
Miniver coughed, and called it fate,
   And kept on drinking.

                              Edwin Arlington Robinson (1869–1935)

QUESTIONS

1. Vocabulary: *khaki* (22). The phrase "on the town" (15) means "on charity" or "down and out."
2. Identify Thebes, Camelot (11), Priam (12), and the Medici (17). What names and what sort of life does each call up? What does Miniver's love of these names tell about him?
3. Discuss the phrase "child of scorn" (1). What does it mean? In how many ways is it applicable to Miniver?
4. What is Miniver's attitude toward material wealth?
5. Identify a Biblical allusion *and* an allusion to Greek mythology in the phrase "rested from his labors" (10). What is the effect of comparing Miniver to the Creator (Genesis 2:2)? To Hercules? Point out other examples of irony in the poem, and discuss their importance.
6. Can we call this a poem about a man whose "fate" was to be "born too late"? Explain your answer.

91. LEDA AND THE SWAN

A sudden blow: the great wings beating still
Above the staggering girl, her thighs caressed
By the dark webs, her nape caught in his bill,
He holds her helpless breast upon his breast.

How can those terrified vague fingers push   5
The feathered glory from her loosening thighs?
And how can body, laid in that white rush,
But feel the strange heart beating where it lies?

A shudder in the loins engenders there
The broken wall, the burning roof and tower   10
And Agamemnon dead.
                          Being so caught up,
So mastered by the brute blood of the air,
Did she put on his knowledge with his power
Before the indifferent beak could let her drop?

William Butler Yeats (1865–1939)

QUESTIONS

1. What is the connection between Leda and "the broken wall, the burning
   roof and tower / And Agamemnon dead"? If you do not know, look up the
   myth of Leda, and, if necessary, the story of Agamemnon.
2. What is the significance of the question asked in the last two lines?

92. JOURNEY OF THE MAGI

"A cold coming we had of it,
Just the worst time of the year
For a journey, and such a long journey:
The ways deep and the weather sharp,
The very dead of winter."   5
And the camels galled, sore-footed, refractory,
Lying down in the melting snow.
There were times we regretted
The summer palaces on slopes, the terraces,
And the silken girls bringing sherbet.   10
Then the camel men cursing and grumbling
And running away, and wanting their liquor and women,
And the night-fires going out, and the lack of shelters,
And the cities hostile and the towns unfriendly
And the villages dirty and charging high prices: 15
A hard time we had of it.
At the end we preferred to travel all night,
Sleeping in snatches,
With the voices singing in our ears, saying
That this was all folly.   20

Then at dawn we came down to a temperate valley,
Wet, below the snow line, smelling of vegetation;
With a running stream and a water-mill beating the darkness,
And three trees on the low sky,
And an old white horse galloped away in the meadow.   25
Then we came to a tavern with vine-leaves over the lintel,
Six hands at an open door dicing for pieces of silver,
And feet kicking the empty wine-skins.
But there was no information, and so we continued
And arrived at evening, not a moment too soon   30
Finding the place; it was (you may say) satisfactory.

    All this was a long time ago, I remember,
And I would do it again, but set down
This set down
This: were we led all that way for   35
Birth or Death? There was a Birth, certainly,
We had evidence and no doubt. I had seen birth and death,
But had thought they were different; this Birth was
Hard and bitter agony for us, like Death, our death.
We returned to our places, these Kingdoms,   40
But no longer at ease here, in the old dispensation,
With an alien people clutching their gods.
I should be glad of another death.

T. S. Eliot (1888–1965)

QUESTIONS

1. The Biblical account of the journey of the Magi, or wise men, to Bethlehem
   is given in Matthew 2:1–12 and has since been elaborated by numerous
   legendary accretions. It has been made familiar through countless pageants
   and Christmas cards. How does this account differ from the familiar one?
   Compare it with the Biblical account. What has been added? What has been
   left out? What is the poet doing? (Lines 1–5 are in quotation marks because
   they are taken, with very slight modification, from a Christmas sermon
   [1622] by the Anglican bishop Lancelot Andrewes.)
2. Who is the speaker? Where and when is he speaking? What is the "old
   dispensation" (41) to which he refers, and why are the people "alien" (42)?
   Why does he speak of the "Birth" as being "like Death" (39)? Of whose
   "Birth" and "Death" is he speaking? How does his life differ from the life
   he lived before his journey? What does he mean by saying that he would be
   "glad of another death"(43)?
3. This poem was written while the poet was undergoing religious conversion.
   (Eliot published it in 1927, the year he was confirmed in the Anglican
   Church.) Could the poem be considered a parable of the conversion experi-

ence? If so, how does this account differ from popular conceptions of this experience?
4. How do the images in the second section differ from those of the first? Do any of them suggest connections with the life of Christ?

93. ABRAHAM TO KILL HIM

Abraham to kill him
Was distinctly told.
Isaac was an urchin,
Abraham was old.

Not a hesitation—   5
Abraham complied.
Flattered by obeisance,
Tyranny demurred.

Isaac, to his children
Lived to tell the tale.   10
Moral: with a mastiff
Manners may prevail.

Emily Dickinson (1830–1886)

QUESTIONS

1. Vocabulary: *obeisance* (7), *demurred* (8).
2. To whom or to what do "Tyranny" (8) and "mastiff" (11) refer? What figure of speech is each?
3. Who are Abraham and Isaac? What, in the context of the original story, does "demurred" mean? If you cannot answer these questions, read Genesis 22:1–18.
4. What is the reaction of the poet toward this Bible story?

94. BELSHAZZAR HAD A LETTER

Belshazzar had a letter.
He never had but one.
Belshazzar's correspondent
Concluded and begun
In that immortal copy
The conscience of us all
Can read without its glasses
On revelation's wall.

Emily Dickinson (1830–1886)

1. Who was Belshazzar? Who was his correspondent? What was the nature of his letter, and where did it appear? If you need help, read Daniel 5.
2. What does the poem say about conscience and revelation?
3. Compare or contrast the tone of this poem with that of the preceding one.

95. IN THE GARDEN

In the garden there strayed
A beautiful maid
As fair as the flowers of the morn;
The first hour of her life
She was made a man's wife,
And was buried before she was born.

Anonymous

QUESTION

Resolve the paradox by identifying the allusion.

EXERCISE

An allusion may be offered as a comparison or parallel, or it may be used as an ironic contrast. In the following examples, is the poet using allusion positively, to extend and enrich the theme, or ironically, to undercut the speaker's ideas?
1. Evans, "When in Rome," No. 14 (allusion to the maxim, "When in Rome, do as the Romans do").
2. Larkin, "A Study of Reading Habits," No. 18 (allusions to the types of cheap fiction read by the speaker).
3. Hardy, "Channel Firing," No. 212 (lines 35–36, allusions identified in the footnote).
4. Keats, "Ode to a Nightingale," No. 219 (line 66, allusion to the Book of Ruth).
5. Ammons, "Providence," No. 190 (allusion to Frost's "Nothing Gold Can Stay," No. 131).

Chapter nine
Meaning and Idea

96. LITTLE JACK HORNER

Little Jack Horner
Sat in a corner
Eating a Christmas pie.
He stuck in his thumb
And pulled out a plum
And said, "What a good boy am I!"

Anonymous

The meaning of a poem is the experience it expresses—nothing less. But readers who, baffled by a particular poem, ask perplexedly, "What does it *mean*?" are usually after something more specific than this. They want something they can grasp entirely with their minds. We may therefore find it useful to distinguish the **total meaning** of a poem—the experience it communicates (and which can be communicated in no other way)—from its **prose meaning**—the ingredient that can be separated out in the form of a prose paraphrase (see Chapter 2). If we make this distinction, however, we must be careful not to confuse the two kinds of meaning. The prose meaning is no more the poem than a plum is a pie or than a prune is a plum.

The prose meaning will not necessarily or perhaps even usually be an idea. It may be a story, it may be a description, it may be a statement of emotion, it may be a presentation of human character, or it may be some combination of these. "The Mill" (by Robinson, No. 16) tells a story; "The Eagle" (No. 1) and "A Hummingbird" (No. 45) are primarily descriptive; "Bereft" (No. 41) and "Those Winter Sundays" (No. 35) are expressions of emotion; "A Study of Reading Habits" (No. 18) and "My Last Duchess" (No. 83) are accounts of human character. None of these poems is directly concerned with ideas. Message hunters will be baffled and disappointed by poetry of this kind, for they will not find what they are looking for, and they may attempt to read some idea into the poem that is really not there. Yet ideas are also part of human experience, and therefore many poems are concerned, at least partially, with presenting ideas. But with these poems message-hunting is an even more dangerous activity, for the message hunters are likely to think that the whole object of reading the poem is to find the message—that the idea is really the only important thing in it. Like Little Jack Horner, they will reach in and pluck out the idea and say, "What a good boy am I!" as if the pie existed for the plum.

The idea in a poem is only part of the total experience that it communicates. The value and worth of the poem are determined by the value of the total experience, not by the truth or the nobility of the idea itself. This is not to say that the truth of the idea is unimportant, or that its validity should not be examined and appraised. But a good idea alone will not make a good poem, nor need an idea with which the reader does not agree ruin one. Good readers of poetry are receptive to all kinds of experience. They are able to make that "willing suspension of disbelief" that Coleridge characterized as constituting poetic faith. When one attends a performance of *Hamlet*, one is willing to forget for the time being that such a person as Hamlet never existed and that the events on the stage are fictions. The reader of poetry should also be willing to entertain imaginatively, for the time being, ideas he objectively regards as untrue. It is one way of understanding these ideas better and of enlarging the reader's own experience. The person who believes in God should be able to enjoy a good poem expressing atheistic ideas, just as the atheist should be able to appreciate a good poem in praise of God. The optimist should be able to find pleasure in pessimistic poetry, and the pessimist in optimistic poetry. The teetotaler should be able to enjoy "The Rubáiyát of Omar Khayyám," and the winebibber a good poem in praise of austerity. The primary value of a poem depends not so much on the truth of the idea presented as on the power with which it is communicated and on its being made a convincing part of a meaningful total experience. We must feel that the idea has been truly and deeply *felt* by the poet, and that the poet is doing something more than merely moralizing. The plum must be made part of a pie. If the plum is properly combined with other ingredients and if the pie is well baked, it should be enjoyable even for persons who do not care for the brand of plums from which it is made. Consider, for instance, the following two poems.

97. BARTER

Life has loveliness to sell,
    All beautiful and splendid things,
Blue waves whitened on a cliff,
    Soaring fire that sways and sings,
And children's faces looking up,   5
Holding wonder like a cup.

Life has loveliness to sell,
    Music like a curve of gold,
Scent of pine trees in the rain,
    Eyes that love you, arms that hold,   10
And for your spirit's still delight,
Holy thoughts that star the night.

Spend all you have for loveliness,
    Buy it and never count the cost;
For one white singing hour of peace   15
    Count many a year of strife well lost,
And for a breath of ecstasy
Give all you have been, or could be.

Sara Teasdale (1884–1933)

98. STOPPING BY WOODS ON A SNOWY EVENING

Whose woods these are I think I know.
His house is in the village though;
He will not see me stopping here
To watch his woods fill up with snow.

My little horse must think it queer   5
To stop without a farmhouse near
Between the woods and frozen lake
The darkest evening of the year.

He gives his harness bells a shake
To ask if there is some mistake.   10
The only other sound's the sweep
Of easy wind and downy flake.

The woods are lovely, dark and deep,
But I have promises to keep,
And miles to go before I sleep,   15
And miles to go before I sleep.

Robert Frost (1874–1963)

QUESTIONS

1. How do these two poems differ in idea?
2. What contrasts are suggested between the speaker in the second poem and
   (a) his horse and (b) the owner of the woods?

Both of these poems present ideas, the first more or less explicitly, the second symbolically. Perhaps the best way to get at the idea of the second poem is to ask two questions. First, why does the speaker stop? Second, why does he go on? He stops, we answer, to watch the woods fill up with snow—to observe a scene of natural beauty. He goes on, we answer, because he has "promises to keep"—that is, he has obligations to fulfill. He is momentarily torn between his love of beauty and these other various and complex claims that life has upon him. The small conflict in the poem is symbolic of a larger conflict in life. One part of the sensitive thinking person would like to give up his life to the enjoyment of beauty and art. But another part is aware of larger duties and responsibilities—responsibilities owed, at least in part, to other human beings. The speaker in the poem would like to satisfy both impulses. But when the two conflict, he seems to suggest, the "promises" must be given precedence.

The first poem also presents a philosophy but an opposed one. For this poet, beauty is of such supreme value that any conflicting demand should be sacrificed to it. "Spend all you have for loveliness, / Buy it and never count the cost . . . And for a breath of ecstasy / Give all you have been, or could be." Thoughtful readers will have to choose between these two philosophies—to commit themselves to one or the other—but this commitment should not destroy for them their enjoyment of either poem. If it does, they are reading for plums and not for pies.

Nothing so far said in this chapter should be construed as meaning that the truth or falsity of the idea in a poem is a matter of no importance. *Other things being equal,* good readers naturally will, and properly should, value more highly the poem whose idea they feel to be more mature and nearer to the heart of human experience. Some ideas, moreover, may seem so vicious or so foolish or so beyond the pale of normal human decency as to discredit *by themselves* the poems in which they are found. A rotten plum may spoil a pie. But good readers strive for intellectual flexibility and tolerance, and are able to entertain sympathetically ideas other than their own. They will often like a poem whose idea they disagree with better than one with an idea they accept. And, above all, they will not confuse the prose meaning of any poem with its total meaning. They will not mistake plums for pies.

*　　　　　*　　　　　*

99. TO A WATERFOWL

Whither, midst falling dew,
While glow the heavens with the last steps of day,
Far, through their rosy depths, dost thou pursue
    Thy solitary way?

Vainly the fowler's eye 5
Might mark thy distant flight to do thee wrong,
As, darkly seen against the crimson sky,
    Thy figure floats along.

Seek'st thou the plashy brink
Of weedy lake, or marge of river wide, 10
Or where the rocking billows rise and sink
    On the chafed ocean side?

There is a Power whose care
Teaches thy way along that pathless coast—
The desert and illimitable air— 15
    Lone wandering, but not lost.

All day thy wings have fanned,
At that far height, the cold, thin atmosphere,
Yet stoop not, weary, to the welcome land,
    Though the dark night is near. 20

And soon that toil shall end;
Soon shalt thou find a summer home, and rest,
And scream among thy fellows; reeds shall bend,
    Soon, o'er thy sheltered nest.

Thou'rt gone, the abyss of heaven   25
Hath swallowed up thy form; yet, on my heart
Deeply has sunk the lesson thou hast given,
    And shall not soon depart.

He who, from zone to zone,
Guides through the boundless sky thy certain flight,   30
In the long way that I must tread alone,
    Will lead my steps aright.

William Cullen Bryant (1794–1878)

QUESTIONS

1. Vocabulary: *fowler* (5), *desert* (15), *stoop* (19).
2. What figure of speech unifies the poem?
3. Where is the waterfowl flying? Why? What is "that pathless coast" (14)?
4. What "Power" (13) "guides" (30) the waterfowl to its destination? How does it do so?
5. What lesson does the poet derive from his observations?

100. DESIGN

I found a dimpled spider, fat and white,
On a white heal-all, holding up a moth
Like a white piece of rigid satin cloth—
Assorted characters of death and blight
Mixed ready to begin the morning right,   5
Like the ingredients of a witches' broth—
A snow-drop spider, a flower like a froth,
And dead wings carried like a paper kite.

What had that flower to do with being white,
The wayside blue and innocent heal-all?   10
What brought the kindred spider to that height,
Then steered the white moth thither in the night?
What but design of darkness to appall?—
If design govern in a thing so small.

Robert Frost (1874–1963)

QUESTIONS

1. Vocabulary: *characters* (4).
2. The heal-all is a wildflower, usually blue or violet but occasionally white, found blooming along roadsides in the summer. It was once supposed to have healing qualities, hence its name. Of what significance, scientific and poetic, is the fact that the spider, the heal-all, and the moth are all white? Of what poetic significance is the fact that the spider is "dimpled" and "fat" and like a "snow-drop," and that the flower is "innocent" and named "heal-all"?
3. The "argument from design"—that the manifest existence of design in the universe implies the existence of a Great Designer—was a favorite eighteenth-century argument for the existence of God. What twist does Frost give the argument? What answer does he suggest to the question in lines 11–13? How comforting is the apparent concession in line 14?
4. Contrast Frost's poem in content and emotional effect with "To a Waterfowl." Is it possible to like both?

101. THE INDIFFERENT

I can love both fair and brown,
Her whom abundance melts, and her whom want betrays,
Her who loves loneness best, and her who masks and plays,
Her whom the country formed, and whom the town,
    Her who believes, and her who tries,°   tests 5
    Her who still weeps with spongy eyes,
And her who is dry cork and never cries;
I can love her, and her, and you, and you;
I can love any, so she be not true.°   faithful

Will no other vice content you?   10
Will it not serve your turn to do as did your mothers?
Or have you all old vices spent, and now would find out others?
Or doth a fear that men are true torment you?
    Oh, we are not; be not you so.
    Let me, and do you, twenty know.   15
Rob me, but bind me not, and let me go.
Must I, who came to travail thorough° you,   through
Grow your fixed subject because you are true?

Venus heard me sing this song,
And by love's sweetest part, variety, she swore   20
She heard not this till now, and that it should be so no more.
    She went, examined, and returned ere long,
        And said, "Alas, some two or three
        Poor heretics in love there be,

Which think to 'stablish dangerous constancy,   25
But I have told them, 'Since you will be true,
You shall be true to them who are false to you.' "

John Donne (1572–1631)

QUESTIONS

1. Vocabulary: *indifferent* (title), *know* (15), *travail* (17).
2. Who is the speaker? To whom is he speaking? About what is he "indifferent"? What one qualification does he insist on in a lover? Why?
3. Of what vice does he accuse the women of his generation in line 10? How, in his opinion, do they differ from their mothers? Why?
4. Why does Venus investigate the speaker's complaint? Does her investigation confirm or refute his accusation? Who are the "heretics in love" whom she discovers? What punishment does she decree for them?

102. LOVE'S DEITY

I long to talk with some old lover's ghost
    Who died before the god of love was born.
I cannot think that he who then loved most
    Sunk so low as to love one which did scorn.
But since this god produced a destiny,   5
And that vice-nature, custom, lets it be,
    I must love her that loves not me.

Sure, they that made him god meant not so much,
    Nor he in his young godhead practiced it.
But when an even flame two hearts did touch,   10
    His office was indulgently to fit
Actives to passives. Correspondency
Only his subject was. It cannot be
    Love till I love her that loves me.

But every modern god will° now extend   *wants to* 15
    His vast prerogative as far as Jove.
To rage, to lust, to write to, to commend,
    All is the purlieu of the god of love.
Oh, were we wakened by this tyranny
To ungod this child again, it could not be   20
    I should love her who loves not me.

Rebel and atheist too, why murmur I
    As though I felt the worst that Love could do?
Love might make me leave loving, or might try

A deeper plague, to make her love me too,   25
Which, since she loves before, I am loath to see.
Falsehood is worse than hate, and that must be
If she whom I love should love me.

John Donne (1572–1631)

QUESTIONS

1. Vocabulary: *vice-* (6), *even* (10), *purlieu* (18).
2. Who is the modern "god of love" (2)? Why is he called a "child" (20)? What did "they which made him god" (8) intend to be his duties? How has he gone beyond these duties? Why does the speaker long to talk with some lover's ghost who died before this god was born (1–2)?
3. What is the speaker's situation? Whom does the speaker call "Rebel and atheist" (22)? Why?
4. Why does the speaker rebuke himself for "murmuring" in the final stanza? What two things could Love do to him that have not been done already? Why are they worse? Explain the words "before" (26) and "Falsehood" (27). To what word in the first stanza does "hate" (27) correspond?
5. How does the speaker define "love" in this poem? Is he consistent in his use of the term? How does he differ from the speaker in "The Indifferent" in his conception of love?
6. How do you explain the fact that "Love's Deity" and "The Indifferent," though both by the same poet, express opposite opinions about the value of fidelity in love?

103. THE CAGED SKYLARK

As a dare-gale skylark scanted in a dull cage
  Man's mounting spirit in his bone-house, mean house, dwells—
  That bird beyond the remembering his free fells;
This in drudgery, day-laboring-out life's age.

Though aloft on turf or perch or poor low stage,   5
  Both sing sometimes the sweetest, sweetest spells,
  Yet both droop deadly sometimes in their cells
Or wring their barriers in bursts of fear or rage.

Not that the sweet-fowl, song-fowl, needs no rest—
Why, hear him, hear him babble and drop down to his nest,   10
  But his own nest, wild nest, no prison.

Man's spirit will be flesh-bound when found at best,
But uncumbered: meadow-down is not distressed
  For a rainbow footing it nor he for his bones risen.

Gerard Manley Hopkins (1844–1889)

QUESTIONS

1. Vocabulary: *scanted* (1), *fells* (3). What meanings of "mean" (2) are appropriate here? "Turf" (5) is a piece of sod placed in a cage.
2. This poem, written by a poet-priest, expresses his belief in the orthodox Roman Catholic doctrine of the resurrection of the body. According to this belief, man's immortal soul, after death, will be ultimately reunited with his body; this body, however, will be a weightless, perfected, glorified body, not the gross imperfect body of mortal life. Express the analogy in the poem as a pair of mathematical statements of proportion (in the form $a{:}b = c{:}d$, and $e{:}f = g{:}h = i{:}j$), using the following terms: caged skylark, mortal body, meadow-down, cage, rainbow, spirit-in-life, nest, immortal spirit, wild skylark, resurrected body.
3. Discuss the image of the last two lines as a figure for weightlessness. Why would not a shadow have been as apt as a rainbow for this comparison?

104. AUBADE

I work all day, and get half drunk at night.
Waking at four to soundless dark, I stare.
In time the curtain-edges will grow light.
Till then I see what's really always there:
Unresting death, a whole day nearer now,   5
Making all thought impossible but how
And where and when I shall myself die.
Arid interrogation: yet the dread
Of dying, and being dead,
Flashes afresh to hold and horrify.   10

The mind blanks at the glare. Not in remorse
—The good not done, the love not given, time
Torn off unused—nor wretchedly because
An only life can take so long to climb
Clear of its wrong beginnings, and may never;   15
But at the total emptiness for ever,
The sure extinction that we travel to
And shall be lost in always. Not to be here,
Not to be anywhere,
And soon; nothing more terrible, nothing more true.   20

This is a special way of being afraid
No trick dispels. Religion used to try,
That vast moth-eaten musical brocade
Created to pretend we never die,
And specious stuff that says *No rational being*   25
Can fear a thing it will not feel, not seeing

That this is what we fear—no sight, no sound,
No touch or taste or smell, nothing to think with,
Nothing to love or link with,
The anaesthetic from which none come round.   30

And so it stays just on the edge of vision,
A small unfocused blur, a standing chill
That slows each impulse down to indecision.
Most things may never happen: this one will,
And realization of it rages out   35
In furnace-fear when we are caught without
People or drink. Courage is no good:
It means not scaring others. Being brave
Lets no one off the grave.
Death is no different whined at than withstood.   40

Slowly light strengthens, and the room takes shape.
It stands plain as a wardrobe, what we know,
Have always known, know that we can't escape,
Yet can't accept. One side will have to go.
Meanwhile telephones crouch, getting ready to ring   45
In locked-up offices, and all the uncaring
Intricate rented world begins to rouse.
The sky is white as clay, with no sun.
Work has to be done.
Postmen like doctors go from house to house.   50

Philip Larkin (1922–1985)

QUESTIONS

1. Vocabulary: *remorse* (11), *specious* (25), *stuff* (25), *anaesthetic* (30).
2. The title of this poem, like that of Richard Wilbur's (No. 31), is partially ironic, but the irony arises from a quite different source. What is the irony here?
3. How does the speaker characterize death? Why is 4 A.M. the time when he feels it most intensely?
4. Comment on Larkin's metaphor for religion (23). What are its implications?
5. What is the "specious stuff" characterized by the italicized sentence in lines 25–26?
6. The speaker dismisses courage as a useless remedy for his fear of death (37–40). Is he, then, an utter coward? Does he display *any* kind of courage?
7. Contrast this poem with "The Caged Skylark" in idea and tone. Discuss its merits as a poem.

105. ARS POETICA

A poem should be palpable and mute
As a globed fruit,

Dumb
As old medallions to the thumb,

Silent as the sleeve-worn stone   5
Of casement ledges where the moss has grown—

A poem should be wordless
As the flight of birds.

                              *

A poem should be motionless in time
As the moon climbs,   10

Leaving, as the moon releases
Twig by twig the night-entangled trees,

Leaving, as the moon behind the winter leaves,
Memory by memory the mind—

A poem should be motionless in time   15
As the moon climbs.

                              *

A poem should be equal to:
Not true.

For all the history of grief
An empty doorway and a maple leaf.   20

For love
The leaning grasses and two lights above the sea—

A poem should not mean
But be.

Archibald MacLeish (1892–1982)

QUESTIONS

1. How can a poem be "wordless" (7)? How can it be "motionless in time" (15)?
2. The Latin title, literally translatable as "The Art of Poetry," is a traditional
   title for works on the philosophy of poetry. What is *this* poet's philosophy of
   poetry? What does he mean by saying that a poem should not "mean" and
   should not be "true"?

Chapter ten
Tone

Tone, in literature, may be defined as the writer's or speaker's attitude toward his subject, his audience, or himself. It is the emotional coloring, or the emotional meaning, of the work and is an extremely important part of the full meaning. In spoken language it is indicated by the inflections of the speaker's voice. If, for instance, a friend tells you, "I'm going to get married today," the facts of the statement are entirely clear. But the emotional meaning of the statement may vary widely according to the tone of voice with which it is uttered. The tone may be ecstatic ("Hooray! I'm going to get married today!"); it may be incredulous ("I can't believe it! I'm going to get married today"); it may be despairing ("Horrors! I'm going to get married today"); it may be resigned ("Might as well face it. I'm going to get married today"). Obviously, a correct interpretation of the tone will be an important part of understanding the full meaning. It may even have rather important consequences. If someone calls you a fool, your interpretation of the tone may determine whether you roll up your sleeves for a fight or walk off with your arm around his shoulder. If a woman says "No" to a proposal of marriage, the man's interpretation of her tone may determine whether he asks her again and wins her or starts going with someone else.

In poetry tone is likewise important. We have not really understood a poem unless we have accurately sensed whether the attitude it manifests is playful or solemn, mocking or reverent, calm or excited. But the correct determination of tone in literature is a much more delicate matter than it is with spoken language, for we do not have the speaker's voice to guide us. We must learn to recognize tone by other means. Almost all the elements of poetry help to indicate its tone: connotation, imagery, and metaphor; irony and understatement; rhythm, sentence construction, and formal pattern. There is therefore no simple formula for recognizing tone. It is an end product of all the elements in a poem. The best we can do is illustrate.

Robert Frost's "Stopping by Woods on a Snowy Evening" (No. 98) seems a simple poem, but it has always afforded trouble to beginning readers. A very good student, asked to interpret it, once wrote this: "The poem means that we are forever passing up pleasures to go onward to what we wrongly consider our obligations. We would like to watch the snow fall on the peaceful countryside, but we always have to rush home to supper and other engagements. Frost feels that the average person considers life too short to stop and take time to appreciate true pleasures." This student did a good job in recognizing the central conflict of the poem. He went astray in recognizing its tone. Let's examine why.

In the first place, the fact that the speaker in the poem *does* stop to watch the snow fall in the woods immediately establishes him as a human being with more sensitivity and feeling for beauty than most. He is not one of the people of Wordsworth's sonnet (No. 26) who, "getting and spending," have laid waste their powers and lost the capacity to be stirred by nature. Frost's speaker is contrasted with his horse, who, as a creature of habit and an animal without esthetic perception, cannot understand the speaker's reason for stopping. There is also a suggestion of contrast with the "owner" of the woods, who, if he saw the speaker stopping, might be as puzzled as the horse. (Who most truly "profits" from the woods—its absentee owner or the person who can enjoy its beauty?) The speaker goes on because he has "promises to keep." But the word "promises," though it may here have a wry ironic undertone of regret, has a favorable connotation: people almost universally agree that promises ought to be kept. If the poet had used a different term, say, "things to do," or "business to attend to," or "financial affairs to take care of," or "money to make," the connotations would have been quite different. As it is, the tone of the poem tells us that the poet is sympathetic to the speaker, is endorsing rather than censuring his action. Perhaps we may go even further. In the concluding two lines, because of their climactic position, because they are repeated, and because "sleep" in poetry is often used figuratively to refer to death, there is a suggestion of symbolic interpretation: "and many years to live before I die." If we accept this interpretation, it poses a parallel between giving oneself up to contemplation of the woods and dying. The poet's total implication would seem to be that beauty is a distinctively human value that deserves its place in a full life but that to devote one's life to its pursuit, at the expense of other obligations and duties, is tantamount to one's death as a responsible being. The poet therefore accepts the choice the speaker makes, though not without a touch of regret.

Differences in tone, and their importance, can perhaps be studied best in poems with similar content. Consider, for instance, the following pair.

106. THE VILLAIN

While joy gave clouds the light of stars,
    That beamed where'er they looked;
And calves and lambs had tottering knees,
    Excited, while they sucked;
While every bird enjoyed his song,   5
Without one thought of harm or wrong—
I turned my head and saw the wind,
    Not far from where I stood,
Dragging the corn by her golden hair,
    Into a dark and lonely wood.   10

W. H. Davies (1871–1940)

QUESTIONS

1. Vocabulary: *corn* (9) in British usage.
2. From what realm of literary experience is the title taken? How is this allusion strengthened by the image in lines 9–10, and what implication does it have for the way this image should be taken—that is, for its relation to reality?

107. APPARENTLY WITH NO SURPRISE

Apparently with no surprise
To any happy flower,
The frost beheads it at its play
In accidental power.

The blond assassin passes on,
The sun proceeds unmoved
To measure off another day
For an approving God.

Emily Dickinson (*1830–1886*)

QUESTIONS

1. What is the "blond assassin"?
2. What ironies are involved in this poem?

Both of these poems are concerned with nature; both use contrast as their basic organizing principle—a contrast between innocence and evil, joy and tragedy. But in tone the two poems are sharply different. The first is light and fanciful; its tone is one of delight or delighted surprise. The second, though superficially fanciful, is basically grim, almost savage; its tone is one of horror. Let's examine the difference.

In "The Villain" the images of the first six lines all suggest joy and innocence. The last four introduce the sinister. The poet, on turning his head, sees a villain dragging a beautiful maiden toward a dark wood to commit there some unmentionable deed, or so his metaphor tells us. But our response is one not of horror but of delight, for we realize that the poet does not mean us to take his metaphor seriously. He has actually seen only the wind blowing through the wheat and bending its golden tops gracefully toward a shady wood. The beauty of the scene has delighted him, and he has been further delighted by the fanciful metaphor which he has found to express it. The reader shares his delight both in the scene and in the metaphor.

The second poem makes the same contrast of joyful innocence (the "happy flower . . . at its play") with the sinister ("the blond assassin"). The chief difference would seem to be that the villain is this time the frost rather than the wind. But this time the poet, though her metaphor is no less fanciful, is earnest in what she is saying. For the frost actually *does* kill the flower. What makes the horror of the killing even worse is that nothing else in nature is disturbed over it or seems even to notice it. The sun "proceeds unmoved / To measure off another day." Nothing in nature stops or pauses. The flower itself is not surprised. And even God—the God who we have all been told is benevolent and concerned over the least sparrow's fall—seems to approve of what has happened, for He shows no displeasure, and it was He who created the frost as well as the flower. Further irony lies in the fact that the "assassin" (the word's connotations are of terror and violence) is not dark but "blond," or white (the connotations here are of innocence and beauty). The destructive agent, in other words, is among the most exquisite creations of God's handiwork. The poet, then, is shocked at what has happened, and is even more shocked that nothing else in nature is shocked. What has happened seems inconsistent with a rule of benevolence in the universe. In her ironic reference to an "approving God," therefore, the poet is raising a dreadful question: are the forces that created and govern the universe actually benevolent? And if we think that the poet is unduly disturbed over the death of a flower, we may consider that what is true for the flower is true throughout nature. Death—even early or accidental death, in terrible juxtaposition with beauty—is its constant condition; the fate that befalls the flower befalls us all.

These two poems, then, though superficially similar, are basically as different as night and day. And the difference is primarily one of tone.

Accurate determination of tone, therefore, is extremely important, whether in the reading of poetry or the interpretation of a woman's "No." For the experienced reader it will be instinctive and automatic. For the beginning reader it will require study. But beyond the general suggestions for reading that already have been made, no specific instructions can be given. Recognition of tone requires an increasing familiarity with the meanings and connotations of words, alertness to the presence of irony and other figures, and, above all, careful reading. Poetry cannot be read as one would skim a newspaper or a mystery novel looking merely for facts.

*   *   *

108. THE COMING OF WISDOM WITH TIME

Though leaves are many, the root is one;
Through all the lying days of my youth
I swayed my leaves and flowers in the sun;
Now I may wither into the truth.

William Butler Yeats (1865–1939)

QUESTION

Is the poet exulting over a gain or lamenting over a loss?

109. SINCE THERE'S NO HELP

Since there's no help, come let us kiss and part;
Nay, I have done, you get no more of me,
And I am glad, yea, glad with all my heart
That thus so cleanly I myself can free;
Shake hands forever, cancel all our vows,   5
And when we meet at any time again,
Be it not seen in either of our brows
That we one jot of former love retain.
Now, at the last gasp of Love's latest breath,
When, his pulse failing, Passion speechless lies,   10
When Faith is kneeling by his bed of death,
And Innocence is closing up his eyes,
Now, if thou wouldst, when all have given him over,
From death to life thou mightst him yet recover.

Michael Drayton (1563–1631)

QUESTIONS

1. What difference in tone do you find between the first eight lines and the last six? In which is the speaker more sincere? What differences in rhythm and language help to establish the difference in tone?
2. How many figures are there in the allegorical scene in lines 9–12? What do the pronouns "his" and "him" in lines 10–14 refer to? What is dying? Why? How might the person addressed still restore it from death to life?
3. Define the dramatic situation as precisely as possible, taking into consideration both the man's attitude and the woman's.

110. THE TELEPHONE

"When I was just as far as I could walk
From here today,
There was an hour
All still
When leaning with my head against a flower   5
I heard you talk.
Don't say I didn't, for I heard you say—
You spoke from that flower on the window sill—
Do you remember what it was you said?"

"First tell me what it was you thought you heard."   10

"Having found the flower and driven a bee away,
I leaned my head,
And holding by the stalk,
I listened and I thought I caught the word—
What was it? Did you call me by my name?   15
Or did you say—
Someone said 'Come'—I heard it as I bowed."

"I may have thought as much, but not aloud."

"Well, so I came."

Robert Frost (1874–1963)

QUESTIONS

1. When and where does the above dialogue take place? What is the relationship between the two speakers?
2. How does the title relate to the poem?
3. Characterize the first speaker. Why does he interrupt his narrative to say, "Don't say I didn't" (7)? Why does he not tell her what he heard her say (7–9, 14–16)? Why does he shift to what *"Someone"* said (17)?
4. Characterize the second speaker.
5. What is the poem about? What is its tone?

111. LOVE IN BROOKLYN

"I love you, Horowitz," he said, and blew his nose.
She splashed her drink. "The hell you say," she said.
Then, thinking hard, she lit a cigarette:
"Not *love*. You don't *love* me. You like my legs,
and how I make your letters nice and all.   5
You drunk your drink too fast. You don't love *me*."

"You wanna bet?" he asked. "You wanna bet?
I loved you from the day they moved you up
from Payroll, last July. I watched you, right?
You sat there on that typing chair you have   10
and swung round like a kid. It made me shake.
Like once, in World War II, I saw a tank
slide through some trees at dawn like it was god.
That's how you make me feel. I don't know why."

She turned towards him, then sat back and grinned,   15
and on the bar stool swung full circle round.

"You think I'm like a tank, you mean?" she asked.
"Some fellers tell me nicer things than that."
But then she saw his face and touched his arm
and softly said "I'm only kidding you."   20

He ordered drinks, the same again, and paid.
A fat man, wordless, staring at the floor.
She took his hand in hers and pressed it hard.
And his plump fingers trembled in her lap.

John Wakeman (b. 1928)

QUESTIONS

1. When and where does the above dialogue take place? What is the relationship between the two speakers?
2. Characterize the first speaker. How does he feel toward the other?
3. Characterize the second speaker. How does she feel toward him? Do her
   feelings change? If so, how?
4. Contrast this poem in tone with "The Telephone."

112. ONE DIGNITY DELAYS FOR ALL

One dignity delays for all,
One mitred afternoon.
None can avoid this purple,
None avoid this crown.

Coach it insures, and footmen,   5
Chamber and state and throng;
Bells, also, in the village,
As we ride grand along.

What dignified attendants,
What service when we pause!   10
How loyally at parting
Their hundred hats they raise!

How pomp surpassing ermine
When simple you and I
Present our meek escutcheon   15
And claim the rank to die!

Emily Dickinson (1830–1886)

1. Vocabulary: *mitred* (2), *state* (6), *escutcheon* (15).
2. What is the "dignity" that delays for all? What is its nature? What is being described in stanzas 2 and 3?
3. What figures of speech are combined in "our meek escutcheon" (15)? What metaphorically does it represent?

113. 'TWAS WARM AT FIRST LIKE US

'Twas warm at first like us,
Until there crept upon
A chill, like frost upon a glass,
Till all the scene be gone.

The forehead copied stone,   5
The fingers grew too cold
To ache, and like a skater's brook
The busy eyes congealed.

It straightened—that was all,
It crowded cold to cold,   10
It multiplied indifference
As pride were all it could.

And even when with cords
'Twas lowered like a weight,
It made no signal, nor demurred,   15
But dropped like adamant.

Emily Dickinson (1830–1886)

QUESTIONS

1. Vocabulary: *adamant* (16).
2. What is "It" in the opening line? What is being described in the poem, and between what points in time?
3. How would you describe the tone of this poem? How does it contrast with that of the preceding?

114. CROSSING THE BAR

Sunset and evening star,
    And one clear call for me!
And may there be no moaning of the bar
    When I put out to sea,

But such a tide as moving seems asleep, 5
  Too full for sound and foam,
When that which drew from out the boundless deep
  Turns again home.

Twilight and evening bell,
  And after that the dark! 10
And may there be no sadness of farewell
  When I embark;

For though from out our bourne of Time and Place
  The flood may bear me far,
I hope to see my Pilot face to face 15
  When I have crossed the bar.

Alfred, Lord Tennyson (1809–1892)

QUESTIONS

1. Vocabulary: *bourne* (13).
2. What two sets of figures does Tennyson use for approaching death? What is the precise moment of death in each set?
3. In troubled weather the wind and waves above the sandbar across a harbor's mouth make a moaning sound. What metaphorical meaning has the "moaning of the bar" here (3)? For what kind of death is the poet wishing? Why does he want "no sadness of farewell" (11)?
4. What is "that which drew from out the boundless deep" (7)? What is "the boundless deep"? To what is it opposed in the poem? Why is "Pilot" (15) capitalized?

115. THE OXEN

Christmas Eve, and twelve of the clock.
  "Now they are all on their knees,"
An elder said as we sat in a flock
  By the embers in hearthside ease.

We pictured the meek mild creatures where 5
  They dwelt in their strawy pen,
Nor did it occur to one of us there
  To doubt they were kneeling then.

So fair a fancy few would weave
  In these years! Yet, I feel, 10
If someone said on Christmas Eve,
  "Come; see the oxen kneel

"In the lonely barton° by yonder coomb°   farm; valley
    Our childhood used to know,"
I should go with him in the gloom,   15
    Hoping it might be so.

Thomas Hardy (1840–1928)

QUESTIONS

1. Is the simple superstition referred to in the poem here opposed to, or identified with, religious faith? With what implications for the meaning of the poem?
2. What are "these years" (10) and how do they contrast with the years of the poet's boyhood? What event in intellectual history between 1840 and 1915 (the date of composition of this poem) was most responsible for the change?
3. Both "Crossing the Bar" and "The Oxen" in their last lines use a form of the verb *hope*. By full discussion of tone, establish the precise meaning of hope in each poem. What degree of expectation does it imply? How should the word be handled in reading Tennyson's poem aloud?

116. THE APPARITION

When by thy scorn, O murderess, I am dead,
    And that thou thinkst thee free
From all solicitatiön from me,
Then shall my ghost come to thy bed,
And thee, feigned vestal, in worse arms shall see;   5
Then thy sick taper° will begin to wink,   candle
And he, whose thou art then, being tired before,
Will, if thou stir, or pinch to wake him, think
        Thou call'st for more,
And in false sleep will from thee shrink.   10
And then, poor aspen wretch, neglected, thou,
Bathed in a cold quicksilver sweat, wilt lie
    A verier° ghost than I.   truer
What I will say, I will not tell thee now,
Lest that preserve thee; and since my love is spent,   15
I had rather thou shouldst painfully repent,
Than by my threatenings rest still innocent.

John Donne (1572–1631)

QUESTIONS

1. Vocabulary: *feigned* (5), *aspen* (11), *quicksilver* (13). Are the latter two words used literally or figuratively? Explain.
2. What has been the past relationship between the speaker and the woman

addressed? How does a "solicitatiön" differ from a proposal? Why does he call her a "murderess"? What threat does he make against her?

3. In line 15 the speaker proclaims that his love for the woman "is spent." Does the tone of the poem support this contention? Discuss.

4. In line 5 why does the speaker use the word "vestal" instead of "virgin"? Does he believe her not to be a virgin? Of what is he accusing her? (In ancient Rome the vestal virgins tended the perpetual fire in the temple of Vesta. They entered this service between the ages of six and ten, and served for a term of thirty years, during which they were bound to virginity.)

5. The implied metaphor in line 1—that a woman who will not satisfy her lover's desires is "killing" him—was a cliché of Renaissance poetry. What original twist does Donne give it to make it fresh and new?

6. In the scene imagined by the speaker of his ghost's visit to the woman's bed, he finds her "in worse arms"—worse than whose? In what respect? By what will this other man have been "tired before"? Of what will he think she is calling for "more"? What is the speaker implying about himself and the woman in these lines?

7. Why (according to the speaker) will the woman *really* be trying to wake up her bedmate? Why, when she fails, will she be a "verier" ghost than the speaker?

8. What will the ghost say to her that he will not now reveal lest his telling it "preserve" her? Can we know? Does *he* know? Why does he make this undefined threat?

9. For what does the speaker say he wants the woman to "painfully repent"? Of what crime or sin would she remain "innocent" if he revealed now what his ghost would say? What is the speaker's real objective?

117. THE FLEA

Mark but this flea, and mark in this
How little that which thou deny'st me is;
It sucked me first, and now sucks thee,
And in this flea our two bloods mingled be;
Thou know'st that this cannot be said   5
A sin, nor shame, nor loss of maidenhead;
  Yet this enjoys before it woo,
  And pampered swells with one blood made of two,
  And this, alas, is more than we would do.

Oh stay, three lives in one flea spare,   10
Where we almost, yea more than married are,
This flea is you and I, and this
Our marriage bed and marriage temple is;
Though parents grudge, and you, we are met
And cloistered in these living walls of jet.   15
  Though use° make you apt to kill me,   habit
  Let not to that, self-murder added be,

And sacrilege, three sins in killing three.
Cruel and sudden, hast thou since
Purpled° thy nail in blood of innocence?   crimsoned 20
Wherein could this flea guilty be,
Except in that drop which it sucked from thee?
Yet thou triumph'st and say'st that thou
Find'st not thyself, nor me, the weaker now.
   'Tis true. Then learn how false fears be: 25
   Just so much honor, when thou yield'st to me,
   Will waste, as this flea's death took life from thee.

John Donne (1572–1631)

QUESTIONS

1. In many respects this poem is like a miniature play: it has two characters, dramatic conflict, dialogue (though we hear only one speaker), and stage-action. The action is indicated by stage directions embodied in the dialogue. What has happened just *preceding* the first line of the poem? What happens *between* the first and second stanzas? What happens *between* the second and third? How does the female character behave and what does she say *during* the third stanza?
2. What has been the past relationship of the speaker and the woman? What has she denied him (2)? How has she habitually "killed" him (16)? Why has she done so? How does it happen that he is still alive? What is his objective in the poem?
3. According to a traditional Renaissance belief, the bloods of the participating parties in sexual intercourse were "mingled." What is the speaker's argument in stanza 1? Reduce it to paraphrase. How logical is it?
4. What do "parents grudge, and you" in stanza 2? What are the "living walls of jet"? What three things will the woman kill by crushing the flea? What three sins will she commit?
5. Why and how does the woman "triumph" in stanza 3? What is the speaker's response? How logical is his concluding argument?
6. What action, if any, would you infer, follows the conclusion of the poem?
7. "The Apparition" and "The Flea" may both be classified as "seduction poems." How do they differ in tone?

118. ENGRAVED ON THE COLLAR OF A DOG WHICH I GAVE TO HIS ROYAL HIGHNESS

I am his Highness' dog at Kew;
Pray tell me, sir, whose dog are you?

Alexander Pope (1688–1744)

QUESTIONS

1. What adjective—or noun—best fits the attitude expressed on the dog's collar?
2. Is the dog in any way symbolic? Explain.

119. LOVE

> There's the wonderful love of a beautiful maid,
>   And the love of a staunch true man,
> And the love of a baby that's unafraid—
>   All have existed since time began.
> But the most wonderful love, the Love of all loves,
>   Even greater than the love for Mother,
> Is the infinite, tenderest, passionate love
>   Of one dead drunk for another.

Anonymous

QUESTION

The radical shift in tone makes "Love" come off. If such a shift were unintentional in a poem, what would our view be?

EXERCISES

1. Marvell's "To His Coy Mistress" (No. 51), Housman's "Loveliest of Trees" (No. 53), and Herrick's "To the Virgins, to Make Much of Time" (No. 59) all treat a traditional poetic theme known as the *carpe diem* ("seize the day") theme. They differ sharply, however, in tone. Characterize the tone of each, and point out the differences in poetic management that account for the difference in tone.
2. Describe and account for the differences in tone between the poems in the following pairs:
   a. "A bird came down the walk" (No. 5) and "A narrow fellow in the grass" (No. 33).
   b. "The Lamb" (No. 196) and "The Tiger" (No. 197).
   c. "The Unknown Citizen" (No. 80) and "Departmental" (No. 81).
   d. "Some keep the Sabbath going to church" (No. 180) and "Design" (No. 100).
   e. "It sifts from leaden sieves" (No. 42) and "The Snow Man" (No. 243).
   f. "I taste a liquor never brewed" (No. 201) and "All day I hear" (No. 153).
   g. "The Dead" (No. 62) and "Anthem for Doomed Youth" (No. 151).
   h. "There is a garden in her face" (No. 46) and "The Silken Tent" (No. 47).

Chapter eleven
Musical Devices

Poetry obviously makes a greater use of the "music" of language than does language that is not poetry. The poet, unlike the person who uses language to convey only information, chooses words for sound as well as for meaning, and uses the sound as a means of reinforcing meaning. So prominent is this musical quality of poetry that some writers have made it the distinguishing term in their definitions of poetry. Edgar Allan Poe, for instance, describes poetry as "music . . . combined with a pleasurable idea." Whether or not it deserves this much importance, verbal music, like connotation, imagery, and figurative language, is one of the important resources that enable the poet to do more than communicate mere information. The poet may indeed sometimes pursue verbal music for its own sake; more often, at least in first-rate poetry, it is an adjunct to the total meaning or communication of the poem.

There are two broad ways by which the poet achieves musical quality: by the choice and arrangement of sounds and by the arrangement of accents. In this chapter we will consider one aspect of the first of these.

An essential element in all music is repetition. In fact, we might say that all art consists of giving structure to two elements: repetition and variation. All things we enjoy greatly and lastingly have these two elements. We enjoy the sea endlessly because it is always the same yet always different. We enjoy a baseball game because it contains the same complex combination of pattern and variation. Our love of art, then, is rooted in human psychology. We like the familiar, we like variety, but we like them combined. If we get too much sameness, the result is monotony and tedium; if we get too much variety, the result is bewilderment and confusion. The composer of music, therefore, repeats certain musical tones; repeats them in certain combinations, or chords; and repeats them in certain patterns, or melodies. The poet likewise repeats certain sounds in certain combinations and arrangements, and thus adds musical meaning to verse. Consider the following short example.

120. THE TURTLE

The turtle lives 'twixt plated decks
Which practically conceal its sex.
I think it clever of the turtle
In such a fix to be so fertile.

Ogden Nash (1902–1971)

Here is a little joke, a paradox of animal life to which the author has cleverly drawn our attention. An experiment will show us, however, that much of its appeal lies not so much in what it says as in the manner in which it says it. If, for instance, we recast the verse as prose: "The turtle lives in a shell which almost conceals its sex. It is ingenious of the turtle, in such a situation, to be so prolific," the joke falls flat. Some of its appeal must lie in its metrical form. So now we cast it in unrimed verse:

Because he lives between two decks,
It's hard to tell a turtle's gender.
The turtle is a clever beast
In such a plight to be so fertile.

Here, perhaps, is *some* improvement, but still the piquancy of the original is missing. Much of that appeal must have consisted in the use of rime—the repetition of sound in "decks" and "sex," "turtle" and "fertile." So we try once more.

The turtle lives 'twixt plated decks
Which practically conceal its sex.
I think it clever of the turtle
In such a plight to be so fertile.

But for perceptive readers there is still something missing—they may not at first see what—but some little touch that makes the difference between a good piece of verse and a little masterpiece of its kind. And then they see it: "plight" has been substituted for "fix."

But why should "fix" make such a difference? Its meaning is little different from that of "plight"; its only important difference is in sound. But there we are. The final *x* in "fix" catches up the concluding consonant sound in "sex," and its initial *f* is repeated in the initial consonant sound of "fertile." Not only do these sound recurrences provide a subtle gratification to the ear, but they also give the verse structure; they emphasize and draw together the key words of the piece: "sex," "fix," and "fertile."

Poets may repeat any unit of sound from the smallest to the largest. They may repeat individual vowel and consonant sounds, whole syllables, words, phrases, lines, or groups of lines. In each instance, in a good poem, the repetition will serve several purposes: it will please the ear, it will emphasize the words in which the repetition occurs, and it will give structure to the poem. The popularity and initial impressiveness of such repetitions is evidenced by their becoming in many instances embedded in the language as clichés like "wild and woolly," "first and foremost," "footloose and fancy-free," "penny-wise, pound-foolish," "dead as a doornail," "might and main," "sink or swim," "do or die," "pell-mell," "helter-skelter," "harum-scarum," "hocus-pocus." Some of these kinds of repetition have names, as we will see.

A syllable consists of a vowel sound that may be preceded or followed by consonant sounds. Any of these sounds may be repeated. The repetition of initial consonant sounds, as in "tried and true," "safe and sound," "fish or fowl," "rime or reason," is **alliteration.** The repetition of vowel sounds, as in "mad as a hatter," "time out of mind," "free and easy," "slapdash," is **assonance.** The repetition of final consonant sounds, as in "first and last," "odds and ends," "short and sweet," "a stroke of luck," or Shakespeare's "struts and frets" (No. 85) is **consonance.***

Repetitions may be used alone or in combination. Alliteration and assonance are combined in such phrases as "time and tide," "thick and thin," "kith and kin," "alas and alack," "fit as a fiddle," and Edgar

---

*There is no established terminology for these various repetitions. *Alliteration* is used by some writers to mean any repetition of consonant sounds. *Assonance* has been used to mean the similarity as well as the identity of vowel sounds, or even the similarity of any sounds whatever. *Consonance* has often been reserved for words in which both the initial *and* final consonant sounds correspond, as in *green* and *groan*, *moon* and *mine*. *Rime* (or rhyme) has been used to mean any sound repetition, including alliteration, assonance, and consonance. In the absence of clear agreement on the meanings of these terms, the terminology chosen here has appeared most useful, with support in usage. Labels are useful in analysis. The student should, however, learn to recognize the devices and, more important, to see their function, without worrying too much over nomenclature.

Allan Poe's famous line, "The viol, the violet, and the vine." Alliteration and consonance are combined in such phrases as "crisscross," "last but not least," "lone and lorn," "good as gold," and Housman's "fleet foot" (No. 214) and "Malt does more than Milton can" (No. 8). The combination of assonance and consonance is rime.

Rime is the repetition of the accented vowel sound and all succeeding sounds. It is called **masculine** when the rime sounds involve only one syllable, as in *decks* and *sex* or *support* and *retort*. It is **feminine** when the rime sounds involve two or more syllables, as in *turtle* and *fertile* or *spitefully* and *delightfully*. It is referred to as **internal rime** when one or more riming words are within the line and as **end rime** when the riming words are at the *ends* of lines. End rime is probably the most frequently used and most consciously sought sound repetition in English poetry. Because it comes at the end of the line, it receives emphasis as a musical effect and perhaps contributes more than any other musical resource except rhythm and meter to give poetry its musical effect as well as its structure. There exists, however, a large body of poetry that does not employ rime and for which rime would not be appropriate. Also, there has always been a tendency, especially noticeable in modern poetry, to substitute approximate rimes for perfect rimes at the ends of lines. **Approximate rimes** include words with any kind of sound similarity, from close to fairly remote. Under approximate rime we include alliteration, assonance, and consonance or their combinations when used at the end of the line; half-rime (feminine rimes in which only half of the word rimes—the accented half, as in *lightly* and *frightful*, or the unaccented half, as in *yellow* and *willow*); and other similarities too elusive to name. "A bird came down the walk" (No. 5), "A narrow fellow in the grass" (No. 33), "'Twas warm at first like us" (No. 113), "Toads" (No. 49), and "Mr. Z" (No. 82), to different degrees, all employ various kinds of approximate end rime.

121. THAT NIGHT WHEN JOY BEGAN

> That night when joy began
> Our narrowest veins to flush,
> We waited for the flash
> Of morning's leveled gun.
>
> But morning let us pass,   5
> And day by day relief
> Outgrows his nervous laugh,
> Grown credulous of peace,

As mile by mile is seen
No trespasser's reproach,   10
And love's best glasses reach
No fields but are his own.

W. H. Auden (1907–1973)

QUESTIONS

1. What has been the past experience with love of the two people in the poem?
   What is their present experience? What precisely is the tone of the poem?
2. What basic metaphor underlies the poem? Work it out stanza by stanza.
   What is "the flash of morning's leveled gun"? Does line 10 mean that no
   trespasser reproaches the lovers or that no one reproaches the lovers for
   being trespassers? Does "glasses" (11) refer to spectacles, tumblers, mirrors, or field glasses? Point out three personifications.
3. The rime pattern in the poem is intricate and exact. Work it out, considering
   alliteration, assonance, and consonance.

In addition to the repetition of individual sounds and syllables, the
poet may repeat whole words, phrases, lines, or groups of lines. When
such repetition is done according to some fixed pattern, it is called a
refrain. The refrain is especially common in songlike poetry. Examples
may be found in Shakespeare's "Winter" (No. 2) and Campion's
"There is a garden in her face" (No. 46).

It is not to be thought that we have exhausted the possibilities of
sound repetition by giving names to a few of the more prominent kinds.
The complete study of possible kinds of sound repetition in poetry
would be so complex that it would break down under its own machin-
ery. Some of the subtlest and loveliest effects escape our net of names.
In as short a phrase as this from the prose of John Ruskin—"ivy as light
and lovely as the vine"—we notice alliteration in *light* and *lovely*, assonance in *ivy, light,* and *vine,* and consonance in *ivy* and *lovely,* but we
have no name to connect the *v* in *vine* with the *v*'s in *ivy* and *lovely,* or
the second *l* in *lovely* with the first *l,* or the final syllables of *ivy* and
lovely with each other; but these are all an effective part of the music of
the line. Also contributing to the music of poetry is the linking of
related rather than identical sounds, such as *m* and *n,* or *p* and *b,* or the
vowel sounds in *boat, boot,* and *book.*

These various musical repetitions, for trained readers, will ordinarily make an almost subconscious contribution to their reading of the
poem: readers will feel their effect without necessarily being aware of
what has caused it. There is value, however, in occasionally analyzing a

poem for these devices in order to increase awareness of them. A few words of caution are necessary. First, the repetitions are entirely a matter of sound; spelling is irrelevant. *Bear* and *pair* are rimes, but *through* and *rough* are not. *Cell* and *sin, folly* and *philosophy* alliterate, but *sin* and *sugar, gun* and *gem* do not. Second, alliteration, assonance, consonance, and masculine rime are matters that ordinarily involve only stressed or accented syllables; for only such syllables ordinarily make enough impression on the ear to be significant in the sound pattern of the poem. We should hardly consider *which* and *its* in the second line of "The Turtle," for instance, as an example of assonance, for neither word is stressed enough in the reading to make it significant as a sound. Third, the words involved in these repetitions must be close enough together that the ear retains the sound, consciously or subconsciously, from its first occurrence to its second. This distance varies according to circumstances, but for alliteration, assonance, and consonance the words ordinarily have to be in the same line or adjacent lines. End rime bridges a longer gap.

122. GOD'S GRANDEUR

The world is charged with the grandeur of God.
　　It will flame out, like shining from shook foil;
　　It gathers to a greatness, like the ooze of oil
Crushed. Why do men then now not reck his rod?
Generations have trod, have trod, have trod;　　　　　　　5
　　And all is seared with trade; bleared, smeared with toil;
　　And wears man's smudge and shares man's smell: the soil
Is bare now, nor can foot feel, being shod.

And for all this, nature is never spent;
　　There lives the dearest freshness deep down things;　　10
And though the last lights off the black West went
　　Oh, morning, at the brown brink eastward, springs—
Because the Holy Ghost over the bent
　　World broods with warm breast and with ah! bright wings.

Gerard Manley Hopkins (1844–1889)

QUESTIONS

1. What is the theme of this sonnet?
2. The image in lines 3–4 possibly refers to olive oil being collected in great vats from crushed olives, but the image is much disputed. Explain the simile in line 2 and the symbols in lines 7–8 and 11–12.

3. Explain "reck his rod" (4), "spent" (9), "bent" (13).
4. Using different-colored pencils, encircle and connect examples of alliteration, assonance, consonance, and internal rime. Do these help to carry the meaning?

We should not leave the impression that the use of these musical devices is necessarily or always valuable. Like the other resources of poetry, they can be judged only in the light of the poem's total intention. Many of the greatest works of English poetry—for instance, *Hamlet* and *King Lear* and *Paradise Lost*—do not employ end rime. Both alliteration and rime, especially feminine rime, if used excessively or unskillfully, become humorous or silly. If the intention is humorous, the result is delightful; if not, fatal. Shakespeare, who knew how to use all these devices to the utmost advantage, parodied their unskillful use in lines like "The preyful princess pierced and pricked a pretty pleasing prickett" in *Love's Labor's Lost* and

> Whereat with blade, with bloody, blameful blade,
> He bravely broached his boiling bloody breast

in *A Midsummer Night's Dream*. Swinburne parodied his own highly alliterative style in "Nephelidia" with lines like "Life is the lust of a lamp for the light that is dark till the dawn of the day when we die." Used skillfully and judiciously, however, musical devices provide a palpable and delicate pleasure to the ear and, even more important, add dimension to meaning.

*   *   *

123. WITH RUE MY HEART IS LADEN

> With rue my heart is laden
>   For golden friends I had.
> For many a rose-lipt maiden
>   And many a lightfoot lad.
>
> By brooks too broad for leaping   5
>   The lightfoot boys are laid;
> The rose-lipt girls are sleeping
>   In fields where roses fade.
>
>   *A. E. Housman (1859–1936)*

1. Vocabulary: *rue* (1).
2. What, where, or why are the "brooks too broad for leaping" and the "fields where roses fade"?
3. What are the connotations here of "golden"? Does the use of "golden" (2), "lad" (4), and "girls" (7) remind you of any earlier poem? (If not, see No. 238.) How does this submerged allusion enrich the poem?
4. Point out and discuss the contribution to the poem of alliteration, end rime (masculine and feminine), and other repetitions.

124. WE REAL COOL

The Pool Players.
Seven At The Golden Shovel.

> We real cool. We
> Left school. We
>
> Lurk late. We
> Strike straight. We
>
> Sing sin. We
> Thin gin. We
>
> Jazz June. We
> Die soon.

Gwendolyn Brooks (b. 1917)

QUESTIONS

1. In addition to end rime, what other musical devices does this poem employ?
2. Try reading this poem with the pronouns at the beginning of the lines instead of at the end. What is lost?
3. English teachers in a certain urban school were once criticized for having their students read this poem: it was said to be immoral. Was the criticism justified? Why or why not?

125. AS IMPERCEPTIBLY AS GRIEF

> As imperceptibly as grief
> The summer lapsed away,
> Too imperceptible at last
> To seem like perfidy.

A quietness distilled   5
As twilight long begun,
Or nature spending with herself
Sequestered afternoon.

The dusk drew earlier in,
The morning foreign shone—   10
A courteous, yet harrowing grace,
As guest who would be gone.

And thus, without a wing
Or service of a keel,
Our summer made her light escape   15
Into the beautiful.

Emily Dickinson (1830–1886)

QUESTIONS

1. What are the subject and tone of the poem? Explain its opening simile.
2. Discuss the ways in which the approximate rimes, alliteration, and the consonant sounds in the last stanza contribute to the meaning and tone.
3. What possible meanings have the last two lines?

126. THE HARBOR

Passing through huddled and ugly walls,
By doorways where women haggard
Looked from their hunger-deep eyes,
Haunted with shadows of hunger-hands,
Out from the huddled and ugly walls,   5
I came sudden, at the city's edge,
On a blue burst of lake—
Long lake waves breaking under the sun
On a spray-flung curve of shore;
And a fluttering storm of gulls,   10
Masses of great gray wings
And flying white bellies
Veering and wheeling free in the open.

Carl Sandburg (1878–1967)

QUESTIONS

1. Define as precisely as possible the contrast in content between the first five and the last seven lines of the poem. What qualities are symbolized by the gulls? What judgment is made by means of the contrast?
2. This poem is in free verse (without meter), and does not rime. But you should be able to find examples of assonance in almost every line. Underline or draw circles around the repeated vowels. What vowel sound dominates the first five lines? Does the pattern change in the last seven? If so, what function is served by this change?
3. What consonant sounds are most prominent in the first five lines? Is there a change in the last seven? Why?

127. PARTING, WITHOUT A SEQUEL

She has finished and sealed the letter
At last, which he so richly has deserved,
With characters venomous and hatefully curved,
And nothing could be better.

But even as she gave it   5
Saying to the blue-capped functioner of doom,
"Into his hands," she hoped the leering groom
Might somewhere lose and leave it.

Then all the blood
Forsook the face. She was too pale for tears,   10
Observing the ruin of her younger years.
She went and stood

Under her father's vaunting oak
Who kept his peace in wind and sun, and glistened
Stoical in the rain; to whom she listened   15
If he spoke.

And now the agitation of the rain
Rasped his sere leaves, and he talked low and gentle
Reproaching the wan daughter by the lintel;
Ceasing and beginning again.   20

Away went the messenger's bicycle,
His serpent's track went up the hill forever,
And all the time she stood there hot as fever
And cold as any icicle.

John Crowe Ransom (1888–1974)

QUESTIONS

1. Identify the figures of speech in lines 3 and 22 and discuss their effectiveness. Are there traces of dramatic irony in the poem? Where?
2. Is the oak literal or figurative? Neither? Both? Discuss the meanings of "vaunting" (13), "stoical" (15), "sere" (18), and "lintel" (19).
3. Do you find any trite language in the poem? Where? What does it tell us about the girl's action?
4. W. H. Auden has defined poetry as "the clear expression of mixed feelings." Discuss the applicability of the definition to this poem. Try it out on other poems.
5. A feminine rime that involves two syllables is known also as a **double rime.** Find examples in the poem of both perfect and approximate double rimes. A feminine rime that involves three syllables is a **triple rime.** Find one example of a triple rime. Which lines employ masculine or **single rimes,** either perfect or approximate?

128. ROW

Slap. Clap.
The lake's back
laps the flat
boat. Croak,
goes a frog,   5
croak. Flo-
tillas of vanilla
water lilies
float. Moats
of air flare, filled   10
with day-diamonds,
flame. Tame
turtles lurch
like dreadnoughts
across murky   15
floors. Oars
dig dingles
in the sun-shingled
roof of the water.
Pines shine,   20
singing their green creeds.

Ralph Pomeroy (b. 1926)

QUESTIONS

1. What activity is the speaker engaged in? What meanings has the title?
2. What kinds of imagery prevail in the poem?

3. Find examples of internal rime, alliteration, assonance, consonance, and approximations or combinations thereof. What one line does *not* contain, in itself or in combination with the preceding or following line, one of these sound repetitions? What are the only two words (other than articles and prepositions) used twice in the poem? Where does punctuation generally occur? Have these questions or their answers any significance?
4. What is a "green creed" (21)?

129. COUNTING-OUT RHYME

Silver bark of beech, and sallow
Bark of yellow birch and yellow
   Twig of willow.

Stripe of green in moosewood maple,
Color seen in leaf of apple,   5
   Bark of popple.

Wood of popple pale as moonbeam,
Wood of oak for yoke and barn-beam,
   Wood of hornbeam.

Silver bark of beech, and hollow   10
Stem of elder, tall and yellow
   Twig of willow.

Edna St. Vincent Millay (1892–1950)

QUESTIONS

1. List all instances of alliteration, assonance, consonance, half-rime, internal rime, and word repetition.
2. How serious is the purpose of this poem?
3. What is a "counting-out rhyme"? Can you remember any from your childhood? What here is being counted?

130. TRAVELING THROUGH THE DARK

Traveling through the dark I found a deer
dead on the edge of the Wilson River road.
It is usually best to roll them into the canyon:
that road is narrow; to swerve might make more dead.

By glow of the tail-light I stumbled back of the car   5
and stood by the heap, a doe, a recent killing;
she had stiffened already, almost cold.
I dragged her off; she was large in the belly.

My fingers touching her side brought me the reason—
her side was warm; her fawn lay there waiting, 10
alive, still, never to be born.
Beside that mountain road I hesitated.

The car aimed ahead its lowered parking lights;
under the hood purred the steady engine.
I stood in the glare of the warm exhaust turning red; 15
around our group I could hear the wilderness listen.

I thought hard for us all—my only swerving—,
then pushed her over the edge into the river.

William Stafford (b. 1914)

QUESTIONS

1. State precisely the speaker's dilemma. What kind of person is he? Does he make the right decision? Why does he call his hesitation "my only swerving" (17), and how does this connect with the word "swerve" in line 4?
2. What different kinds of imagery and of image contrasts give life to the poem? Do any of the images have symbolic overtones?
3. At first glance this poem may appear to be without end rime. Looking closer, do you find any correspondences between lines 2 and 4 in each stanza? Between the final words of the concluding couplet? Can you find any line-end in the poem without some connection in sound to another line-end in its stanza?

131. NOTHING GOLD CAN STAY

Nature's first green is gold,
Her hardest hue to hold.
Her early leaf's a flower;
But only so an hour.
Then leaf subsides to leaf.
So Eden sank to grief,
So dawn goes down to day.
Nothing gold can stay.

Robert Frost (1874–1963)

QUESTIONS

1. Explain the paradoxes in lines 1 and 3.
2. Discuss the poem as a series of symbols. What are the symbolic meanings of "gold" in the final line of the poem?
3. Discuss the contributions of alliteration, assonance, consonance, rime, and other repetitions to the effectiveness of the poem.

Chapter twelve
Rhythm and Meter

Our love of rhythm and meter is rooted even deeper in us than our love for musical repetition. It is related to the beat of our hearts, the pulse of our blood, the intake and outflow of air from our lungs. Everything that we do naturally and gracefully we do rhythmically. There is rhythm in the way we walk, the way we swim, the way we ride a horse, the way we swing a golf club or a baseball bat. So native is rhythm to us that we read it, when we can, into the mechanical world around us. Our clocks go tick-tick-tick-tick, but we hear them go tick-tock, tick-tock in an endless trochaic. The click of the railway wheels beneath us patterns itself into a tune in our heads. There is a strong appeal for us in language that is rhythmical.

The term **rhythm** refers to any wavelike recurrence of motion or sound. In speech it is the natural rise and fall of language. All language is to some degree rhythmical, for all language involves some kind of alternation between accented and unaccented syllables. Language varies considerably, however, in the degree to which it exhibits rhythm. In some forms of speech the rhythm is so unobtrusive or so unpatterned that we are scarcely, if at all, aware of it. In other forms of speech the rhythm is so pronounced that we may be tempted to tap our foot to it.

Meter is the kind of rhythm we can tap our foot to. In metrical language the accents are arranged to occur at apparently equal intervals of time, and it is this interval we mark off with the tap of our foot. Metrical language is called **verse**. Nonmetrical language is **prose**. Not all poetry is metrical, nor is all metrical language poetry. *Verse* and *poetry* are not synonymous terms, nor is a *versifier* necessarily a *poet*.

The study of meter is a fascinating but highly complex subject. It is by no means an absolute prerequisite to an enjoyment, even a rich enjoyment, of poetry. But a knowledge of its fundamentals does have certain values. It can make the beginning reader more aware of the rhythmical effects of poetry and of how poetry should be read. It can enable the more advanced reader to analyze how certain effects are achieved, to see how rhythm is adapted to thought, and to explain what makes one poem (in this respect) better than another. The beginning student ought to have at least an elementary knowledge of the subject. It is not so difficult as its terminology might suggest.

In every word of more than one syllable, one syllable is *accented* or *stressed*, that is, given more prominence in pronunciation than the rest.* We say in*ter*, *en*ter, inter*vene*, *en*terprise, in*ter*pret. These accents are indicated in the dictionary, and only rarely are words in good poems accented differently: *only* cannot be pronounced on*ly*. If words of even one syllable are arranged into a sentence, we give certain words or syllables more prominence then the rest. We say: "He *went* to the *store*" or "*Ann* is *driv*ing her *car.*" There is nothing mysterious about this; it is the normal process of language. The only difference between prose and verse is that in prose these accents occur more or less haphazardly; in verse the poet has arranged them to occur at regular intervals.

The word *meter* comes from a word meaning "measure." To measure something we must have a unit of measurement. For measuring length we use the inch, the foot, and the yard; for measuring time we use the second, the minute, and the hour. For measuring verse we use the foot, the line, and (sometimes) the stanza.

The basic metrical unit, the **foot**, consists normally of one accented syllable plus one or two unaccented syllables, though occasionally there may be no unaccented syllables, and very rarely there may be three. For diagramming verse, various systems of visual symbols have been invented. In this book we shall use a short curved line to indicate an unaccented syllable, a short horizontal line to indicate an accented syllable, and a vertical bar to indicate the division between feet. The basic kinds of feet are thus as follows:

*Though the words *accent* and *stress* are generally used interchangeably, as here, a distinction is sometimes made between them in technical discussions. **Accent**, the relative prominence given a syllable in relation to its neighbors, is then said to result from one or more of four causes: *stress*, or force of utterance, producing loudness; *duration;* *pitch;* and *juncture*, the manner of transition between successive sounds. Of these, *stress*, in English verse, is most important.

Examples		Name of foot	Name of meter*	
ĭn-*ter*,⁻	thĕ *sun*	Iamb	Iambic ⎫	
— ̆	— ̆		⎬ Duple meters	
en-ter,	*went* to	Trochee	Trochaic ⎭	
̆ ̆ —	̆ ̆ —			
in-ter-*vene*,	in a *hut*	Anapest	Anapestic ⎫	
— ̆ ̆	— ̆ ̆		⎬ Triple meters	
en-ter-*prise*,	*col*-or of	Dactyl	Dactylic ⎭	
true-*blue*		Spondee	(Spondaic)	
truth		Monosyllabic foot		

The secondary unit of measurement, the **line**, is measured by naming the number of feet in it. The following names are used:

Monometer	one foot	Pentameter	five feet
Dimeter	two feet	Hexameter	six feet
Trimeter	three feet	Heptameter	seven feet
Tetrameter	four feet	Octameter	eight feet

The third unit, the **stanza**, consists of a group of lines whose metrical pattern is repeated throughout the poem. Since not all verse is written in stanzas, we shall save our discussion of this unit till a later chapter.

The process of measuring verse is referred to as **scansion**. To *scan* any specimen of verse, we do three things: (1) we identify the prevailing foot, (2) we name the number of feet in a line—if this length follows any regular pattern, and (3) we describe the stanza pattern—if there is one. We may try out our skill on the following poem.

132. VIRTUE

> Sweet day, so cool, so calm, so bright,
> The bridal of the earth and sky;
> The dew shall weep thy fall to night,
> For thou must die.

---

*In the spondee the accent is thought of as being distributed equally or almost equally over the two syllables and is sometimes referred to as a hovering accent. No whole poems are written in spondees or monosyllabic feet; hence there are only four basic meters: iambic, trochaic, anapestic, and dactylic. Iambic and trochaic are **duple meters** because they employ two-syllable feet; anapestic and dactylic are **triple meters** because they employ three-syllable feet.

Sweet rose, whose hue, angry and brave,   5
   Bids the rash gazer wipe his eye;
Thy root is ever in its grave,
   And thou must die.

Sweet spring, full of sweet days and roses,
   A box where sweets compacted lie;   10
My music shows ye have your closes,
   And all must die.

Only a sweet and virtuous soul,
   Like seasoned timber, never gives;
But though the whole world turn to coal,   15
   Then chiefly lives.

George Herbert (1593–1633)

QUESTIONS

1. Vocabulary: *bridal* (2), *brave* (5), *closes* (11).
2. How are the four stanzas interconnected? How do they build to a climax?
How does the fourth contrast with the first three?

The first step in scanning a poem is to read it normally according to
its prose meaning, listening to where the accents fall, and perhaps beating time with the hand. If we have any doubt about how a line should
be marked, we should skip it temporarily and go on to lines where we
feel greater confidence—that is, to those lines which seem most regular, with accents that fall unmistakably at regular intervals. In "Virtue"
lines 3, 10, and 14 clearly fall into this category, as do also the short
lines 4, 8, and 12. Lines 3, 10, and 14 may be marked as follows:

The dew | shall weep | thy fall | to night, | 3

A box | where sweets | com- pact- | ed lie; | 10

Like sea- | soned tim- | ber, nev- | er gives. | 14

Lines 4, 8, and 12 are so nearly identical that we may let line 4 represent
all three:

For thou | must die. | 4

Surveying what we have done so far, we may with some confidence
say that the prevailing metrical foot of the poem is iambic; and we may
reasonably hypothesize that the second and third lines of each stanza

are tetrameter (four-foot) lines and the fourth line dimeter. What about the first line? Line 1 contains eight syllables, and the last six are clearly iambic:

Sweet day,ˈsŏ co͞ol,ˈsŏ ca͞lm,ˈsŏ bri͞ght.ˈ   1

This too, then, is a tetrameter line, and the only question is whether to mark the first foot as another iamb or as a spondee. Many metrists, emphasizing the priority of pattern, would mark it as an iamb. Clearly, however, the word "Sweet" is more important and receives more emphasis in a sensitive reading than the three "so's" in the line. Other metrists, therefore, would give it equal emphasis with "day" and mark the first foot as a spondee. Neither marking can be called incorrect. It is a matter of the reader's personal judgment or of his metrical philosophy. Following my own preference, I mark it as a spondee, and mark the first foot in lines 5 and 9 correspondingly. Similar choices occur at several points in the poem (lines 11, 15, and 16). Many readers will quite legitimately perceive line 16 as parallel to lines 4, 8, and 12. Others, however, may argue that the word "Then"—emphasizing what happens to the virtuous soul when everything else has perished—has an importance that should be reflected in both the reading and the scansion and will therefore mark the first foot of this line as a spondee:

Th͞en chief-ˈlў li͞ves.ˈ   16

These readers will also see the third foot in line 15 as a spondee:

Bŭt thou͞ghˈthĕ who͞leˈwo͞rld tu͞rnˈtŏ co͞al.ˈ   15

Lines 2 and 7 introduce a different problem. Most readers, encountering these lines in a paragraph of prose, would read them thus:

Thĕ bri͞- dăl o͞f thĕ e͞arth ănd sk͞y,   2

Thў ro͞ot ĭs e͞v- ĕr ĭn ĭts gra͞ve.   7

But this reading leaves us with an anomalous situation. First, we have only three accents where our hypothetical pattern calls for four. Second, we have three unaccented syllables occurring together, a situation almost never encountered in verse of duple meter. From this situation we learn an important principle. Though normal reading of the sentences in a poem establishes its metrical pattern, the metrical pattern so established in turn influences the reading. A circular process is at work. In this poem the pressure of the pattern will cause most sensitive readers to stress the second of the three unaccented syllables slightly more than those on either side of it. In scansion we recognize this slight increase of stress by promoting the syllable to the status of an accented syllable. Thus we mark lines 2 and 7 respectively thus:

The bri-ˈ dal ofˈ the earthˈ and sky,ˈ   2

Thy rootˈ is ev-ˈ er inˈ its grave.ˈ   7

Line 5 presents a situation about which there can be no dispute. The word "angry," though it occurs in a position where we would expect an iamb, *must* be accented on the first syllable, and thus must be marked as a trochee:

Sweet rose,ˈ whose hue,ˈ an- gryˈ and brave.ˈ   5

There is little question also that the following line begins with a trochee in the first foot, followed by a spondee:

Bids theˈ rash gaz-ˈ er wipeˈ his eye.ˈ   6

Similarly, the word "Only," beginning line 13, is accented on the first syllable, thus introducing a trochaic substitution in the first foot of that line. Line 13 presents also another problem. A modern reader perceives the word "virtuous" as a three-syllable word, but the poet (writing in the seventeenth century, when metrical requirements were stricter than they are today) would probably have meant the word to be pronounced as two syllables (*ver-tyus*). Following the tastes of my century, I mark it as three, thus introducing an anapest instead of the expected iamb in the last foot:

On- lyˈa sweetˈand vir-ˈtu- ous soul.ˈ   13

In doing this, however, I am consciously "modernizing"—altering the intention of the poet for the sake of a contemporary audience.

One problem remains. In the third stanza, lines 9 and 11 differ from the other lines of the poem in two respects: (a) they contain nine rather than eight syllables; (b) they end on unaccented syllables.

Sweet spring,ˈ full ofˈ sweet daysˈ and ros-ˈ es,   9

My mu-ˈ sic showsˈ ye haveˈ your clos-ˈ es.   11

Such left-over unaccented syllables are not counted in identifying and naming the meter. These lines are both tetrameter, and if we tap our foot while reading them, we shall tap it four times. Metrical verse will often have one and sometimes two left-over unaccented syllables. In iambic and anapestic verse they will come at the end of lines; in trochaic and dactylic at the beginning.

Our metrical analysis of "Virtue" is completed. Though (mainly for ease of discussion) we have skipped about eccentrically, we have indicated a scansion for all its lines. "Virtue" is written in iambic meter (meaning that most of its feet are iambs), and is composed of four-line stanzas, the first three lines tetrameter, and the final line dimeter. We are now ready to make a few generalizations about scansion.

1. Good readers will not ordinarily stop to scan a poem they are reading, and they certainly will not read a poem with the exaggerated emphasis on accented syllables that we sometimes give them in order to make the scansion more apparent. However, occasional scansion of a poem has value, as will become more apparent in the next chapter, which discusses the relation of sound and meter to sense. Just one example here. The structure of meaning in "Virtue" is unmistakable. It consists of three parallel stanzas concerning things that die, followed by a contrasting fourth stanza concerning the one thing that does not die. The first three stanzas all begin with the word "Sweet" preceding a noun, and the first metrical foot in these stanzas—whether we consider it iamb or spondee—is the same. The contrasting fourth stanza, however, begins with a trochee, thus departing both from the previous pattern and from the basic meter of the poem. This departure is significant, for the word "Only" is the hinge upon which the structure of the poem turns, and the metrical reversal gives it emphasis. Thus meter serves meaning.

2. Scansion is at best a gross way of describing the rhythmical quality of a poem. It depends on classifying all syllables into either accented or unaccented categories and on ignoring the sometimes considerable difference between degrees of accent. Whether we call a syllable accented or unaccented depends, moreover, on its degree of accent relative to the syllables on either side of it. In lines 2 and 7 of "Virtue," the accents on "of" and "in" are obviously much lighter than on the other accented syllables in the line. Unaccented syllables also vary in weight. In line 5 "whose" is clearly heavier than "-gry" and "and," and is arguably heavier even than the accented "of" and "in" of lines 2 and 7. The most ardent champion of spondees, moreover, would concede that the accentual weight is not really equivalent in "Sweet rose": the noun shoulders more of the burden. Scansion is thus incapable of dealing with the subtlest rhythmical effects in poetry. It is nevertheless a useful and serviceable tool. Any measurement device more refined or sensitive would be too complicated to be widely serviceable.

3. Scansion is not an altogether exact science. Within certain limits we may say that a certain scansion is right or wrong, but beyond these limits there is legitimate room for disagreement between qualified read-

ers. Line 11 of "Virtue" provides the best example. Many metrists—those wanting scansion to reflect as closely as possible the underlying pattern—would mark it as perfectly regular: a succession of four iambs. Others—those wishing the scansion to reveal more nearly the nuances of a sensitive reading—would find that three sensitive readers might read this line in three different ways. One might stress "ye"; a second, "your"; and a third, both. The result is four possible scansions for this line:

My mu- | sic shows | ye have | your close- | es,   11

My mu- | sic shows | ye have | your close- | es,   11

My mu- | sic shows | ye have | your close- | es,   11

My mu- | sic shows | ye have | your close- | es.   11

Notice that the divisions between feet have no meaning except to help us identify the meter. They do not correspond to real divisions in the line; indeed, they fall often in the middle of a word. We place them where we do only to yield the most possible of a single kind of foot; in other words, to reveal regularity. If line 14 is marked

Like sea- | soned tim- | ber, nev- | er gives, | 14

it yields four regular iambs. If it were marked

Like | sea- soned | tim- ber, | nev- er | gives | 14

there would be an unaccented "left-over" syllable, three trochees, and a monosyllabic foot. The basic pattern of the poem would be obscured.

4. Finally—and this is the most important generalization of all—perfect regularity of meter is no criterion of merit. Beginning students sometimes get the notion that it is. If the meter is smooth and perfectly regular, they feel that the poet has handled the meter successfully and deserves all credit for it. Actually there is nothing easier than for any moderately talented versifier to make language go ta-*dum* ta-*dum* ta-*dum*. But there are two reasons why this is not generally desirable. The first is that, as we have said, all art consists essentially of repetition and variation. If a meter alternates too regularly between light and heavy beats, the result is to banish variation; the meter becomes mechanical and, for any sensitive reader, monotonous. The second is that, once a basic meter has been established, any deviations from it become highly significant and provide a means by which the poet can use meter to reinforce meaning. If a meter is too perfectly regular, the probability is that the poet, instead of adapting rhythm to meaning, has simply forced the meaning into a metrical straitjacket.

Actually what gives the skillful use of meter its greatest effectiveness is that it consists, not of one rhythm, but of two. One of these is the *expected* rhythm. The other is the *heard* rhythm. Once we have determined the basic meter of a poem, say, iambic tetrameter, we expect that this rhythm will continue. Thus a silent drumbeat is set up in our minds, and this drumbeat constitutes the expected rhythm. But the actual rhythm of the words—the heard rhythm—will sometimes confirm this expected rhythm and sometimes not. Thus the two rhythms are counterpointed, and the appeal of the verse is magnified just as when two melodies are counterpointed in music or as when we see two swallows flying together and around each other, following the same general course but with individual variations and making a much more eye-catching pattern than one swallow flying alone. If the heard rhythm conforms too closely to the expected rhythm, the meter becomes dull and uninteresting. If it departs too far from the expected rhythm, there ceases to be an expected rhythm. If the irregularity is too great, meter disappears and the result is prose rhythm or free verse.

There are several ways by which variation can be introduced into the poet's use of meter. The most obvious way is by the substitution of other kinds of feet for regular feet. In our scansion of line 9 of "Virtue," for instance, we found a spondee, a trochee, and another spondee substituted for the expected iambs in the first three feet (plus an unexpected unaccented syllable left over at the end of the line). A less obvious but equally important means of variation is through simple phrasing and variation of degrees of accent. Though we began our scansion of "Virtue" by marking lines 3, 10, and 14 as perfectly regular, there is actually a considerable difference among them. Line 3 is quite regular, for the phrasing corresponds with the metrical pattern, and the line can be read ta-*dum* ta-*dum* ta-*dum* ta-*dum*. Line 10 is less regular, for the three-syllable word "compacted" cuts across the division between two feet. We should read it ta-*dum* ta-*dum* ta-*dump*-ty *dum*. Line 14 is the least regular of the three, for here there is no correspondence between phrasing and metrical division. We should read this line ta-*dump*-ty *dump*-ty, *dump*-ty *dum*. Finally, variation can be introduced by grammatical and rhetorical pauses. The comma in line 14, by introducing a grammatical pause, provides an additional variation from its perfect regularity. Probably the most violently irregular line in the poem is line 5,

Sweet rose, whose hue, an- gry and brave,   5

for here the spondaic substitution in the first foot, and the unusual trochaic substitution in the middle of a line in the third foot, are set off and emphasized by grammatical pauses, and also (as we have noted) the unaccented "whose" is considerably heavier than the other two unaccented syllables in the line. It is worth noting that the violent irregularity of this line (only slightly diminished in the next) corresponds with, and reinforces, the most violent image in the poem. Again, meter serves meaning.

The uses of rhythm and meter are several. Like the musical repetitions of sound, the musical repetitions of accent can be pleasing for their own sake. In addition, rhythm works as an emotional stimulus and serves, when used skillfully, to heighten our attention and awareness to what is going on in a poem. Finally, by choice of meter, and by skillful use of variation within the metrical framework, the poet can adapt the sound of verse to its content and thus make meter a powerful reinforcement of meaning. We should avoid, however, the notion that there is any mystical correspondence between certain meters and certain emotions. There are no "happy" meters and no "melancholy" ones. The poet's choice of meter is probably less important than how he handles it after he has chosen it. However, some meters are swifter than others, some slower; some are more lilting than others, some more dignified. The poet can choose a meter that is appropriate or one that is inappropriate to his content, and by his handling of it can increase the appropriateness or inappropriateness. If he chooses a swift, lilting meter for a serious and grave subject, the meter will probably act to keep the reader from feeling any really deep emotion. But if he chooses a more dignified meter, it will intensify the emotion. In all great poetry, meter works intimately with the other elements of the poem to produce the appropriate total effect.

We must not forget, of course, that poetry need not be metrical at all. Like alliteration and rime, like metaphor and irony, like even imagery, meter is simply one resource the poet may or may not use. His job is to employ his resources to the best advantage for the object he has in mind—the kind of experience he wishes to express. And on no other basis can we judge him.

SUPPLEMENTAL NOTE

Of the four standard meters, iambic is by far the most common. Perhaps 80 percent of metered poetry in English is iambic. Anapestic meter (examples: "The Chimney Sweeper," No. 74, and "In the garden," No. 95) is next most common. Trochaic meter (example: "Counting-Out Rhyme," No. 129) is relatively infrequent. Dactylic meter is so rare as to be almost a museum specimen ("Bedtime Story," No. 222, in stanzas of three tetrameter lines followed by a dimeter line, is the sole example in this book).

Because of the predominance of iambic and anapestic meters in English verse, and because most anapestic poems have a high percentage of iambic substitutions, Robert Frost has written that in our language there are virtually but two meters: "strict iambic and loose iambic."* This is, of course, an overstatement; but, like many overstatements, it contains a good deal of truth. "Strict iambic" is strictly duple meter: it admits no trisyllabic substitutions. Trochees, spondees, and, occasionally, monosyllabic feet may be substituted for the expected iambs, but not anapests or dactyls. The presence of a triple foot has such a conspicuous effect in speeding or loosening up a line that the introduction of a few of them quite alters the nature of the meter. Herbert's "Virtue" is written in "strict iambic" (most of its feet are iambic; and, with the dubious exception of "virtuous," it contains no trisyllabic feet). "In the garden" and "The Chimney Sweeper" (after its difficult first stanza) are anapestic (most of their feet are anapests). But e.e. cummings's "if everything happens that can't be done" (No. 136), though by actual count it has more iambic feet than anapestic, *sounds* more like "The Chimney Sweeper" than it does like "Virtue." It would be impossible to define what percentage of anapestic feet a poem must have before it ceases seeming iambic and begins seeming anapestic, but it would be considerably less than 50 percent and might be more like 25 percent. At any rate, a large number of poems fall into an area between "strict iambic" and "prevailingly anapestic," and they might be fittingly described as iambic-anapestic (what Frost called "loose iambic").

Finally, the importance of the final paragraph preceding this note must be underscored: *poetry need not be metrical at all.* Following the prodigious example of Walt Whitman in the nineteenth century, more and more twentieth-century poets have turned to the writing of *free verse.* **Free verse**, by our definition, is not verse at all; that is, it is not metrical. It may be rimed or unrimed (but is most often unrimed). The only difference between free verse and rhythmical prose is that free verse introduces one additional rhythmical unit, the line. The arrangement into lines divides the material into rhythmical units, or cadences. Beyond its line arrangement there are no necessary differences between

*"The Figure a Poem Makes," *Selected Prose of Robert Frost* (New York: Holt, 1966), pp. 17–18.

it and rhythmical prose. Probably more than 50 percent of published contemporary poetry is written in free verse.

To add one further variation, a number of contemporary poets have begun writing "prose poems," or poems in prose (example: Carolyn Forché's "The Colonel," No. 206). It is too early to determine whether this is a passing fashion or will be a lasting development.

EXERCISES

1. An important term which every student of poetry should know (and should be careful not to confuse with *free verse*) is *blank verse*. **Blank verse** has a very specific meter: it is *iambic pentameter, unrimed*. It has a special name because it is the principal English meter, that is, the meter that has been used for a large proportion of the greatest English poetry, including the tragedies of Shakespeare and the epics of Milton. Iambic pentameter in English seems especially suitable for the serious treatment of serious themes. The natural movement of the English language tends to be iambic. Lines shorter than pentameter tend to be songlike, not suited to sustained treatment of serious material. Lines longer than pentameter tend to break up into shorter units, the hexameter line being read as two three-foot units, the heptameter line as a four-foot and a three-foot unit, and so on. Rime, while highly appropriate to most short poems, often proves a handicap for a long and lofty work. (The word *blank* implies that the end of the line is "blank," that is, bare of rime.)

Of the following poems, four are in blank verse, four are in free verse, and two are in other meters. Determine in which category each belongs.
   a. Portrait d'une Femme (No. 24).
   b. Last Stand (No. 89).
   c. Ulysses (No. 63).
   d. Base Details (No. 28).
   e. Excerpt from *Macbeth* (No. 85).
   f. "Out, Out—" (No. 84).
   g. Journey of the Magi (No. 92).
   h. The Telephone (No. 110).
   i. Mirror (No. 17).
   j. Love Song: I and Thou (No. 65).
2. Another useful distinction is that between end-stopped lines and run-on lines. An **end-stopped line** is one in which the end of the line corresponds with a natural speech pause; a **run-on line** is one in which the sense of the line hurries on into the next line. (There are, of course, all degrees of end-stop and run-on. A line ending with a period or semicolon is heavily end-stopped. A line without punctuation at the end is normally considered a run-on line, but it is less forcibly run-on if it ends at a natural speech pause— as between subject and predicate—than if it ends, say, between an article and its noun, between an auxiliary and its verb, or between a preposition and its object.) The use of run-on lines is one way the poet can make use of grammatical or rhetorical pauses to vary his basic meter.

a. Examine "Sound and Sense" (No. 147) and "My Last Duchess" (No. 83). Both are written in the same meter: iambic pentameter, rimed in couplets. Is their general rhythmical effect quite similar or markedly different? What accounts for the difference? Does the contrast support our statement that the poet's choice of meter is probably less important than the way he handles it?

b. Examine "The Hound" (No. 40) and "The Dance" (No. 155). Which is the more forcibly run-on in the majority of its lines? Describe the difference in effect.

* * *

133. "INTRODUCTION" TO *SONGS OF INNOCENCE*

Piping down the valleys wild,
Piping songs of pleasant glee,
On a cloud I saw a child,
And he laughing said to me:

"Pipe a song about a Lamb."   5
So I piped with merry cheer.
"Piper, pipe that song again."
So I piped; he wept to hear.

"Drop thy pipe, thy happy pipe;
Sing thy songs of happy cheer."   10
So I sung the same again
While he wept with joy to hear.

"Piper, sit thee down and write
In a book that all may read."
So he vanished from my sight,   15
And I plucked a hollow reed,

And I made a rural pen,
And I stained the water clear,
And I wrote my happy songs
Every child may joy to hear.   20

William Blake (1757–1827)

QUESTIONS

1. Poets have traditionally been thought of as inspired by one of the Muses (Greek female divinities whose duties were to nurture the arts). Blake's

Songs of Innocence, a book of poems about childhood and the state of innocence, includes "The Chimney Sweeper" (No. 74) and "The Lamb" (No. 196). In this introductory poem to the book, what function is played by the child upon a cloud?
2. What is symbolized by "a Lamb" (5)?
3. What three stages of poetic composition are suggested in stanzas 1–2, 3, and 4–5 respectively?
4. What features of the poems in his book does Blake indicate in this "Introduction"? Name at least four.
5. Mark the stressed and unstressed syllables in lines 1–2 and 9–10. Do they establish the basic meter of the poem? If so, is that meter iambic or trochaic? Or could it be either? Some metrists have discarded the distinction between iambic and trochaic, and between anapestic and dactylic, as being artificial. The important distinction, they feel, is between duple and triple meters. Does this poem support their claim?

134. IT TAKES ALL SORTS

It takes all sorts of in- and outdoor schooling
To get adapted to my kind of fooling.

Robert Frost (1874–1963)

QUESTIONS

1. What is the poet saying about the nature of his poetry?
2. Scan the poem. Is it iambic or trochaic? Or could it be either? How does this poem differ from Blake's "Introduction" in illustrating the ambiguity of the distinction between the two meters?

135. EPITAPH ON AN ARMY OF MERCENARIES

These, in the day when heaven was falling,
   The hour when earth's foundations fled,
Followed their mercenary calling
   And took their wages and are dead.

Their shoulders held the sky suspended;   5
   They stood, and earth's foundations stay;
What God abandoned, these defended,
   And saved the sum of things for pay.

A. E. Housman (1859–1936)

1. The Battle of Ypres (October 31, 1914), early in World War I, pitted a small army of British "regulars" against a much larger force of German volunteers. German newspapers described the conflict as one between young German volunteers and British "mercenaries." Housman first published this poem in the London *Times* on October 31, 1917, the third anniversary of the battle. Who are "These" (1)? Is the tone of the poem one of tribute or one of cynical scorn for "These"? How does the poet use the word "mercenary"?
2. In scanning Herbert's "Virtue," we discovered two lines that had an unaccented syllable left over at the end which we did not count in determining the meter. How does this poem differ from "Virtue" in its use of such lines? The meter of this poem is iambic tetrameter. Does this sufficiently describe its metrical form?

136. IF EVERYTHING HAPPENS THAT CAN'T BE DONE

if everything happens that can't be done
(and anything's righter
than books
could plan)
the stupidest teacher will almost guess   5
(with a run
skip
around we go yes)
there's nothing as something as one

one hasn't a why or because or although   10
(and buds know better
than books
don't grow)
one's anything old being everything new
(with a what   15
which
around we come who)
one's everyanything so

so world is a leaf so tree is a bough
(and birds sing sweeter   20
than books
tell how)
so here is away and so your is a my
(with a down
up   25
around again fly)
forever was never till now

now i love you and you love me
(and books are shuter
than books   30
can be)
and deep in the high that does nothing but fall
(with a shout
each
around we go all)   35
there's somebody calling who's we

we're anything brighter than even the sun
(we're everything greater
than books
might mean)   40
we're everyanything more than believe
(with a spin
leap
alive we're alive)
we're wonderful one times one   45

e. e. cummings (1894–1962)

QUESTIONS

1. Explain the last line. Of what very familiar idea is this poem a fresh treatment?
2. The poem is based on a contrast between heart and mind, or love and learning. Which does the poet prefer? What symbols does he use for each?
3. What is the tone of the poem?
4. Which lines of each stanza regularly rime with each other (either perfect or approximate rime)? How does the poet link the stanzas?
5. What is the basic metrical scheme of the poem? What does the meter contribute to the tone? What line (in the fourth stanza) most clearly states the subject and occasion of the poem? How does meter underline its significance?
6. Can you suggest any reason why the poet did not write lines 2–4 and 6–8 of each stanza as one line each? What metrical variations does the poet use in lines 6–8 of each stanza and with what effect?
7. In scanning "Virtue" (No. 132) we spoke of a circular process in which normal reading establishes the metrical pattern which then partially determines how the poem should be read. Whether, for instance, we read a word like *fire* as one syllable (riming with *hire*) or two syllables (riming with *liar*) may depend on the meter. The word *every* can be pronounced as having two syllables (*ev'ry*) or three (*ev-er-y*). How should it be pronounced in lines 14 and 38? In lines 18 and 41?

137. OH WHO IS THAT YOUNG SINNER

Oh who is that young sinner with the handcuffs on his wrists?
And what has he been after that they groan and shake their fists?
And wherefore is he wearing such a conscience-stricken air?
Oh they're taking him to prison for the color of his hair.

'Tis a shame to human nature, such a head of hair as his;   5
In the good old time 'twas hanging for the color that it is;
Though hanging isn't bad enough and flaying would be fair
For the nameless and abominable color of his hair.

Oh a deal of pains he's taken and a pretty price he's paid
To hide his poll or dye it of a mentionable shade;   10
But they've pulled the beggar's hat off for the world to see and stare,
And they're taking him to justice for the color of his hair.

Now 'tis oakum for his fingers and the treadmill for his feet,
And the quarry-gang on Portland in the cold and in the heat,
And between his spells of labor in the time he has to spare   15
He can curse the God that made him for the color of his hair.

A. E. Housman (1859–1936)

QUESTIONS

1. Vocabulary: *poll* (10), *oakum* (13). Portland (14), an English peninsula, is the site of a famous criminal prison.
2. What kind of irony does the poem exhibit? Explain.
3. What symbolic meanings are suggested by "the color of his hair"?
4. This poem represents a kind of meter that we have not yet discussed. It *may* be scanned as iambic heptameter:

Ŏh who | ĭs that | yŏung sin-|nĕr with | thĕ hand-|cŭffs on | hĭs wrists?

But you will probably find yourself reading it as a four-beat line:

Ŏh who | ĭs thăt yŏung sin-|nĕr wĭth thĕ hand-|cŭffs ŏn hĭs wrists?

Although the meter is duple insofar as there is an alternation between unaccented and accented syllables, there is also an alternation in the degree of stress on the accented syllables: the first, third, fifth, and seventh stresses being heavier than the second, fourth, and sixth; the result is that the two-syllable feet tend to group themselves into larger units. We may scan it as follows, using a short line for a light accent, a longer one for a heavy accent:

Oh who is that young sin-ner with the hand-cuffs on his wrists?
And what has he been af-ter that they groan and shake their fists?
And where-fore is he wear-ing such a con-science strick-en air?
Oh they're tak-ing him to pris-on for the col-or of his hair.

This kind of meter, in which there is an alternation between heavy and light stresses, is known as **dipodic** (two-footed) **verse**. The alternation may not be perfect throughout, but it will be frequent enough to establish a pattern in the reader's mind. Now scan the last three stanzas. For another example of dipodic verse, see "Midway" (No. 223).

138. DOWN BY THE SALLEY GARDENS

Down by the salley gardens my love and I did meet;
She passed the salley gardens with little snow-white feet.
She bid me take love easy, as the leaves grow on the tree;
But I, being young and foolish, with her would not agree.
In a field by the river my love and I did stand,
And on my leaning shoulder she laid her snow-white hand.
She bid me take life easy, as the grass grows on the weirs;
But I was young and foolish, and now am full of tears.

William Butler Yeats (1865–1939)

QUESTIONS

1. Vocabulary: *salley* (1), *weirs* (7).
2. This poem introduces an additional kind of metrical variation—the metrical pause or rest. Unlike grammatical and rhetorical pauses, the metrical pause affects scansion. If you beat out the rhythm of this poem with your hand, you will find that the fourth beat of each line (possibly excepting lines 3 and 7) regularly falls *between* syllables. A **metrical pause**, then, is a pause that replaces an accented syllable. It is usually found in verse that has a pro-nounced lilt or swing. The first line of Yeats's poem may be scanned as follows (the metrical pause is represented with an *x*):

Down by the sal-ley gar-dens^x my love and I did meet.

The third line might be scanned in several ways, as the following alternatives suggest:

She bid me take love eas-y, as the leaves grow on the tree,
She bid me take love eas-y,^{x} as the leaves grow on the tree.

Scan the rest of the poem.

139. HAD I THE CHOICE

Had I the choice to tally greatest bards,
To limn their portraits, stately, beautiful, and emulate at will,
Homer with all his wars and warriors—Hector, Achilles, Ajax,
Or Shakespeare's woe-entangled Hamlet, Lear, Othello—Tennyson's
    fair ladies,
Meter or wit the best, or choice conceit to wield in perfect rhyme,
    delight of singers;
These, these, O sea, all these I'd gladly barter,
Would you the undulation of one wave, its trick to me transfer,
Or breathe one breath of yours upon my verse,
And leave its odor there.

Walt Whitman (1819–1892)

QUESTIONS

1. Vocabulary: *tally* (1), *limn* (2), *conceit* (5).
2. What poetic qualities does Whitman propose to barter in exchange for what?
   What qualities do the sea and its waves symbolize?
3. What kind of "verse" is this? Why does Whitman prefer it to "meter" and
   "perfect rhyme"?

140. THE AIM WAS SONG

Before man came to blow it right
    The wind once blew itself untaught,
And did its loudest day and night
    In any rough place where it caught.

Man came to tell it what was wrong: 5
    It hadn't found the place to blow;
It blew too hard—the aim was song.
    And listen—how it ought to go!

He took a little in his mouth,
    And held it long enough for north   10
To be converted into south,
    And then by measure blew it forth.

By measure. It was word and note,
    The wind the wind had meant to be—
A little through the lips and throat.   15
    The aim was song—the wind could see.

Robert Frost (1874–1963)

1. Frost invents a myth about the origin of poetry. What implications does it suggest about the relation of man to nature and of poetry to nature?
2. Contrast the thought and form of this poem with Whitman's.
3. Scan the poem and identify its meter. How does the poet give variety to a regular metrical pattern?

141. METRICAL FEET

Tro-chee trips from long to short.

From long to long in sol-emn sort

Slow Spon-dee stalks; strong foot! yet ill a-ble

Ev-er to come up with Dac-tyl tri-syl-la-ble.

I-am-bics march from short to long;

With a leap and a bound the swift An-a-pests throng.

Samuel Taylor Coleridge (1772–1834)

QUESTIONS

1. The scansion markings for lines 1–3 have been deliberately left incomplete by your editors. Why? How would you complete the marking?
2. The meter of this poem cannot be fully named because there is no prevailing foot. (Two lines, however, are metrically identical. Which two?) *Can* the poem be assigned a consistent line length—trimeter, tetrameter, or pentameter?
3. If you have trouble remembering the metrical feet, memorize this.

EXERCISE

The following passage, a scene in the Garden of Eden, is excerpted from Milton's epic *Paradise Lost*. The poem is written in blank verse, but the *visual* signs of its metrical form (line spacing, capital letters at line beginnings) are here removed. Using your ear and your knowledge of the poem's meter, decide where the line breaks occur, and indicate them with a slash mark.

Now came still Evening on, and Twilight gray had in her sober livery all things clad; Silence accompanied, for beast and bird, they to their grassy couch, these to their nests were slunk, all but the wakeful nightingale; she all night long her amorous descant sang; Silence was pleased; now glowed the firmament with living sapphires: Hesperus that led the starry host, rode brightest, till the Moon rising in cloudy majesty, at length apparent Queen, unveiled her peerless light, and o'er the dark her silver mantle threw.

Chapter thirteen
Sound and Meaning

Rhythm and sound cooperate to produce what we call the music of poetry. This music, as we have pointed out, may serve two general functions: it may be enjoyable in itself; it may be used to reinforce meaning and intensify the communication.

Pure pleasure in sound and rhythm exists from a very early age in the human being—probably from the age the baby first starts cooing in its cradle, certainly from the age that children begin chanting nursery rimes and skipping rope. The appeal of the following verse, for instance, depends almost entirely on its "music":

142.   Pease por-ridge hot,
          Pease por-ridge cold,
          Pease por-ridge in the pot
          Nine days old.

There is very little sense here; the attraction comes from the emphatic rhythm, the emphatic rimes (with a strong contrast between the short vowel and short final consonant of *hot-pot* and the long vowel and long final consonant combination of *cold-old*), and the heavy alliteration (exactly half the words begin with *p*). From nonsense rimes such as this, many of us graduate into a love of more meaningful poems whose appeal resides largely in the sound they make. Much of the pleasure that we find in poems like Vachel Lindsay's "The Congo" and Edgar Allan Poe's "The Bells" lies in their musical qualities.

The peculiar function of poetry as distinguished from music, however, is to convey not sounds but meaning or experience *through* sounds. In third- and fourth-rate poetry, sound and rhythm sometimes distract attention from sense. In first-rate poetry the sound exists, not for its own sake, not for mere decoration, but as a medium of meaning. Its function is to support the leading player, not to steal the scene.

There are numerous ways in which the poet may reinforce meaning through sound. Without claiming to exhaust them, perhaps we can include most of the chief means under four general headings.

First, the poet can choose words whose sound in some degree suggests their meaning. In its narrowest sense this is called onomatopoeia. **Onomatopoeia,** strictly defined, means the use of words which, at least supposedly, sound like what they mean, such as *hiss, snap,* and *bang.*

143. SONG: HARK, HARK!

Hark, hark!
Bow-wow.
The watch-dogs bark!
Bow-wow.
Hark, hark! I hear
The strain of strutting chanticleer
Cry, "Cock-a-doodle-doo!"

William Shakespeare (1564–1616)

In these lines, "bark," "bow-wow," and "cock-a-doodle-doo" are onomatopoetic words. In addition, Shakespeare has reinforced the onomatopoetic effect with the repeated use of "hark," which sounds like "bark." The usefulness of onomatopoeia, of course, is strictly limited, because it can be used only where the poet is describing sound, and most poems do not describe sound. And the use of pure onomatopoeia, as in the preceding example, is likely to be fairly trivial except as it forms an incidental part of a more complex poem. But by combining onomatopoeia with other devices that help convey meaning, the poet can achieve subtle and beautiful effects whose recognition is one of the keenest pleasures in reading poetry.

In addition to onomatopoetic words there is another group of words, sometimes called **phonetic intensives,** whose sound, by a process as yet obscure, to some degree connects with their meaning. An initial *fl-* sound, for instance, is often associated with the idea of moving light, as in *flame, flare, flash, flicker, flimmer.* An initial *gl-* also frequently accompanies the idea of light, usually unmoving, as in *glare,* *gleam, glint, glow, glisten.* An initial *sl-* often introduces words meaning "smoothly wet," as in *slippery, slick, slide, slime, slop, slosh, slobber, slushy.* An initial *st-* often suggests strength, as in *staunch, stalwart, stout, sturdy, stable, steady, stocky, stern, strong, stubborn, steel.* Short *-i-* often goes with the idea of smallness, as in *inch, imp, thin, slim, little, bit, chip, sliver, chink, slit, sip, whit, tittle, snip, wink, glint, glimmer, flicker, pigmy, midge, chick, kid, kitten, minikin, miniature.* Long *-o-* or *-oo-* may suggest melancholy or sorrow, as in *moan, groan, woe, mourn, forlorn, toll, doom, gloom, moody.* Final *-are* sometimes goes with the idea of a big light or noise, as *flare, glare, stare, blare.* Medial *-att-* suggests some kind of particled movement, as in *spatter, scatter, shatter, chatter, rattle, prattle, clatter, batter.* Final *-er* and *-le* indicate repetition, as in *glitter, flutter, shimmer, whisper, jabber, chatter, clatter, sputter, flicker, twitter, mutter,* and *ripple, bubble, twinkle, sparkle, rattle, rumble, jingle.* None of these various sounds is invariably associated with the idea that it seems to suggest, and, in fact, a short *-i-* is found in *thick* as well as *thin,* in *big* as well as *little.* Language is a complex phenomenon. But there is enough association between these sounds and ideas to suggest some sort of intrinsic if obscure relationship, and a word like *flicker,* though not onomatopoetic, for it does not refer to sound, would seem somehow to suggest its sense, the *fl-* suggesting moving light, the *-i-* suggesting smallness, the *-ck-* suggesting sudden cessation of movement (as in *crack, peck, pick, hack,* and *flick*), and the *-er* suggesting repetition. The above list of sound-idea correspondences is only a very partial one. A complete list, though it would involve only a small proportion of words in the language, would probably be a longer list than that of the more strictly onomatopoetic words, to which they are related.

144. SPLINTER

The voice of the last cricket
across the first frost
is one kind of good-by.
It is so thin a splinter of singing.

Carl Sandburg (1878–1967)

QUESTIONS

1. Why is "so thin a splinter" a better choice of metaphor than *so small an atom* or *so meager a morsel?*
2. How does the poet intensify the effect of the two phonetic intensives in line 4?

A second way that the poet can reinforce meaning through sound is to choose sounds and group them so that the effect is smooth and pleasant sounding *(euphonious)* or rough and harsh sounding *(cacophonous)*. The vowels are in general more pleasing than the consonants, for the vowels are musical tones, whereas the consonants are merely noises. A line with a high percentage of vowel sounds in proportion to consonant sounds will therefore tend to be more melodious than one in which the proportion is low. The vowels and consonants themselves differ considerably in quality. The "long" vowels, such as those in *fate, reed, rime, coat, food,* and *dune* are fuller and more resonant than the "short" vowels, as in *fat, red, rim, cot, foot,* and *dun.* Of the consonants, some are fairly mellifluous, such as the "liquids," *l, m, n,* and *r;* the soft *v* and *f* sounds; the semivowels *w* and *y;* and such combinations as *th* and *wh.* Others, such as the "plosives," *b, d, g, k, p,* and *t,* are harsher and sharper in their effect. These differences in sound are the poet's materials. Good poets, however, will not necessarily seek out the sounds that are pleasing and attempt to combine them in melodious combinations. Rather, they will use **euphony** and **cacophony** as they are appropriate to content. Consider, for instance, the following poem.

145. UPON JULIA'S VOICE

So smooth, so sweet, so silvery is thy voice,
As, could they hear, the Damned would make no noise,
But listen to thee (walking in thy chamber)
Melting melodious words to Lutes of Amber.

Robert Herrick (1591–1674)

QUESTION

Literally, an amber lute is as nonsensical as a silver voice. What connotations do "Amber" and "silvery" have that contribute to the meaning of this poem?

There are no strictly onomatopoetic words in this poem, and yet the sound seems marvelously adapted to the sense. Especially remarkable are the first and last lines, those most directly concerned with Julia's voice. In the first line the sounds that most strike the ear are the unvoiced *s*'s and the soft *v*'s, supported by *th:* "So smoo*th,* so *s*weet, so *s*ilvery is *th*y *v*oice." In the fourth line the predominating sounds are the liquid consonants *m, l,* and *r,* supported by a *w:* "*Me*lting *me*lodious *w*ords to *L*utes of *A*mber." The least euphonious line in the poem, on the other hand, is the second, where the subject is the tormented in hell, not Julia's voice. Here the prominent sounds are the *d*'s, supported by a voiced *s* (a voiced *s* buzzes, unlike the sibilant unvoiced *s*'s in line 1), and two *k* sounds: "A*s*, *could* they hear, the *D*amne*d* would ma*k*e no noi*s*e." Throughout the poem there is a remarkable correspondence between the pleasant-sounding and the pleasant in idea, the unpleasant-sounding and the unpleasant in idea.

A third way in which a poet can reinforce meaning through sound is by controlling the speed and movement of the lines by the choice and use of meter, by the choice and arrangement of vowel and consonant sounds, and by the disposition of pauses. In meter the unaccented syllables usually go faster than the accented syllables; hence the triple meters are swifter than the duple. But the poet can vary the tempo of any meter by the use of substitute feet. Generally, whenever two or more unaccented syllables come together, the effect will be to speed up the pace of the line; when two or more accented syllables come together, the effect will be to slow it down. This pace will also be affected by the vowel lengths and by whether the sounds are easily run together. The long vowels take longer to pronounce than the short ones. Some words are easily run together, while others demand that the position of the mouth be re-formed before the next word is uttered. It takes much longer, for instance, to say, "Watch dogs catch much meat" than to say, "My aunt is away," though the number of syllables is the same. And finally the poet can slow down the speed of a line through the introduction of grammatical and rhetorical pauses. Consider lines 54–56 from Tennyson's "Ulysses" (No. 63):

The lights be-gin to twin-kle from the rocks;

The long day wanes; the slow moon climbs; the deep   55

Moans round with man-y voi-ces . . .

In these lines Tennyson wished the movement to be slow, in accordance with the slow waning of the long day and the slow climbing of the moon. His meter is iambic pentameter. This is not a swift meter, but in lines 55–56 he slows it down, (1) by introducing three spondaic feet, thus bringing three accented syllables together in three separate places; (2) by choosing for his accented syllables words that have long vowel sounds or dipthongs that the voice hangs on to: "long," "day," "wanes," "slow," "moon," "climbs," "deep," "moans," "round"; (3) by choosing words that are not easily run together (except for "day" and "slow," each of these words begins and ends with consonant sounds that demand varying degrees of readjustment of the mouth before pronunciation is continued); (4) by introducing two grammatical pauses, after "wanes" and "climbs," and a rhetorical pause after "deep." The result is an extremely effective use of the movement of the verse to accord with the movement suggested by the words.*

A fourth way for a poet to fit sound to sense is to control both sound and meter in such a way as to emphasize words that are important in meaning. This can be done by highlighting such words through alliteration, assonance, consonance, or rime; by placing them before a pause; or by skillfully placing or displacing them in the metrical scheme. We have already seen how Ogden Nash uses alliteration and consonance to emphasize and link the three major words ("sex," "fix," and "fertile") in his little verse "The Turtle" (No. 120), and how George Herbert pivots the structure of meaning in "Virtue" (No. 132) on a trochaic substitution in the initial foot of his final stanza. For an additional example, let us look again at "Since there's no help" (No. 109). This poem is a sonnet—fourteen lines of iambic pentameter—in which a lover threatens to leave his sweetheart forever if she will not go to bed with him. In the first eight lines he pretends to be *glad* that they are breaking off their relationship so cleanly. In the last six lines, however, he paints a vivid picture of the death of his personified Love/Passion for her but intimates that even at this last moment ("Now") she could restore it to life again—by satisfying his sexual desires.

Now, at the last gasp of Love's latest breath,

When, his pulse failing, Passion speechless lies,　　　　10

When Faith is kneeling by his bed of death,

And Innocence is closing up his eyes.

Now, if thou wouldst, when all have given him over,†

From death to life thou mightst him yet recover.

---

*In addition, Tennyson uses one onomatopoetic word ("moans") and one phonetic intensive ("twinkle").

†Drayton probably intended "given" to be pronounced as one syllable (*giv'n*), and most sixteenth-century readers would have pronounced it thus in this poem.

The emphasis is on *Now*. In a matter of seconds, the speaker indicates, it will be too late: his Love/Passion will be dead, and he himself will be gone. The word "Now" begins line 9. It also begins a new sentence and a new direction in the poem. It is separated from what has gone before by a period at the end of the preceding line. Metrically it initiates a trochee, thus breaking away from the poem's basic iambic meter (line 8 is perfectly regular). In all these ways—its initial position in line, sentence, and thought, and its metrical irregularity—the word "Now" is given extraordinary emphasis appropriate to its importance in the context. Its repetition in line 13 reaffirms this importance, and there again it is given emphasis by its positional and metrical situation. It begins both a line and the final riming couplet, is separated by punctuation from the line before, and participates in a metrical inversion. (The lines before and after are metrically regular.)

While Herbert and Drayton use metrical deviation to give emphasis to important words, Tennyson, in the concluding line of "Ulysses," uses marked regularity, plus skillful use of grammatical pauses, to achieve the same effect:

> We are | not now | that strength | which in old | days |
> Moved earth | and heav-en, | that | which we are, | we are: |
> One e- | qual tem-per of | he-ro-ic hearts, |
> Made weak | by time | and fate, | but strong | in will |
> To strive, | to seek, | to find, | and not | to yield. |

The blank verse rhythm throughout "Ulysses" is remarkably subtle and varied, but the last line is not only regular in its scansion but heavily regular, for a number of reasons. First, all the words are monosyllables: no words cross over the divisions between feet. Second, the unaccented syllables are all very small and unimportant words—four "to's" and one "and," whereas the accented syllables consist of four important verbs and a very important "not." Third, each of the verbs is followed by a grammatical pause pointed off by a mark of punctuation. The result is to cause a pronounced alternation between light and heavy syllables that brings the accent down on the four verbs and the "not" with sledgehammer blows. The line rings out like a challenge, which it is.

146. THE SPAN OF LIFE

The old dog barks backward without getting up.
I can remember when he was a pup.

Robert Frost (1874–1963)

QUESTIONS

1. Is the dog a dog only or also a symbol?
2. The first line presents a visual and auditory image; the second line makes a comment. But does the second line *call up images?* Does it suggest more than it says? Would the poem have been more or less effective if the second line had been, "He was frisky and lively when he was a pup"?

We may well conclude our discussion of the adaptation of sound to sense by analyzing this very brief poem. It consists of one riming anapestic tetrameter couplet. Its content is a contrast between the decrepitude of an old dog and his friskiness as a pup. The scansion is as follows:

The old | dog barks back-|ward with-out | get-ting up.

I | can re-mem-|ber when he | was a pup.

How is sound fitted to sense? In the first place, the triple meter chosen by the poet is a swift meter, but in the first line he has jammed it up in a remarkable way by substituting a kind of foot so rare that we do not even have a name for it. It might be called a triple spondee: at any rate it is a foot in which the accent is distributed over three syllables. This foot, following the accented syllable in the first foot, creates a situation where four accented syllables are pushed up together. In addition, each of these accented syllables begins and ends with a strong consonant sound or cluster of consonant sounds, so that they cannot be run together in pronunciation: the mouth must be re-formed between syllables: "The ol*d dog barks back*ward." The result is to slow down the line drastically, to damage its rhythmical quality severely, and to make it difficult to utter. Indeed, the line is as decrepit as the old dog who turns his head to greet his master but does not get up. When we get to the second line, however, the contrast is startling. The rhythm is swift and regular, the syllables end in vowels or liquid consonants and are easily run together, the whole line ripples fluently off the tongue. In addition, where the first line has a high proportion of explosive and cacophonous

consonants—"The old dog barks backward without getting up"—the
second line contains predominantly consonants which are smoother and
more graceful—"I can remember when he was a pup." Thus the motion
and the sound of the lines are remarkably in accord with the visual images they suggest. In addition, in the first line the poet has supported the
onomatopoetic word barks with a near echo back, so that the sound reinforces the auditory image. If the poem does a great deal in just two lines,
this skillful adaptation of sound to sense is one very important reason.

In analyzing verse for correspondence between sound and sense, we
need to be very cautious not to make exaggerated claims. A great deal of
nonsense has been written about the moods of certain meters and the
effects of certain sounds, and it is easy to suggest correspondences that
exist really only in our imaginations. Nevertheless, the first-rate poet
has nearly always an instinctive tact about handling sound so that it in
some degree supports meaning; the inferior poet is usually obtuse to
these correspondences. One of the few absolute rules that can be applied to the judgment of poetry is that the form should be adequate to
the content. This rule does not mean that there must always be a close
and easily demonstrable correspondence. It does mean that there will
be no glaring discrepancies. Poor poets, and even good poets in their
third-rate work, sometimes go horribly wrong.

The two selections that introduce this chapter illustrate, first, the
use of sound in verse almost purely for its own sake ("Pease porridge
hot"), and, second, the use of sound in verse almost purely to *imitate*
meaning ("Hark, hark! Bow-wow"), and they are, as significant poetry, perhaps the most trivial pieces in the whole book. But in between
these extremes there is an abundant range of poetic possibilities where
sound is pleasurable for itself without violating meaning and where
sound to varying degrees corresponds with and corroborates meaning;
and in this rich middle range, for the reader who can learn to perceive
them, lie many of the greatest pleasures of reading poetry.

EXERCISE

In each of the following paired quotations, the named poet wrote the version
that more successfully adapts sound to sense. As specifically as possible, account for the superiority of the better version.

1. a. Go forth—and Virtue, ever in your sight,
      Shall be your guide by day, your guard by night.
   b. Go forth—and Virtue, ever in your sight,
      Shall point your way by day, and keep you safe at night.
                                                    Charles Churchill

2. a. How charming is divine philosophy!
      Not harsh and rough as foolish men suppose
      But musical as is the lute of Phoebus.
   b. How charming is divine philosophy!
      Not harsh and crabbed as dull fools suppose
      But musical as is Apollo's lute.   *John Milton*

3. a. All day the fleeing crows croak hoarsely over the snow.
   b. All day the out-cast crows croak hoarsely across the whiteness.
                                                          Elizabeth Coatsworth

4. a. Your talk attests how bells of singing gold
      Would sound at evening over silent water.
   b. Your low voice tells how bells of singing gold
      Would sound at twilight over silent water.   *Edwin Arlington Robinson*

5. a. A thousand streamlets flowing through the lawn,
      The moan of doves in gnarled ancient oaks,
      And quiet murmuring of countless bees.
   b. Myriads of rivulets hurrying through the lawn,
      The moan of doves in immemorial elms,
      And murmuring of innumerable bees.   *Alfred, Lord Tennyson*

6. a. It is the lark that sings so out of tune,
      Straining harsh discords and unpleasing sharps.
   b. It is the lark that warbles out of tune
      In harsh discordant tones with doleful flats.   *William Shakespeare*

7. a. "Artillery" and "armaments" and "implements of war"
      Are phrases too severe to please the gentle Muse.
   b. Bombs, drums, guns, bastions, batteries, bayonets, bullets,—
      Hard words, which stick in the soft Muses' gullets.   *Lord Byron*

8. a. The hands of the sisters Death and Night incessantly softly wash
         again, and ever again, this soiled world.
   b. The hands of the soft twins Death and Night repeatedly wash
         again, and ever again, this dirty world.   *Walt Whitman*

9. a. The curfew sounds the knell of parting day,
      The lowing cattle slowly cross the lea,
      The plowman goes wearily plodding his homeward way,
      Leaving the world to the darkening night and me.
   b. The curfew tolls the knell of parting day,
      The lowing herd wind slowly o'er the lea,
      The plowman homeward plods his weary way,
      And leaves the world to darkness and to me.   *Thomas Gray*

10. a. Let me chastise this odious, gilded bug,
       This painted son of dirt, that smells and bites.
    b. Yet let me flap this bug with gilded wings,
       This painted child of dirt, that stinks and stings.   *Alexander Pope*

*   *   *

147. SOUND AND SENSE

True ease in writing comes from art, not chance,
As those move easiest who have learned to dance.
'Tis not enough no harshness gives offense,
The sound must seem an echo to the sense:
Soft is the strain when Zephyr gently blows,   5
And the smooth stream in smoother numbers flows;
But when loud surges lash the sounding shore,
The hoarse, rough verse should like the torrent roar;
When Ajax strives some rock's vast weight to throw,
The line too labors, and the words move slow;   10
Not so, when swift Camilla scours the plain,
Flies o'er the unbending corn, and skims along the main.
Hear how Timotheus' varied lays surprise,
And bid alternate passions fall and rise!

Alexander Pope (1688–1744)

QUESTIONS

1. Vocabulary: *numbers* (6), *lays* (13).
2. This excerpt is from a long poem (called *An Essay on Criticism*) on the arts of writing and judging poetry. Which line is the topic sentence of the passage?
3. There are four classical allusions: Zephyr (5) was god of the west wind; Ajax (9), a Greek warrior noted for his strength; Camilla (11), a legendary queen reputedly so fleet of foot that she could run over a field of grain without bending the blades or over the sea without wetting her feet; Timotheus (13), a famous Greek rhapsodic poet. Does the use of these allusions enable Pope to achieve greater economy?
4. Copy the passage and scan it. Then, considering both meter and sounds, show how Pope practices what he preaches. (Incidentally, on which syllable should "alternate" in line 14 be accented? Does the meter help you to know the pronunciation of "Timotheus'" in line 13?)

148. I LIKE TO SEE IT LAP THE MILES

I like to see it lap the miles,
And lick the valleys up,
And stop to feed itself at tanks;
And then, prodigious, step

Around a pile of mountains,   5
And, supercilious, peer
In shanties by the sides of roads;
And then a quarry pare

To fit its ribs,
And crawl between,   10
Complaining all the while
In horrid, hooting stanza;
Then chase itself down hill

And neigh like Boanerges;
Then, punctual as a star,   15
Stop—docile and omnipotent—
At its own stable door.

Emily Dickinson (1830–1886)

QUESTIONS

1. Vocabulary: *prodigious* (4), *supercilious* (6), *Boanerges* (14).
2. What basic metaphor underlies the poem? Identify the literal and the metaphorical terms and explain how you were able to make both identifications.
3. What additional figures of speech do you find in lines 8, 12, 15, 16, and 17?
   Explain their appropriateness.
4. Point out examples of alliteration, assonance, and consonance. Does this
   poem have a rime scheme?
5. Considering such things as sounds and sound repetitions, grammatical
   pauses, run-on lines, monosyllabic and polysyllabic words, onomatopoeia,
   and meter, explain in detail how sound is fitted to sense in this poem.

149. WIND

This house has been far out at sea all night,
The woods crashing through darkness, the booming hills,
Winds stampeding the fields under the window
Floundering black astride and blinding wet

Till day rose; then under an orange sky   5
The hills had new places, and wind wielded
Blade-like, luminous black and emerald,
Flexing like the lens of a mad eye.

At noon I scaled along the house-side as far as
The coal-house door. I dared once to look up—   10
Through the brunt wind that dented the balls of my eyes
The tent of the hills drummed and strained its guyrope,

The fields quivering, the skyline a grimace,
At any second to bang and vanish with a flap:
The wind flung a magpie away and a black-   15
Back gull bent like an iron bar slowly. The house

Rang like some fine green goblet in the note
That any second would shatter it. Now deep
In chairs, in front of the great fire, we grip
Our hearts and cannot entertain book, thought,   20

Or each other. We watch the fire blazing,
And feel the roots of the house move, but sit on,
Seeing the window tremble to come in,
Hearing the stones cry out under the horizons.

Ted Hughes (b. 1930)

QUESTIONS

1. Explain the images, or metaphors, in lines 1, 3, 6, 7–8, 12–14, 15–16, 22.
   What kind of weather is the poem describing?
2. Discuss the adaptation of sound to sense.

150. HEAVEN-HAVEN

A Nun Takes the Veil

> I have desired to go
>   Where springs not fail,
> To fields where flies no sharp and sided hail
> And a few lilies blow.
>
> And I have asked to be
>   Where no storms come,
> Where the green swell is in the havens dumb,
> And out of the swing of the sea.

Gerard Manley Hopkins (1844–1889)

QUESTIONS

1. Vocabulary: *blow* (4).
2. Who is the speaker and what is the situation? Explain the metaphors that
   form the substance of the poem. What things are being compared?
3. Comment on the meaning of "springs" (2) and on the effectiveness of the
   poet's choice of "lilies" (4).
4. How do the sound repetitions of the title reinforce the meaning? Are there
   other instances in the poem where sound reinforces meaning?
5. Scan the poem. (The meter is basically iambic, but there is a great deal of

variation.) How does the meter reinforce meaning, especially in the last line? What purpose is served by the displacement of "not" (2) from its normal order?

151. ANTHEM FOR DOOMED YOUTH

What passing-bells for these who die as cattle?
Only the monstrous anger of the guns.
Only the stuttering rifles' rapid rattle
Can patter out their hasty orisons.
No mockeries now for them; no prayers nor bells,   5
Nor any voice of mourning save the choirs—
The shrill, demented choirs of wailing shells;
And bugles calling for them from sad shires.

What candles may be held to speed them all?
Not in the hands of boys, but in their eyes   10
Shall shine the holy glimmers of good-byes.
The pallor of girls' brows shall be their pall;
Their flowers the tenderness of patient minds,
And each slow dusk a drawing-down of blinds.

Wilfred Owen (1893–1918)

QUESTIONS

1. Vocabulary: *passing-bells* (1), *orisons* (4), *shires* (8), *pall* (12).
2. How do the octave and the sestet of this sonnet differ in (a) geographical setting, (b) subject matter, (c) kind of imagery used, and (d) tone? Who are the "boys" (10) and "girls" (12) referred to in the sestet? It was the custom during World War I to draw down the blinds in homes where a son had been lost (14).
3. What central metaphorical image runs throughout the poem? What secondary metaphors build up the central one?
4. Why are the "doomed youth" said to die "as cattle"? Why would prayers, bells, and so on, be "mockeries" for them (5)?
5. Show how sound is adapted to sense throughout the poem.

152. EIGHT O'CLOCK

He stood, and heard the steeple
   Sprinkle the quarters on the morning town.
One, two, three, four, to market-place and people
   It tossed them down.

Strapped, noosed, nighing his hour,
He stood and counted them and cursed his luck;
And then the clock collected in the tower
Its strength, and struck.

A. E. Housman (1859–1936)

QUESTIONS

1. Vocabulary: *quarters* (2).
2. Eight A.M. was the traditional hour in England for putting condemned men to death. Discuss the force of "morning" (2) and "struck" (8). Discuss the appropriateness of the image of the clock collecting its strength. Can you suggest any reason for the use of "nighing" (5) rather than *nearing?*
3. Scan the poem and note its musical devices. Comment on the adaptation of sound to sense.

153. ALL DAY I HEAR

All day I hear the noise of waters
    Making moan,
Sad as the sea-bird is, when going
    Forth alone,
He hears the winds cry to the waters'   5
    Monotone.

The grey winds, the cold winds are blowing
    Where I go.
I hear the noise of many waters
    Far below.   10
All day, all night, I hear them flowing
    To and fro.

James Joyce (1882–1941)

QUESTIONS

1. What is the central purpose of the poem? Is it primarily descriptive?
2. What kinds of imagery does the poem contain?
3. Discuss the adaptation of sound to meaning, commenting on the use of onomatopoeia, phonetic intensives, alliteration, consonance, rime, vowel quality, stanzaic structure, the counterpointing of the rhythmically varied long lines with the rhythmically regular short lines.

154. I HEARD A FLY BUZZ WHEN I DIED

I heard a fly buzz when I died.
The stillness in the room
Was like the stillness in the air
Between the heaves of storm.

The eyes around had wrung them dry,   5
The breaths were gathering firm
For that last onset when the king
Be witnessed in the room.

I willed my keepsakes, signed away
What portion of me be   10
Assignable; and then it was
There interposed the fly

With blue, uncertain, stumbling buzz
Between the light and me;
And then the windows failed, and then   15
I could not see to see.

Emily Dickinson (1830–1886)

QUESTIONS

1. It is important to understand the sequence of events in this death-bed scene. Arrange the following events in correct chronological order: (a) the willing of keepsakes, (b) the weeping of mourners, (c) the appearance of the fly, (d) the preternatural stillness in the room.
2. What or who are the "eyes" and the "breaths" in lines 5–6? What figures of speech are involved in these lines? Is the speaker making out her will in lines 11–13? What *is* she doing?
3. What sort of expectation is set up by phrases like "last onset," "the king," and "be witnessed"?
4. Explain "the windows failed" (15) and "I could not see to see" (16).
5. What is the rime scheme? What kinds of rime are employed? Explain the marvelous effectiveness of line 13, in terms of both imagery and sound.
6. Explain the point of the poem. How do you interpret the fly?

155. THE DANCE

In Breughel's great picture, The Kermess,
the dancers go round, they go round and
around, the squeal and the blare and the
tweedle of bagpipes, a bugle and fiddles

tipping their bellies (round as the thick-   5
sided glasses whose wash they impound)
their hips and their bellies off balance
to turn them. Kicking and rolling about
the Fair Grounds, swinging their butts, those
shanks must be sound to bear up under such   10
rollicking measures, prance as they dance
in Breughel's great picture, The Kermess.

William Carlos Williams (1883–1963)

QUESTION

Peter Breughel, the Elder, was a sixteenth-century Flemish painter of peasant life. A *kermess* is an annual outdoor festival or fair. How do the form, the meter, and the sounds of this poem reinforce its content?

EXERCISE

Follow the instructions for the exercise on page 196, of which this is a continuation.

11. a. Like an iron-clanging anvil banged / With hammers.
    b. Like a massive iron anvil hit / With sledges. *Alfred, Lord Tennyson*

12. a. I am quiet sand / In an hourglass.
    b. I am soft sift / In an hourglass. *Gerard Manley Hopkins*

13. a. Dress! arm! mount!—away!
       Save my castle before the day
       Turns to blue from silver gray.
    b. Boot, saddle, to horse, and away!
       Rescue my cattle before the hot day
       Brightens to blue from its silvery gray. *Robert Browning*

14. a. The lilies and languors of virtue,
       . . . the roses and raptures of vice.
    b. The lilies and boredom of virtue,
       . . . the roses and pleasures of evil. *Algernon Charles Swinburne*

15. a. And still she lullèd him asleep.
    b. And yet she conjured him to sleep. *Anonymous*

Chapter fourteen
Pattern

Art, ultimately, is organization. It is a searching after order, after form. The primal artistic act was God's creation of the universe out of chaos, shaping the formless into form; and every artist since, on a lesser scale, has sought to imitate Him—by selection and arrangement to reduce the chaotic in experience to a meaningful and pleasing order. For this reason we evaluate a poem partially by the same criteria that an English instructor uses to evaluate a theme—by its unity, its coherence, and its proper placing of emphasis. In a well-constructed poem there is neither too little nor too much; every part of the poem belongs where it is and could be placed nowhere else; any interchanging of two stanzas, two lines, or even two words, would to some extent damage the poem and make it less effective. We come to feel, with a truly first-rate poem, that the choice and placement of every word is inevitable, that it could not be otherwise.

In addition to the internal ordering of materials—the arrangement of ideas, images, and thoughts, which we may refer to as the poem's **structure**—the poet may impose some external pattern on a poem, may give it not only an inside logical order but an outside symmetry, or **form**. Such formality appeals to the human instinct for design, the instinct that has prompted people, at various times, to tattoo and paint their bodies, to decorate their swords and armor with beautiful and complex tracery, and to choose patterned fabrics for their clothing, carpets, curtains, and wallpapers. The poet appeals to our love of the shapely.

In general, there are three broad kinds of form into which a poem may be cast: continuous form, stanzaic form, and fixed form. In **continuous form,** as illustrated by "The Harbor" (No. 126), "After Apple-Picking" (No. 32), "Ulysses" (No. 63), and "My Last Duchess" (No. 83), the element of design is slight. The lines follow each other without formal grouping, the only breaks being dictated by units of meaning, as paragraphs are in prose. But even here there are degrees of pattern. "The Harbor" has neither regular meter nor rime. "After Apple-Picking," on the other hand, is metrical; it has no regularity in length of line, but the meter is prevailingly iambic; also every line rimes with another, though not according to any fixed pattern. "Ulysses" is regular in both meter and length of line: it is unrimed iambic pentameter, or blank verse. And to these regularities "My Last Duchess" adds regularity of rime, for it is written in riming pentameter couplets. Thus, in increasing degrees, the authors of "After Apple-Picking," "Ulysses," and "My Last Duchess" have chosen a predetermined pattern in which to cast their work.

In **stanzaic form** the poet writes in a series of **stanzas,** that is, repeated units having the same number of lines, usually the same metrical pattern, and often an identical rime scheme. The poet may choose some traditional stanza pattern (for poetry, like colleges, is rich in tradition) or invent an original one. The traditional stanza patterns (for example, terza rima, ballad meter, rime royal, Spenserian stanza) are many, and the student specializing in literature will wish to become familiar with some of them; the general student should know that they exist. Often the use of one of these traditional stanza forms constitutes a kind of literary allusion. The reader who is conscious of its traditional use or of its use by a previous great poet will be aware of subtleties in the communication that a less well-read reader may miss.

As with continuous form, there are degrees of formal pattern in stanzaic form. The poem "in Just-" (No. 86) is divided into alternating stanzas of four lines and one line, but neither the four-line stanzas nor the one-line stanzas have any resemblance to each other. In "Poem in October" (No. 161) the stanzas are alike in length of line but are without a regular pattern of rime. In "The Aim Was Song" (No. 140) a rime pattern is added to a metrical pattern. In Shakespeare's "Winter" (No. 2) a refrain is employed in addition to the patterns of meter and rime. The following poem illustrates additional elements of design:

156. THE GREEDY THE PEOPLE

the greedy the people
(as if as can yes)
they sell and they buy
and they die for because
though the bell in the steeple   5
says Why

the chary the wary
(as all as can each)
they don't and they do
and they turn to a which   10
though the moon in her glory
says Who

the busy the millions
(as you're as can i'm)
they flock and they flee   15
through a thunder of seem
though the stars in their silence
say Be

the cunning the craven
(as think as can feel)   20
they when and they how
and they live for until
though the sun in his heaven
says Now

the timid the tender   25
(as doubt as can trust)
they work and they pray
and they bow to a must
though the earth in her splendor
says May   30

e. e. cummings (1894–1962)

QUESTIONS

1. This poem is a constellation of interlocking patterns. To appreciate them
   fully, read it first in the normal fashion, one line after another, then read all
   the first lines of the stanzas, followed by the second lines, the third lines,
   and so on. Having done this, describe (a) the rime scheme; (b) the metrical
   design; (c) the sound pattern (how are the two main words in each of the first

lines related?); (d) the syntactical pattern. Prepare a model of the poem in which the recurring words are written out, blanks are left for varying words, and recurring parts of speech are indicated in parentheses. The model for the third lines would be: *they [verb] and they [verb]*. Describe the pattern of meaning. How do the last two lines of each stanza relate to the first four? What blanks in your model are to be filled in by words related in meaning?

2. A trademark of e. e. cummings as a poet is his imaginative freedom with parts of speech. For instance, in line 21 he uses conjunctions as verbs. What different parts of speech does he use as nouns in the fourth line of each stanza? Can you see meanings for these unusual nouns? Explain the contrast between the last words in the fourth and sixth lines of each stanza. What two meanings has the final word of the poem?

3. Sum up briefly the meaning of the poem.

A stanza form may be described by designating four things: the rime scheme (if there is one), the position of the refrain (if there is one), the prevailing metrical foot, and the number of feet in each line. Rime scheme is traditionally designated by using letters of the alphabet to indicate the riming lines, and x for unrimed lines. Refrain lines may be indicated by a capital letter, and the number of feet in the line by a numerical exponent after the letter. Thus the stanza pattern of Browning's "Meeting at Night" (No. 29) is iambic tetrameter $abccba$ (or iambic $abccba^4$); that of cummings's "if everything happens that can't be done" (No. 136) is anapestic $a^4x^2x^1a^1b^4x^1x^1b^2a^3$; that of Donne's "A Hymn to God the Father" (No. 27) is iambic $abab^5A^4B^2$.

A **fixed form** is a traditional pattern that applies to a whole poem. In French poetry many fixed forms have been widely used: rondeaus, rondels, villanelles, triolets, sestinas, ballades, double ballades, and others. In English poetry, though most of the fixed forms have been experimented with, perhaps only two—the limerick and the sonnet—have really taken hold.

The **limerick,** though really a subliterary form, will serve to illustrate the fixed form in general. Its pattern is anapestic $aa^3bb^2a^3$:

157.   I sat next the Duch-ess at tea.

It was just as I feared it would be:

Her rum-blings ab-dom-i-nal

Were sim-ply a-bom-i-na-ble

And eve-ry-one thought it was me!

Anonymous

The limerick form freely allows the use of a substitute foot in the first foot of any line but insists as a rule upon strict adherence to anapestic meter thereafter. The preceding limerick, by these standards, is defective, for one too many unaccented syllables has been squeezed in at the end of line 4; moreover, *abdominal* and *abominable* are imperfect rimes (because of the second *b* in *abominable*). Both of these flaws disappear if *abominable* is replaced by *phenomenal*, or if *internal* and *infernal* are chosen as the rimes in lines 3–4. In the face of such appropriate substitutions, can you make a case for preferring the defective version?

The limerick form is used exclusively for humorous and nonsense verse, for which, with its swift catchy meter, short lines, and emphatic rimes, it is particularly suitable. By trying to recast these little jokes and bits of nonsense in a different meter and pattern or into prose, we may discover how much of their effect they owe particularly to the limerick form. There is, of course, no magical or mysterious identity between certain forms and certain types of content, but there may be more or less correspondence. A form may be appropriate or inappropriate. The limerick form is inappropriate for the serious treatment of serious material.

The **sonnet** is less rigidly prescribed than the limerick. It must be fourteen lines in length, and it almost always is iambic pentameter, but in structure and rime scheme there may be considerable leeway. Most sonnets, however, conform more or less closely to one of two general models or types, the Italian and the English.

The **Italian** or *Petrarchan* **sonnet** (so called because the Italian poet Petrarch practiced it so extensively) is divided usually between eight lines called the octave, using two rimes arranged *abbaabba,* and six lines called the sestet, using any arrangement of either two or three rimes: *cdcdcd* and *cdecde* are common patterns. Usually in the Italian sonnet, corresponding to the division between octave and sestet indicated by the rime scheme (and sometimes marked off in printing by a space), there is a division of thought. The octave presents a situation and the sestet a comment, or the octave an idea and the sestet an example, or the octave a question and the sestet an answer. Thus the form reflects the structure.

158. ON FIRST LOOKING INTO CHAPMAN'S HOMER

> Much have I traveled in the realms of gold,
>   And many goodly states and kingdoms seen;
>   Round many western islands have I been
> Which bards in fealty to Apollo hold.

Oft of one wide expanse had I been told 5
That deep-browed Homer ruled as his demesne;
Yet did I never breathe its pure serene
Till I heard Chapman speak out loud and bold:
Then felt I like some watcher of the skies
When a new planet swims into his ken; 10
Or like stout Cortez when with eagle eyes
He stared at the Pacific—and all his men
Looked at each other with a wild surmise—
Silent, upon a peak in Darien.

John Keats (1795–1821)

QUESTIONS

1. Vocabulary: *fealty* (4), *Apollo* (4), *demesne* (6), *ken* (10). *Darien* (14) is an ancient name for the isthmus of Panama.
2. John Keats, at twenty-one, could not read Greek and was probably acquainted with Homer's *Iliad* and *Odyssey* only through the translations of Alexander Pope, which to him probably seemed prosy and stilted. Then one day he and a friend found a vigorous poetic translation by the Elizabethan poet George Chapman. Keats and his friend, enthralled, sat up late at night excitedly reading aloud to each other from Chapman's book. Toward morning Keats walked home and, before going to bed, wrote the above sonnet and sent it to his friend. What common ideas underlie the three major figures of speech in the poem?
3. What is the rime scheme? What division of thought corresponds to the division between octave and sestet?
4. Balboa, not Cortez, discovered the Pacific. How seriously does this mistake detract from the value of the poem?

The **English** or *Shakespearean* **sonnet** (invented by the English poet Surrey and made famous by Shakespeare) is composed of three quatrains and a concluding couplet, riming *abab cdcd efef gg*. Again, there is often a correspondence between the units marked off by the rimes and the development of the thought. The three quatrains, for instance, may present three examples and the couplet a conclusion or (as in the following example) three metaphorical statements of one idea plus an application.

159. THAT TIME OF YEAR

That time of year thou mayst in me behold
When yellow leaves, or none, or few, do hang
Upon those boughs which shake against the cold,
Bare ruined choirs where late the sweet birds sang.

In me thou see'st the twilight of such day 5
As after sunset fadeth in the west,
Which by and by black night doth take away,
Death's second self, that seals up all in rest.
In me thou see'st the glowing of such fire,
That on the ashes of his youth doth lie 10
As the deathbed whereon it must expire,
Consumed with that which it was nourished by.
This thou perceivest, which makes thy love more strong,
To love that well which thou must leave ere long.

William Shakespeare (1564–1616)

QUESTIONS

1. What are the three major images introduced by the three quatrains? What do they have in common? Can you see any reason for presenting them in this particular order, or might they be rearranged without loss?
2. Each of the images is to some degree complicated rather than simple. For instance, what additional image is introduced by "bare ruined choirs" (4)? Explain its appropriateness.
3. What additional comparisons are introduced in the second and third quatrains? Explain line 12.
4. Whom does the speaker address? What assertion does he make in the concluding couplet, and with what degree of confidence? Paraphrase these lines so as to state their meaning as clearly as possible.

At first glance it may seem absurd that a poet should choose to confine himself in an arbitrary fourteen-line mold with prescribed meter and rime scheme. He does so partly from the desire to carry on a tradition, as all of us carry out certain traditions for their own sake, else why should we bring a tree indoors at Christmas time? But, in addition, the tradition of the sonnet has proved useful because, like the limerick, it seems effective for certain types of subject matter and treatment. Though this area cannot be as narrowly limited or as rigidly described as for the limerick, the sonnet is usually most effective when used for the serious treatment of love but has also been used for the discussion of death, religion, political situations, and related subjects. Again, there is no magical affinity between form and subject, or treatment, and excellent sonnets have been written outside these traditional areas. The sonnet tradition has also proved useful because it has provided a challenge to the poet. The inferior poet, of course, is often defeated by that challenge: he will use unnecessary words to fill out the meter or inappropriate words for the sake of rime. The good poet is inspired by the challenge: it will call forth ideas and images that might not otherwise have come. He will subdue the form rather than be subdued by it; he will make it do his will. There is no doubt that the presence of a net makes good tennis players more precise in their shots than they otherwise would be. And finally, there is in all form the pleasure of form itself.

EXERCISES

1. Reread the following sonnets; classify each (when possible) as primarily Italian or primarily English; then specify how closely each sticks to or how far it departs from (in form and structure) the polarities represented by "On First Looking into Chapman's Homer" and "That time of year":
   a. The world is too much with us (No. 26).
   b. The Caged Skylark (No. 103).
   c. Design (No. 100).
   d. From *Romeo and Juliet* (No. 163).
   e. The Silken Tent (No. 47).
   f. Since there's no help (No. 109).
   g. The Dead (No. 62).
   h. Batter my heart, three-personed God (No. 76).
   i. Ozymandias (No. 75).
   j. Mowing (No. 11).
2. "The Story We Know" (No. 165), "One Art" (No. 194), "The Waking" (No. 237) and "Do not go gentle" (No. 246) are all examples of a French fixed form known as the *villanelle*. After studying their formal features, formulate a definition for the villanelle. *Hint:* Start with No. 246, the "purest" example of the form; then examine the extent to which the others confirm or depart from that norm.

*   *   *

160. A HANDFUL OF LIMERICKS

There was a young lady from Niger
Who smiled as she rode on a tiger;
   They returned from the ride
   With the lady inside
And the smile on the face of the tiger.

Anonymous

There was a young lady of Lynn
Who was so uncommonly thin
    That when she essayed
    To drink lemonade
She slipped through the straw and fell in.
                  Anonymous

A tutor who tooted the flute
Tried to teach two young tooters to toot.
    Said the two to the tutor,
    "Is it harder to toot, or
To tutor two tooters to toot?"
              Carolyn Wells (1862–1942)

There was a young maid who said, "Why
Can't I look in my ear with my eye?
    If I put my mind to it,
    I'm sure I can do it.
You never can tell till you try."
                  Anonymous

A goat on a stroll near a brook
Found an old movie film and partook.
    "Was it good?" asked his mate.
    Said the goat, "Second-rate!
Not nearly as good as the book!"
           Martin Bristow Smith (b. 1916)

A decrepit old gas man named Peter,
While hunting around for the meter,
    Touched a leak with his light.
    He arose out of sight,
And, as anyone can see by reading this, he
    also destroyed the meter.
                  Anonymous

Well, it's partly the shape of the thing
That gives the old limerick wing;
    These accordion pleats
    Full of airy conceits
Take it up like a kite on a string.
              David McCord (b. 1897)

161. POEM IN OCTOBER

It was my thirtieth year to heaven
Woke to my hearing from harbor and neighbor wood
    And the mussel pooled and the heron
            Priested shore
            The morning beckon   5
With water praying and call of seagull and rook
And the knock of sailing boats on the net webbed wall
            Myself to set foot
                That second
    In the still sleeping town and set forth.   10

    My birthday began with the water-
Birds and the birds of the winged trees flying my name
    Above the farms and the white horses
                And I rose
            In rainy autumn   15
And walked abroad in a shower of all my days.
High tide and the heron dived when I took the road
            Over the border
            And the gates
    Of the town closed as the town awoke.   20

    A springful of larks in a rolling
Cloud and the roadside bushes brimming with whistling
    Blackbirds and the sun of October
                Summery
            On the hill's shoulder,   25
Here were fond climates and sweet singers suddenly
Come in the morning where I wandered and listened
            To the rain wringing
            Wind blow cold
    In the woods faraway under me.   30

    Pale rain over the dwindling harbor
And over the sea wet church the size of a snail
    With its horns through mist and the castle
            Brown as owls
            But all the gardens   35
Of spring and summer were blooming in the tall tales
Beyond the border and under the lark full cloud.
            There could I marvel
            My birthday
    Away but the weather turned around.   40

It turned away from the blithe country
And down the other air and the blue altered sky
Streamed again a wonder of summer
With apples
Pears and red currants 45
And I saw in the turning so clearly a child's
Forgotten mornings when he walked with his mother
Through the parables
Of sun light
And the legends of the green chapels 50

And the twice told fields of infancy
That his tears burned my cheeks and his heart moved in mine.
These were the woods the river and sea
Where a boy
In the listening 55
Summertime of the dead whispered the truth of his joy
To the trees and the stones and the fish in the tide.
And the mystery
Sang alive
Still in the water and singingbirds. 60

And there could I marvel my birthday
Away but the weather turned around. And the true
Joy of the long dead child sang burning
In the sun.
It was my thirtieth 65
Year to heaven stood there then in the summer noon
Though the town below lay leaved with October blood.
O may my heart's truth
Still be sung
On this high hill in a year's turning. 70

Dylan Thomas (1914–1953)

QUESTIONS

1. The setting is a small fishing village on the coast of Wales. The poet's first
   name in Welsh means "water" (12). Trace the poet's walk in relation to the
   village, the weather, and the time of day.
2. "The weather turned around" is an expression indicating a change in the
   weather or the direction of the wind. In what psychological sense does the
   weather turn around during the poet's walk? Who is "the long dead child"
   (63), and what kind of child was he? With what wish does the poem close?
3. Explain "thirtieth year to heaven" (1), "horns" (33), "tall tales" (36),
   "green chapels" (50), "October blood" (67).

4. The elaborate stanza pattern in this poem is based not on the meter (which is very free) but on a syllable count. How many syllables are there in each line of the stanza? (In line 1 "thirtieth" may be counted as only two syllables.) Notice that stanzas 1 and 3 consist of exactly one sentence each.
5. The poem makes a considerable use of approximate rime, though not according to a regular pattern. Point out examples.

162. TWO JAPANESE HAIKU

The lightning flashes!
And slashing through the darkness,
A night-heron's screech.

A lightning gleam:
into darkness travels
a night heron's scream.

Matsuo Bashō (1644–1694)

The falling flower
I saw drift back to the branch
Was a butterfly.

Fallen flowers rise
back to the branch—I watch:
oh . . . butterflies!

Moritake (1452–1540)

QUESTION

The *haiku*, a Japanese form, consists of three lines with five, seven, and five syllables respectively. The translators of the versions on the left (Earl Miner and Babette Deutsch respectively) preserve this syllable count; the translator of the right-hand versions (Harold G. Henderson) seeks to preserve the sense of formal structure by making the first and last lines rime. Moritake's haiku, as Miss Deutsch points out, "refers to the Buddhist proverb that the fallen flower never returns to the branch; the broken mirror never again reflects." From these two examples, what would you say are the characteristics of effective haiku?

163. FROM *ROMEO AND JULIET*

ROMEO If I profane with my unworthiest hand
This holy shrine, the gentle sin is this;
My lips, two blushing pilgrims, ready stand
To smooth that rough touch with a tender kiss.

JULIET Good pilgrim, you do wrong your hand too much,   5
Which mannerly devotion shows in this;
For saints have hands that pilgrims' hands do touch,
And palm to palm is holy palmers' kiss.

ROMEO Have not saints lips, and holy palmers too?

JULIET Ay, pilgrim, lips that they must use in prayer.   10

ROMEO	O! then, dear saint, let lips do what hands do;
	They pray, Grant thou, lest faith turn to despair.
JULIET	Saints do not move,° though grant for prayers' propose,
	sake. instigate
ROMEO	Then move not, while my prayers' effect I take.

William Shakespeare (1564–1616)

QUESTIONS

1. These fourteen lines have been lifted out of Act I, scene 5, of Shakespeare's play. They are the first words exchanged between Romeo and Juliet, who are meeting, for the first time, at a masquerade ball given by her father. Romeo is dressed as a pilgrim. Struck by Juliet's beauty, he has come up to greet her. What stage action accompanies this passage?
2. What is the basic metaphor employed? How does it affect the tone of the relationship between Romeo and Juliet?
3. What play on words do you find in lines 8 and 13–14? What two meanings has line 11?
4. By meter and rime scheme, these lines form a sonnet. Do you think this was coincidental or intentional on Shakespeare's part? Discuss.

164. DEATH, BE NOT PROUD

Death, be not proud, though some have callèd thee
Mighty and dreadful, for thou art not so;
For those whom thou think'st thou dost overthrow
Die not, poor death, nor yet canst thou kill me.
From rest and sleep, which but thy pictures be,   5
Much pleasure—then, from thee much more must flow;
And soonest° our best men with thee do go,   readiest
Rest of their bones and soul's delivery.
Thou art slave to fate, chance, kings, and desperate men,
And dost with poison, war, and sickness dwell;   10
And poppy or charms can make us sleep as well,
And better than thy stroke. Why swell'st thou then?
One short sleep passed, we wake eternally,
And death shall be no more; death, thou shalt die.

John Donne (1572–1631)

QUESTIONS

1. What two figures of speech dominate the poem?
2. Why should death not be proud? List the speaker's major reasons. Are they consistent? Logical? Persuasive?

3. Discuss the tone of the poem. Is the speaker (a) a man of assured faith with a firm conviction that death is not to be feared, (b) a man desperately trying to convince himself that there is nothing in death to be feared, or (c) other?
4. In form this sonnet blends the English and Italian models. Explain. Is its organization of thought more like that of the Italian or the English sonnet?

165. THE STORY WE KNOW

The way to begin is always the same. Hello,
Hello. Your hand, your name. So glad, Just fine,
and Good-bye at the end. That's every story we know,

and why pretend? But lunch tomorrow? No?
Yes? An omelette, salad, chilled white wine?   5
The way to begin is simple, sane, Hello,

and then it's Sunday, coffee, the *Times*, a slow
day by the fire, dinner at eight or nine
and Good-bye. In the end, this is a story we know

so well we don't turn the page, or look below   10
the picture, or follow the words to the next line:
The way to begin is always the same Hello.

But one night, through the latticed window, snow
begins to whiten the air, and the tall white pine.
Good-bye is the end of every story we know   15

that night, and when we close the curtains, oh,
we hold each other against that cold white sign
of the way we all begin and end. *Hello*,
Good-bye is the only story. We know, we know.

Martha Collins (b. 1940)

QUESTIONS

1. What have lines 1, 6, 12, and 18 in common? What have lines 3, 9, 15, and 19 in common?
2. What is the rime scheme?
3. Show how the words "Hello" and "Good-bye" acquire deeper meanings as the poem progresses. What do they refer to or symbolize in the last two lines? Why is the phrase "We know" repeated in the last line?
4. This poem is an example of a French fixed form called a **villanelle**. For further material about villanelles, see Exercise on page 212.

166. AS HE LAY DYING

As he lay dying, two fat crows
    Sat perched above in a strangling vine,
    And one crow called to the other:
        "Brother,
    Harvest his eyes, his tongue is mine."   5

As he lay dying, two lithe hawks
    Caressed the wind and spied two crows;
    And one hawk hissed to the other:
        "Brother,
    Mine is the sleekest one of those."   10

As he lay dying, two eagles passed
    And saw two hawks that hung in flying,
    And one said soft to the other:
        "Brother,
    Mark your prey." As he lay dying.   15

Randolph Stow (b. 1935)

QUESTIONS

1. Diagram the repetitions and parallels that organize this poem in wording, action, and stanza pattern. Do these patterns serve a useful purpose?
2. What is the central theme of the poem?

167. EDWARD

"Why dois° your brand° sae drap wi bluid,   does; sword
    Edward, Edward,
Why dois your brand sae drap wi bluid,
    And why sae sad gang° yee O?"   go
"O I hae killed my hauke sae guid,   5
    Mither, mither,
O I hae killed my hauke sae guid,
    And I had nae mair bot hee O."

"Your haukis bluid was nevir sae reid,
    Edward, Edward,   10
Your haukis bluid was nevir sae reid,
    My deir son I tell thee O."
"O I hae killed my reid-roan steid,
    Mither, mither,
O I hae killed my reid-roan steid,   15
    That erst° was sae fair and frie° O."   formerly; spirited

"Your steid was auld, and ye hae got mair,
　　　　Edward, Edward,
Your steid was auld, and ye hae got mair,
　　Sum other dule° ye drie° O."　　　　　　grief; suffer　20
"O I hae killed my fadir deir,
　　　　Mither, mither,
O I hae killed my fadir deir,
　　Alas, and wae is mee O!"

"And whatten penance wul ye drie for that,　　　　　　25
　　　　Edward, Edward,
And whatten penance wul ye drie for that?
　　My deir son, now tell me O."
"Ile set my feit in yonder boat,
　　　　Mither, mither,　　　　　　　　　　　　　　30
Ile set my feit in yonder boat,
　　And Ile fare ovir the sea O."

"And what wul ye doe wi your towirs and your ha,°　　hall
　　　　Edward, Edward,
And what wul ye doe wi your towirs and your ha,　　35
　　That were sae fair to see O?"
"Ile let thame stand tul they doun fa,°　　　　　　fall
　　　　Mither, mither,
Ile let thame stand tul they doun fa,
　　For here nevir mair maun° I bee O."　　　　must　40

"And what wul ye leive to your bairns° and your wife,　children
　　　　Edward, Edward,
And what wul ye leive to your bairns and your wife,
　　Whan ye gang ovir the sea O?"
"The warldis° room, late them beg thrae° life,　world's; through　45
　　　　Mither, mither,
The warldis room, late them beg thrae life,
　　For thame nevir mair wul I see O."

"And what wul ye leive to your ain mither deir,
　　　　Edward, Edward?　　　　　　　　　　　　　50
And what wul ye leive to your ain mither deir?
　　My deir son, now tell me O."
"The curse of hell frae me sall ye beir,
　　　　Mither, mither,
The curse of hell frae me sall ye beir,　　　　　　55
　　Sic° counseils ye gave to me O."　　　　　　Such

Anonymous

1. What has Edward done and why? Where do the two climaxes of the poem come?
2. Tell as much as you can about Edward and his feelings toward what he has done. From what class of society is he? Why does he at first give false answers to his mother's questions? What reversal of feelings and loyalties has he undergone? Do his answers about his hawk and steed perhaps indicate his present feelings toward his father? How do you explain his behavior to his wife and children? What are his present feelings toward his mother?
3. Tell as much as you can about Edward's mother. Why does she ask what Edward has done—doesn't she already know? Is there any clue as to the motivation of her deed? How skillful is she in her questioning? What do we learn about her from her dismissal of Edward's steed as "auld" and only one of many (17)? From her asking Edward what penance *he* will do for his act (25)? From her reference to herself as Edward's "ain mither deir" (49)?
4. Structure and form are both important in this poem. Could any of the stanzas be interchanged without loss, or do they build up steadily to the two climaxes? What effect has the constant repetition of the two short refrains, "Edward, Edward" and "Mither, mither"? What is the effect of the final "O" at the end of each speech? Does the repetition of each question and answer simply waste words or does it add to the suspense and emotional intensity? (Try reading the poem omitting the third and seventh lines of each stanza. Is it improved or weakened?)
5. Much of what happened is implied, much is omitted. Does the poem gain anything in power from what is *not* told?

168. 400-METER FREESTYLE

THE GUN full swing the swimmer catapults and cracks

         s
         i
         x
feet away onto that perfect glass he catches at   5
a
n
d
throws behind him scoop after scoop cunningly moving
         t   10
         h
         e
water back to move him forward. Thrift is his wonderful

                    s
                    e
                    c   15
ret; he has schooled out all extravagance. No muscle
                                        r
                                          i
                                        p   20
ples without compensation wrist cock to heel snap to
h
i
                    s
mobile mouth that siphons in the air that nurtures   25
                                        h
                                          i
                                        m
at half an inch above sea level so to speak.
T   30
h
e
astonishing whites of the soles of his feet rise
                                        a
                                          n   35
                                        d
salute us on the turns. He flips, converts, and is gone
a
l
l   40
in one. We watch him for signs. His arms are steady at
                                        t
                                          h
                                        e
catch, his cadent feet tick in the stretch, they know   45
t
h
e
lesson well. Lungs know, too; he does not list for
                                        a   50
                                          i
                                        r
he drives along on little sips carefully expended
b
u   55
t

that plum red heart pumps hard cries hurt how soon

                                                    i

                                                    t

                                                    s   60
near one more and makes its final surge TIME: 4:25.9

Maxine Kumin (b. 1925)

QUESTIONS

1. To what quality or qualities does this poem essentially pay tribute? What
   sentence in the poem most nearly expresses its theme?
2. Does the poem itself exhibit the qualities which it praises? Discuss.
3. How does the visual form of the poem reflect its content?

169. A CHRISTMAS TREE

Star,
If you are
A love compassionate,
You will walk with us this year.
We face a glacial distance, who are here
Huddld
At your feet.

William Burford (b. 1927)

QUESTION

Why do you think the author misspelled "huddled" in line 6?

EXERCISE

The typographical shape of a poem on the page (whether, for example, it is
printed with a straight left-hand margin or with a system of indentations) is
determined sometimes by the poet, sometimes by the printer, sometimes by an
editor. Examine each of the following poems and try to deduce what *principle* (if
any) determined its typographical design:

1. The Mill (Robinson, No. 16)
2. To a Waterfowl (No. 99)
3. With rue my heart is laden (No. 123)
4. To His Coy Mistress (No. 51)
5. Poem in October (No. 161)

Chapter fifteen

Bad Poetry and Good

The attempt to evaluate a poem should never be made before the poem is understood; and, unless one has developed the capacity to feel some poetry deeply, any judgments one makes will be worthless. A person who likes no wines can hardly be a judge of them. But the ability to make judgments, to discriminate between good and bad, great and good, good and half-good, is surely a primary object of all liberal education, and one's appreciation of poetry is incomplete unless it includes discrimination. Of the mass of verse that appears each year in print, as of all literature, most is "stale, flat, and unprofitable"; a very, very little is of any enduring value.

In judging a poem, as in judging any work of art, we need to ask three basic questions: (1) *What is its central purpose?* (2) *How fully has this purpose been accomplished?* (3) *How important is this purpose?* We need to answer the first question in order to understand the poem. Questions 2 and 3 are those by which we evaluate it. Question 2 measures the poem on a scale of perfection. Question 3 measures it on a scale of significance. And, just as the area of a rectangle is determined by multiplying its measurements on two scales, breadth and height, so the greatness of a poem is determined by multiplying its measurements on two scales, perfection and significance. If the poem measures well on the first of these scales, we call it a good poem, at least of its kind. If it measures well on both scales, we call it a great poem.*

---

* As indicated in the footnote on page 21, some objection has been made to the use of the term "purpose" in literary criticism. For the two criteria suggested above may be substituted these two: (1) How thoroughly are the materials of the poem integrated or unified? (2) How many and how diverse are the materials that it integrates? Thus a poem becomes successful in proportion to the tightness of its organization—that is, according to the degree to which all its elements work together and require each other to produce the total effect—and it becomes great in proportion to its scope—that is, according to the amount and diversity of the material it amalgamates into unity.

The measurement of a poem is a much more complex process, of course, than is the measurement of a rectangle. It cannot be done as exactly. Agreement on the measurements will never be complete. Yet over a period of time the judgments of qualified readers* tend to coalesce: there comes to be more agreement than disagreement. There is almost universal agreement, for instance, that Shakespeare is the greatest of English poets. Although there might be sharp disagreements among qualified readers as to whether Donne or Keats is the superior poet—or Wordsworth or Chaucer, or Shelley or Pope—there is almost universal agreement among them that each of these is superior to Kipling or Longfellow. And there is almost universal agreement that Kipling and Longfellow are superior to James Whitcomb Riley or Rod McKuen.

But your problem is to be able to discriminate, not between already established reputations, but between poems—poems you have not seen before and of which, perhaps, you do not even know the author. Here, of course, you will not always be right—even the most qualified readers occasionally go badly astray—but you should, we hope, be able to make broad distinctions with a higher average of success than you could when you began this book. And, unless you allow yourself to petrify, your ability to do this should improve throughout your college years and beyond.

For answering the first of our evaluative questions, *How fully has the poem's purpose been accomplished?* there are no easy yardsticks that we can apply. We cannot ask, Is the poem melodious? Does it have smooth meter? Does it use good grammar? Does it contain figures of speech? Are the rimes perfect? Excellent poems exist without any of these attributes. We can judge any element in a poem only as it contributes or fails to contribute to the achievement of the central purpose; and we can judge the total poem only as these elements work together to form an integrated whole. But we can at least attempt a few generalizations. In a perfect poem there are no excess words, no words that do not bear their full weight in contributing to the total meaning, and no words used just to fill out the meter. Each word is the best word for expressing the total meaning: there are no inexact words forced by the rime scheme or the metrical pattern. The word order is the best order for expressing the author's total meaning; distortions or departures from normal order are for emphasis or some other meaningful purpose. The diction, the im-

---

* Throughout this discussion the term "qualified reader" is of utmost importance. By a qualified reader we mean briefly a person with considerable experience of literature and considerable experience of life: a person of intelligence, sensitivity, and knowledge.

ages, and the figures of speech are fresh, not trite (except, of course, when the poet uses trite language deliberately for purposes of irony). There are no clashes between the sound of the poem and its sense, or its form and its content; and in general both sound and pattern are used to support meaning. The organization of the poem is the best possible organization: images and ideas are so effectively arranged that any re-arrangement would be harmful to the poem. We will always remember, however, that a good poem may have flaws. We should never damn a poem for its flaws if these flaws are amply compensated for by positive excellence.

If a poem is to have true excellence, it must be in some sense a "new" poem; it must exact a fresh response from the qualified reader. It will not be merely imitative of previous literature nor appeal to stock, preestablished ways of thinking and feeling that in some read-ers are automatically stimulated by words like *mother, baby, home, country, faith,* or *God,* as a coin put into a slot always gets an expected reaction.

And here, perhaps, may be discussed the kinds of poems that most frequently "fool" inexperienced readers (and occasionally a few experi-enced ones) and achieve sometimes a tremendous popularity without winning the respect of most good readers. These poems are frequently published on greeting cards or in anthologies entitled *Poems of Inspira-tion, Poems of Courage,* or *Heart-Throbs.* The people who write such poems and the people who like them are often the best of people, but they are not poets or lovers of poetry in any genuine sense. They are lovers of conventional ideas or sentiments or feelings, which they like to see expressed with the adornment of rime and meter, and which, when so expressed, they respond to in predictable ways.

Of the several varieties of inferior poetry, we shall concern ourselves with three: the sentimental, the rhetorical, and the purely didactic. All three are perhaps unduly dignified by the name of poetry. They might more aptly be described as verse.

Sentimentality is indulgence in emotion for its own sake, or expres-sion of more emotion than an occasion warrants. A sentimental *person* is gushy, stirred to tears by trivial or inappropriate causes; he weeps at all weddings and all funerals; he is made ecstatic by manifestations of young love; he clips locks of hair, gilds baby shoes, and talks baby talk; he grows compassionate over hardened criminals when he hears of their being punished. His opposite is the callous or unfeeling person. The ideal is the person who responds sensitively on appropriate occasions and feels deeply on occasions that deserve deep feeling, but who has nevertheless a certain amount of emotional reserve, a certain command over his feelings. Sentimental *literature* is *"tear-jerking"* literature. It aims primarily at stimulating the emotions directly rather than at communicating experience truly and freshly; it depends on trite and well-tried formulas for exciting emotion; it revels in old oaken buckets, rocking chairs, mother love, and the pitter-patter of little feet; it oversimplifies; it is unfaithful to the full complexity of human experience. In our book the best example of sentimental verse is the first seven lines of the anonymous "Love" (No. 119). If this verse had ended as it began, it would have been pure sentimentalism. The eighth line redeems it by making us realize that the writer is not serious and thus transfers the piece from the classification of sentimental verse to that of humorous verse. In fact, the writer is poking fun at sentimentality by showing that in its most maudlin form it is characteristic of drunks.

Rhetorical poetry uses a language more glittering and high flown than its substance warrants. It offers a spurious vehemence of language—language without a corresponding reality of emotion or thought underneath. It is oratorical, overelegant, artificially eloquent. It is superficial and, again, often basically trite. It loves rolling phrases like "from the rocky coast of Maine to the sun-washed shores of California" and "our heroic dead" and "Old Glory." It deals in generalities. At its worst it is bombast. In this book an example is offered by the two lines quoted from the play-within-a-play in Shakespeare's *A Midsummer Night's Dream:*

> Whereat with blade, with bloody, blameful blade,
> He bravely broached his boiling bloody breast.

Another example may be found in the player's recitation in *Hamlet* (in Act II, scene 2):

> Out, out, thou strumpet Fortune! All you gods,
> In general synod take away her power,
> Break all the spokes and fellies from her wheel,
> And bowl the round nave down the hill of heaven
> As low as to the fiends!

Didactic poetry has as a primary purpose to teach or preach. It is probable that all the very greatest poetry teaches in subtle ways, without being expressly didactic; and much expressly didactic poetry ranks high in poetic excellence: that is, it accomplishes its teaching without ceasing to be poetry. But when the didactic purpose supersedes the poetic purpose, when the poem communicates information or moral instruction only, then it ceases to be didactic poetry and becomes didactic verse. Such verse appeals to people who go to poetry primarily for noble thoughts or inspiring lessons and like them prettily expressed. It is recognizable often by its lack of any specific situation, the flatness of its diction, the poverty of its imagery and figurative language, its emphasis on moral platitudes, its lack of poetic freshness. It is either very trite or has little to distinguish it from informational prose except rime or meter. Bryant's "To a Waterfowl" (No. 99) is an example of didactic *poetry*. The familiar couplet

> Early to bed and early to rise,
> Makes a man healthy, wealthy, and wise

is more aptly characterized as didactic *verse*.

Undoubtedly, so far in this chapter, we have spoken too categorically, have made our distinctions too sharp and definite. All poetic excellence is a matter of degree. There are no absolute lines between sentimentality and true emotion, artificial and genuine eloquence, didactic verse and didactic poetry. Though the difference between extreme examples is easy to recognize, subtler discriminations are harder to make. But a primary distinction between the educated person and the ignorant one is the ability to make informed judgments.

A final caution to students. In making judgments on literature, always be honest. Do not pretend to like what you really do not like. Do not be afraid to admit a liking for what you do like. A genuine enthusiasm for the second-rate is much better than false enthusiasm or no enthusiasm at all. Be neither hasty nor timorous in making your judgments. When you have attentively read a poem and thoroughly considered it, decide what you think. Do not hedge, equivocate, or try to find out others' opinions before forming your own. Having formed an opinion and expressed it, do not allow it to petrify. Compare your opinion *then* with the opinions of others; allow yourself to change it when convinced of its error: in this way you learn. Honesty, courage, and humility are the necessary moral foundations for all genuine literary judgment.

In the poems for comparison in this chapter, the distinction to be made is not always between bad and good; it may be between varying degrees of poetic merit.

*　　　　*　　　　*

170. GOD'S WILL FOR YOU AND ME

Just to be tender, just to be true,
Just to be glad the whole day through,
Just to be merciful, just to be mild,
Just to be trustful as a child,
Just to be gentle and kind and sweet,   5
Just to be helpful with willing feet,
Just to be cheery when things go wrong,
Just to drive sadness away with a song,
Whether the hour is dark or bright,
Just to be loyal to God and right,   10
Just to believe that God knows best,
Just in his promises ever to rest—
Just to let love be our daily key,
That is God's will for you and me.

171. PIED BEAUTY

Glory be to God for dappled things—
    For skies of couple-color as a brinded cow;
        For rose-moles all in stipple upon trout that swim;
Fresh-firecoal chestnut-falls; finches' wings;
    Landscape plotted and pieced—fold, fallow and plow;   5
        And all trades, their gear and tackle and trim.

All things counter, original, spare, strange;
    Whatever is fickle, freckled (who knows how?)
        With swift, slow; sweet, sour; adazzle, dim;
He fathers-forth whose beauty is past change: 10
        Praise him.

QUESTION

Which is the superior poem? Explain in full.

172. PITCHER

His art is eccentricity, his aim
How not to hit the mark he seems to aim at,

His passion how to avoid the obvious,
His technique how to vary the avoidance.

The others throw to be comprehended. He 5
Throws to be a moment misunderstood.

Yet not too much. Not errant, arrant, wild,
But every seeming aberration willed.

Not to, yet still, still to communicate
Making the batter understand too late. 10

173. THE OLD-FASHIONED PITCHER

How dear to my heart was the old-fashioned hurler
   Who labored all day on the old village green.
He did not resemble the up-to-date twirler
   Who pitches four innings and ducks from the scene.
The up-to-date twirler I'm not very strong for; 5
   He has a queer habit of pulling up lame.
And that is the reason I hanker and long for
   The pitcher who started and finished the game.

      The old-fashioned pitcher,
        The iron-armed pitcher, 10
      The stout-hearted pitcher
        Who finished the game.

QUESTION

Which poem is the more interesting and more meaningful? Why?

174. COME UP FROM THE FIELDS FATHER

Come up from the fields father, here's a letter from our Pete,
And come to the front door mother, here's a letter from thy dear son.

Lo, 'tis autumn,
Lo, where the trees, deeper green, yellower and redder,
Cool and sweeten Ohio's villages with leaves fluttering in the moderate
   wind, 5
Where apples ripe in the orchards hang and grapes on the trellised
   vines,
(Smell you the smell of the grapes on the vines?
Smell you the buckwheat where the bees were lately buzzing?)

Above all, lo, the sky so calm, so transparent after the rain, and with
   wondrous clouds,
Below too, all calm, all vital and beautiful, and the farm prospers
   well.   10

Down in the fields all prospers well,
But now from the fields come father, come at the daughter's call,
And come to the entry mother, to the front door come right away.

Fast as she can she hurries, something ominous, her steps trembling,
She does not tarry to smooth her hair nor adjust her cap.   15

Open the envelope quickly,
O this is not our son's writing, yet his name is signed,
O a strange hand writes for our dear son, O stricken mother's soul!
All swims before her eyes, flashes with black, she catches the main
   words only,
Sentences broken, *gunshot wound in the breast, cavalry skirmish, taken to
   hospital,*   20
At present low, but will soon be better.

Ah now the single figure to me,
Amid all teeming and wealthy Ohio with all its cities and farms,
Sickly white in the face and dull in the head, very faint,
By the jamb of a door leans.   25

Grieve not so, dear mother (the just-grown daughter speaks through her
   sobs,
The little sisters huddle around speechless and dismayed),
See, dearest mother, the letter says Pete will soon be better.

Alas poor boy, he will never be better (nor maybe needs to be better,
   that brave and simple soul),
While they stand at home at the door he is dead already,   30
The only son is dead.

But the mother needs to be better,
She with thin form presently dressed in black,
By day her meals untouched, then at night fitfully sleeping, often
   waking,
In the midnight waking, weeping, longing with one deep longing,   35
O that she might withdraw unnoticed, silent from life escape and
   withdraw,
To follow, to seek, to be with her dear dead son.

175. THE FADED COAT OF BLUE

My brave lad he sleeps in his faded coat of blue,
In a lonely grave unknown lies that heart that beat so true;
He sank faint and hungry among the famished brave,
And they laid him sad and lonely within his nameless grave.

No more the bugle calls that weary one,   5
Rest, noble spirit, in the grave unknown;
I'll find you, and know you, among the good and true,
When a robe of white is given for the faded coat of blue.

He cried, "Give me water, and just a little crumb,
And my mother she will bless you through all the years to come— 10
Oh! tell my sweet sister, so gentle, good and true,
That I'll meet her up in Heaven, in my faded coat of blue."

No more the bugle calls that weary one,
Rest, noble spirit, in the grave unknown;
I'll find you, and know you, among the good and true,   15
When a robe of white is given for the faded coat of blue.

He said, "My dear comrades, you cannot take me home,
But you'll mark my grave for mother, she'll find it if she comes;
I fear she'll not know me among the good and true,
When I meet her up in Heaven in my faded coat of blue."   20

No more the bugle calls that weary one,
Rest, noble spirit, in the grave unknown;
I'll find you, and know you, among the good and true,
When a robe of white is given for the faded coat of blue.

No one was nigh him to close his sweet eyes,   25
And no gentle one was by him to give sweet replies;
No stone marks the sod o'er my lad so brave and true,
In his lonely grave he's sleeping in his faded coat of blue.

No more the bugle calls that weary one,
Rest, noble spirit, in the grave unknown;   30
I'll find you, and know you, among the good and true,
When a robe of white is given for the faded coat of blue.

QUESTION

Compare this poem with "Come Up From the Fields Father," also a Civil War
poem. Which treats its subject more honestly? Which is guilty of sentimentality? Explain in full.

176. A POISON TREE

I was angry with my friend:
I told my wrath, my wrath did end.
I was angry with my foe:
I told it not, my wrath did grow.

And I watered it in fears,   5
Night and morning with my tears;
And I sunnèd it with smiles,
And with soft deceitful wiles.

And it grew both day and night
Till it bore an apple bright;   10
And my foe beheld it shine,
And he knew that it was mine,

And into my garden stole
When the night had veiled the pole:°   sky
In the morning glad I see   15
My foe outstretched beneath the tree.

177. THE MOST VITAL THING IN LIFE

When you feel like saying something
   That you know you will regret,
Or keenly feel an insult
   Not quite easy to forget,
That's the time to curb resentment   5
   And maintain a mental peace,
For when your mind is tranquil
   All your ill-thoughts simply cease.

It is easy to be angry
   When defrauded or defied,   10
To be peeved and disappointed
   If your wishes are denied;
But to win a worthwhile battle
   Over selfishness and spite,
You must learn to keep strict silence   15
   Though you know you're in the right.

So keep your mental balance
   When confronted by a foe,
Be it enemy in ambush
   Or some danger that you know.   20

If you are poised and tranquil
When all around is strife,
Be assured that you have mastered
The most vital thing in life.

QUESTION

Which poem has more poetic merit? Explain.

178. ON A DEAD CHILD

Man proposes, God in His time disposes,
    And so I wandered up to where you lay,
A little rose among the little roses,
    And no more dead than they.

It seemed your childish feet were tired of straying,   5
    You did not greet me from your flower-strewn bed,
Yet still I knew that you were only playing—
    Playing at being dead.

I might have thought that you were really sleeping,
    So quiet lay your eyelids to the sky,   10
So still your hair, but surely you were peeping;
    And so I did not cry.

God knows, and in His proper time disposes,
    And so I smiled and gently called your name,
Added my rose to your sweet heap of roses,   15
    And left you to your game.

179. BELLS FOR JOHN WHITESIDE'S DAUGHTER

There was such speed in her little body,
And such lightness in her footfall,
It is no wonder her brown study
Astonishes us all.

Her wars were bruited in our high window.   5
We looked among orchard trees and beyond
Where she took arms against her shadow,
Or harried unto the pond

The lazy geese, like a snow cloud
Dripping their snow on the green grass, 10
Tricking and stopping, sleepy and proud,
Who cried in goose, Alas,

For the tireless heart within the little
Lady with rod that made them rise
From their noon apple-dreams and scuttle 15
Goose-fashion under the skies!

But now go the bells, and we are ready,
In one house we are sternly stopped
To say we are vexed at her brown study,
Lying so primly propped. 20

QUESTIONS

1. Vocabulary: *brown study* (3, 19), *bruited* (5).
2. Which is the sentimental poem? Which is the honest one? Explain.

180. SOME KEEP THE SABBATH GOING TO CHURCH

Some keep the Sabbath going to church;
I keep it staying at home,
With a bobolink for a chorister,
And an orchard for a dome.

Some keep the Sabbath in surplice; 5
I just wear my wings,
And instead of tolling the bell for church,
Our little sexton sings.

God preaches,—a noted clergyman,—
And the sermon is never long; 10
So instead of getting to heaven at last,
I'm going all along!

181. MY CHURCH

My church has but one temple,
Wide as the world is wide,
Set with a million stars,
Where a million hearts abide.

My church has no creed to bar   5
    A single brother man
But says, "Come thou and worship"
    To every one who can.

My church has no roof nor walls,
    Nor floors save the beautiful sod—   10
For fear, I would seem to limit
    The love of the illimitable God.

QUESTION

Which is the better poem, and why?

182. THE LONG VOYAGE

Not that the pines were darker there,
nor mid-May dogwood brighter there,
nor swifts more swift in summer air;
    it was my own country,

having its thunderclap of spring,   5
its long midsummer ripening,
its corn hoar-stiff at harvesting,
    almost like any country,

yet being mine; its face, its speech,
its hills bent low within my reach,   10
its river birch and upland beech
    were mine, of my own country.

Now the dark waters at the bow
fold back, like earth against the plow;
foam brightens like the dogwood now   15
    at home, in my own country.

183. BREATHES THERE THE MAN

Breathes there the man, with soul so dead,
Who never to himself hath said,
    This is my own, my native land!
Whose heart hath ne'er within him burned,
As home his footsteps he hath turned,   5
    From wandering on a foreign strand?

If such there breathe, go, mark him well;
For him no minstrel raptures swell;
High though his titles, proud his name,
Boundless his wealth as wish can claim—   10
Despite those titles, power, and pelf,
The wretch, concentered all in self,
Living, shall forfeit fair renown,
And, doubly dying, shall go down
To the vile dust from whence he sprung,   15
Unwept, unhonored, and unsung.

QUESTION

Which poem communicates the more genuine poetic emotion? Which is more
rhetorical? Justify your answer.

184. LITTLE BOY BLUE

The little toy dog is covered with dust,
    But sturdy and staunch he stands;
And the little toy soldier is red with rust,
    And his musket moulds in his hands.
Time was when the little toy dog was new,   5
    And the soldier was passing fair;
And that was the time when our Little Boy Blue
    Kissed them and put them there.

"Now, don't you go till I come," he said,
    "And don't you make any noise!"   10
So, toddling off to his trundle-bed,
    He dreamt of the pretty toys;
And, as he was dreaming, an angel song
    Awakened our Little Boy Blue—
Oh! the years are many, the years are long,   15
    But the little toy friends are True!

Ay, faithful to Little Boy Blue they stand
    Each in the same old place—
Awaiting the touch of a little hand,
    The smile of a little face;   20
And they wonder, as waiting the long years through
    In the dust of that little chair,
What has become of our Little Boy Blue,
    Since he kissed them and put them there.

185. THE TOYS

My little Son, who looked from thoughtful eyes
And moved and spoke in quiet grown-up wise,
Having my law the seventh time disobeyed,
I struck him, and dismissed
With hard words and unkissed,   5
His Mother, who was patient, being dead.
Then, fearing lest his grief should hinder sleep,
I visited his bed,
But found him slumbering deep,
With darkened eyelids, and their lashes yet   10
From his late sobbing wet.
And I, with moan,
Kissing away his tears, left others of my own;
For, on a table drawn beside his head,
He had put, within his reach,   15
A box of counters and a red-veined stone,
A piece of glass abraded by the beach,
And six or seven shells,
A bottle with bluebells,
And two French copper coins, ranged there with careful art,   20
To comfort his sad heart.
So when that night I prayed
To God, I wept, and said:
Ah, when at last we lie with trancèd breath,
Not vexing Thee in death,   25
And thou rememberest of what toys
We made our joys,
How weakly understood
Thy great commanded good,
Then, fatherly not less   30
Than I whom Thou hast moulded from the clay,
Thou'lt leave Thy wrath, and say,
"I will be sorry for their childishness."

QUESTION

One of these poems has an obvious appeal for the beginning reader. The other
is likely to have more meaning for the mature reader. Try to explain in terms of
sentimentality and honesty.

Chapter sixteen
Good Poetry and Great

If a poem has successfully met the test in the question, *How fully has it accomplished its purpose?* we are ready to subject it to our second question, *How important is its purpose?*

Great poetry must, of course, be good poetry. Noble intent alone cannot redeem a work that does not measure high on the scale of accomplishment; otherwise the sentimental and purely didactic verse of much of the last chapter would stand with the world's masterpieces. But once a work has been judged as successful on the scale of execution, its final standing will depend on its significance of purpose.

Suppose, for instance, we consider three poems in our text: the limerick "A tutor who tooted the flute" by Carolyn Wells (No. 160); the poem "It sifts from leaden sieves" by Emily Dickinson (No. 42), and Shakespeare's sonnet "That time of year" (No. 159). Each of these would probably be judged by competent critics as highly successful in what it sets out to do. Wells has attempted a tongue-twister in strict limerick form, and she succeeds magnificently. Her poem is filled with a tooting of *oo*'s, a clatter of *t*'s, and a swarming of *-or*'s and *-er*'s. Every foot of the poem contains at least one of these sounds; most contain several. Moreover, this astounding feat is accomplished in verse which has no unnecessary or inappropriate words, no infelicities of grammar or syntax. We are delighted by its sheer technical virtuosity. But what is this limerick *about*? Nothing of the slightest interest. It makes no attempt to communicate significant human experience. Its true subject is the ingenuity of its wordplay. Like an ornately decorated Easter egg, its value lies in its shell rather than in its content. Indeed, we should hardly call it poetry at all; it is highly accomplished, brilliantly clever *verse*. Emily Dickinson's poem, in contrast, *is* poetry, and very good poetry. It appeals richly to our senses and to our imaginations, and it succeeds excellently in its purpose: to convey the appearance and the quality of falling and newly fallen snow as well as a sense of the magic and the mystery of nature. Yet, when we compare this excellent poem with Shakespeare's, we again see important differences. Although the first poem engages the senses and the imagination and may affect us with wonder and cause us to meditate on nature, it does not deeply engage the emotions or the intellect. It does not come as close to the core of human living and suffering as does Shakespeare's sonnet. In fact, it is concerned primarily with that staple of small talk, the weather. On the other hand, Shakespeare's sonnet is concerned with the universal human tragedy of growing old, with approaching death, and with love. Of these three selections, then, Shakespeare's is the greatest. It "says" more than Emily Dickinson's poem or the limerick; it communicates a richer experience; it successfully accomplishes a more significant purpose. The discriminating reader will get from it a deeper enjoyment, because it is nourishing as well as delightful.

Great poetry engages the whole person—senses, imagination, emotion, intellect; it does not touch us merely on one or two sides of our nature. Great poetry seeks not merely to entertain us but to bring us—along with pure pleasure—fresh insights, or renewed insights, and important insights, into the nature of human experience. Great poetry, we might say, gives us a broader and deeper understanding of life, of our fellows, and of ourselves, always with the qualification, of course, that the kind of insight literature gives is not necessarily the kind that can be summed up in a simple "lesson" or "moral." It is *knowledge—felt* knowledge, *new* knowledge—of the complexities of human nature and of the tragedies and sufferings, the excitements and joys, that characterize human experience.

Is Shakespeare's sonnet a *great* poem? It is, at least, a great *sonnet*. Greatness, like goodness, is relative. If we compare any of Shakespeare's sonnets with his greatest plays—*Macbeth, Othello, Hamlet, King Lear*—another big difference appears. What is undertaken and accomplished in these tragedies is enormously greater, more difficult, and more complex than could ever be undertaken or accomplished in a single sonnet. Greatness in literature, in fact, cannot be entirely dissociated from size. In literature, as in basketball and football, a good big player is better than a good little player. The greatness of a poem is in proportion to the range and depth and intensity of experience that it brings to us: its amount of life. Shakespeare's plays offer us a multiplicity of life and a depth of living that could never be compressed into the fourteen lines of a sonnet. They organize a greater complexity of life and experience into unity.

Yet, after all, we have provided no easy yardsticks or rule-of-thumb measures for literary judgment. There are no mechanical tests. The final measuring rod can be only the responsiveness, the maturity, the taste and discernment of the cultivated reader. Such taste and discernment are partly a native endowment, partly the product of experience, partly the achievement of conscious study, training, and intellectual effort. They cannot be achieved suddenly or quickly; they can never be achieved in perfection. The pull is a long and a hard one. But success, even relative success, brings enormous rewards in enrichment and command of life.

*   *   *

186. THE CANONIZATION

For God's sake, hold your tongue, and let me love!
   Or chide my palsy or my gout,
My five gray hairs or ruined fortune flout;
With wealth your state, your mind with arts improve,
    Take you a course,° get you a place,   career 5
    Observe his honor° or his grace,°   judge; bishop
Or the king's real or his stamped face°   on a coin
    Contemplate; what you will, approve,°   try out
    So you will let me love.

Alas, alas, who's injured by my love?   10
    What merchant ships have my sighs drowned?
Who says my tears have overflowed his ground?
When did my colds a forward° spring remove?   early
    When did the heats which my veins fill
    Add one more to the plaguy bill?   15
Soldiers find wars, and lawyers find out still
    Litigious men which quarrels move,
    Though she and I do love.

Call us what you will, we are made such by love.
　　Call her one, me another fly;°　　　　　　　　moth　20
We are tapers too, and at our own cost die;
And we in us find the eagle and the dove;
　　The phoenix riddle hath more wit°　　　　　meaning
　　By us; we two, being one, are it.
So to one neutral thing both sexes fit.　　　　　　25
　　We die and rise the same, and prove
　　　　Mysterious by this love.

We can die by it, if not live by love,
　　And if unfit for tombs and hearse
Our legend be, it will be fit for verse;　　　　　　30
And if no piece of chronicle° we prove,　　　　history
　　We'll build in sonnets pretty rooms:
　　As well a well-wrought urn becomes
The greatest ashes as half-acre tombs,
　　And by these hymns all shall approve°　　　confirm　35
　　　　Us canonized for love,

And thus invoke us: "You whom reverend love
　　Made one another's hermitage,
You to whom love was peace, that now is rage,
Who did the whole world's soul contract, and drove　　40
　　Into the glasses of your eyes
　　(So made into such mirrors and such spies
That they did all to you epitomize)
　　Countries, towns, courts: beg from above
　　　　A pattern of your love!"　　　　　　　　45

John Donne (1572–1631)

QUESTIONS

1. Vocabulary: *Canonization* (title), *tapers* (21), *phoenix* (23), *invoke* (37), *epitomize* (43). "*Real*" (7), pronounced as two syllables, puns on *royal*. The "plaguy bill" (15) is a list of plague victims. The word "die" (21, 26, 28) in seventeenth-century slang meant to experience the sexual climax. To understand lines 21 and 28, one also needs to be familiar with the Renaissance superstition that every act of sexual intercourse shortened one's life by one day. The "eagle" and the "dove" (22) are symbols for strength and mildness. "Pattern" (45) is a model which one can copy.
2. Who is the speaker and what is his condition? How old is he? To whom is he speaking? What has his auditor been saying to him before the opening of the poem? What sort of values can we ascribe to the auditor by inference from the first stanza? What value does the speaker oppose to these? How does the stanzaic pattern of the poem emphasize this value?

3. The sighs and tears, the fevers and chills, in the second stanza, were commonplace in the love poetry of Donne's time. How does Donne make them fresh? What is the speaker's argument in this stanza? How does it begin to turn from pure defense to offense in the last three lines of the stanza?
4. How are the things to which the lovers are compared in the third stanza *arranged*? Does it reflect in any way the arrangement of the whole poem? Elucidate line 21. Elucidate or paraphrase lines 23–27.
5. Elucidate the first line of the fourth stanza. What status does the speaker claim for himself and his beloved in the last line of this stanza?
6. In what sense is the last stanza an invocation? Who speaks in it? To whom? What powers are ascribed to the lovers in it?
7. What do the following words from the poem have in common: "mysterious" (27), "hymns" (35), "canonized" (36), "reverend" (37), "hermitage" (38)? What judgment about love does the speaker make by the use of these words?

187. HOME BURIAL

He saw her from the bottom of the stairs
Before she saw him. She was starting down,
Looking back over her shoulder at some fear.
She took a doubtful step and then undid it
To raise herself and look again. He spoke   5
Advancing toward her: "What is it you see
From up there always?—for I want to know."
She turned and sank upon her skirts at that,
And her face changed from terrified to dull.
He said to gain time: "What is it you see?"   10
Mounting until she cowered under him.
"I will find out now—you must tell me, dear."
She, in her place, refused him any help,
With the least stiffening of her neck and silence.
She let him look, sure that he wouldn't see,   15
Blind creature; and awhile he didn't see.
But at last he murmured, "Oh," and again, "Oh."

"What is it—what?" she said.

                "Just that I see."

"You don't," she challenged. "Tell me what it is."

"The wonder is I didn't see at once.   20
I never noticed it from here before.
I must be wonted to it—that's the reason.
The little graveyard where my people are!
So small the window frames the whole of it.
Not so much larger than a bedroom, is it?   25

There are three stones of slate and one of marble,
Broad-shouldered little slabs there in the sunlight
On the sidehill. We haven't to mind *those*.
But I understand: it is not the stones,
But the child's mound—"

                     "Don't, don't, don't,
   don't," she cried.   30

She withdrew, shrinking from beneath his arm
That rested on the banister, and slid downstairs;
And turned on him with such a daunting look,
He said twice over before he knew himself:
"Can't a man speak of his own child he's lost?"   35

"Not you!—Oh, where's my hat? Oh, I don't need it!
I must get out of here. I must get air.—
I don't know rightly whether any man can."

"Amy! Don't go to someone else this time.
Listen to me. I won't come down the stairs."   40
He sat and fixed his chin between his fists.
"There's something I should like to ask you, dear."

"You don't know how to ask it."

                       "Help me, then."

Her fingers moved the latch for all reply.

"My words are nearly always an offense.   45
I don't know how to speak of anything
So as to please you. But I might be taught,
I should suppose. I can't say I see how.
A man must partly give up being a man
With womenfolk. We could have some arrangement   50
By which I'd bind myself to keep hands off
Anything special you're a-mind to name.
Though I don't like such things 'twixt those that love.
Two that don't love can't live together without them.
But two that do can't live together with them."   55
She moved the latch a little. "Don't—don't go.
Don't carry it to someone else this time.
Tell me about it if it's something human.
Let me into your grief. I'm not so much
Unlike other folks as your standing there   60
Apart would make me out. Give me my chance.

I do think, though, you overdo it a little.
What was it brought you up to think it the thing
To take your mother-loss of a first child
So inconsolably—in the face of love.   65
You'd think his memory might be satisfied—"

"There you go sneering now!"

                              "I'm not, I'm not!
You make me angry. I'll come down to you.
God, what a woman! And it's come to this,
A man can't speak of his own child that's dead."   70

"You can't because you don't know how to speak.
If you had any feelings, you that dug
With your own hand—how could you?—his little grave;
I saw you from that very window there,
Making the gravel leap and leap in air,   75
Leap up, like that, like that, and land so lightly
And roll back down the mound beside the hole.
I thought, Who is that man? I didn't know you.
And I crept down the stairs and up the stairs
To look again, and still your spade kept lifting.   80
Then you came in. I heard your rumbling voice
Out in the kitchen, and I don't know why,
But I went near to see with my own eyes.
You could sit there with the stains on your shoes
Of the fresh earth from your own baby's grave   85
And talk about your everyday concerns.
You had stood the spade up against the wall
Outside there in the entry, for I saw it."

"I shall laugh the worst laugh I ever laughed.
I'm cursed. God, if I don't believe I'm cursed."   90

"I can repeat the very words you were saying:
'Three foggy mornings and one rainy day
Will rot the best birch fence a man can build.'
Think of it, talk like that at such a time!
What had how long it takes a birch to rot   95
To do with what was in the darkened parlor?
You *couldn't* care! The nearest friends can go
With anyone to death, comes so far short
They might as well not try to go at all.
No, from the time when one is sick to death,   100
One is alone, and he dies more alone.

Friends make pretense of following to the grave,
But before one is in it, their minds are turned
And making the best of their way back to life
And living people, and things they understand.   105
But the world's evil. I won't have grief so
If I can change it. Oh, I won't, I won't!"

"There, you have said it all and you feel better.
You won't go now. You're crying. Close the door.
The heart's gone out of it: why keep it up?   110
Amy! There's someone coming down the road!"

"*You*—oh, you think the talk is all. I must go—
Somewhere out of this house. How can I make you—"

"If—you—do!" She was opening the door wider.
"Where do you mean to go? First tell me that.   115
I'll follow and bring you back by force. I *will!*—"

Robert Frost (1874–1963)

QUESTIONS

1. Vocabulary: *wonted* (22).
2. The poem centers on a conflict between husband and wife. What causes the conflict? Why does Amy resent her husband? What is *his* dissatisfaction with Amy?
3. Characterize the husband and wife respectively. What is the chief difference between them? Does the poem take sides? Is either presented more sympathetically than the other?
4. The poem does not say how long the couple have been married or how long the child has been buried. Does it contain materials from which we may make rough inferences?
5. The husband and wife both generalize on the other's faults during the course of the poem, attributing them to all men or to all women or to people in general. Point out these places. Are the generalizations valid?
6. Finish the unfinished sentences in lines 30, 66, 113, 114.
7. Comment on the function of lines 25, 39, 92–93.
8. Following are three paraphrased and abbreviated versions of statements made in published discussions of the poem. Which would you support? Why?
   a. The young wife is gradually persuaded by her husband's kind yet firm reasonableness to express her feelings in words and to recognize that human nature is limited and cannot sacrifice everything to sorrow. Though she still suffers from excess grief, the crisis is past, and she will eventually be brought back to life.
   b. At the end, the whole poem is epitomized by the door that is neither open nor shut. The wife cannot really leave; the husband cannot really make

her stay. Neither husband nor wife is capable of decisive action, of liber-
ating either himself or the other.

c. Her husband's attempt to talk, since it is the wrong kind of talk, only
leads to her departure at the poem's end.

188. THE LOVE SONG OF J. ALFRED PRUFROCK

S'io credesse che mia risposta fosse
A persona che mai tornasse al mondo,
Questa fiamma staria senza piu scosse.
Ma perciocche giammai di questo fondo
Non torno vivo alcun, s'i'odo il vero,
Senza tema d'infamia ti rispondo.

Let us go then, you and I,
When the evening is spread out against the sky
Like a patient etherized upon a table;
Let us go, through certain half-deserted streets,
The muttering retreats   5
Of restless nights in one-night cheap hotels
And sawdust restaurants with oyster-shells:
Streets that follow like a tedious argument
Of insidious intent
To lead you to an overwhelming question . . .   10
Oh, do not ask, "What is it?"
Let us go and make our visit.

    In the room the women come and go
Talking of Michelangelo.

    The yellow fog that rubs its back upon the window-panes,   15
The yellow smoke that rubs its muzzle on the window-panes
Licked its tongue into the corners of the evening,
Lingered upon the pools that stand in drains,
Let fall upon its back the soot that falls from chimneys,
Slipped by the terrace, made a sudden leap,   20
And seeing that it was a soft October night,
Curled once about the house, and fell asleep.

    And indeed there will be time
For the yellow smoke that slides along the street,
Rubbing its back upon the window-panes;   25
There will be time, there will be time
To prepare a face to meet the faces that you meet;

There will be time to murder and create,
And time for all the works and days of hands
That lift and drop a question on your plate;   30
Time for you and time for me,
And time yet for a hundred indecisions,
And for a hundred visions and revisions,
Before the taking of a toast and tea.

    In the room the women come and go   35
Talking of Michelangelo.

    And indeed there will be time
To wonder, "Do I dare?" and "Do I dare?"
Time to turn back and descend the stair,
With a bald spot in the middle of my hair—   40
(They will say: "How his hair is growing thin!")
My morning coat, my collar mounting firmly to the chin,
My necktie rich and modest, but asserted by a simple pin—
(They will say: "But how his arms and legs are thin!")
Do I dare   45
Disturb the universe?
In a minute there is time
For decisions and revisions which a minute will reverse.

    For I have known them all already, known them all:—
Have known the evenings, mornings, afternoons,   50
I have measured out my life with coffee spoons;
I know the voices dying with a dying fall
Beneath the music from a farther room.
    So how should I presume?

    And I have known the eyes already, known them all—   55
The eyes that fix you in a formulated phrase,
And when I am formulated, sprawling on a pin,
When I am pinned and wriggling on the wall,
Then how should I begin
To spit out all the butt-ends of my days and ways?   60
    And how should I presume?

    And I have known the arms already, known them all—
Arms that are braceleted and white and bare
(But in the lamplight, downed with light brown hair!)
Is it perfume from a dress   65
That makes me so digress?
Arms that lie along a table, or wrap about a shawl.
    And should I then presume?
    And how should I begin?

       *   *   *

Shall I say, I have gone at dusk through narrow streets   70
And watched the smoke that rises from the pipes
Of lonely men in shirt-sleeves, leaning out of windows? . . .

I should have been a pair of ragged claws
Scuttling across the floors of silent seas.

           *   *   *

And the afternoon, the evening, sleeps so peacefully!   75
Smoothed by long fingers,
Asleep . . . tired . . . or it malingers,
Stretched on the floor, here beside you and me.
Should I, after tea and cakes and ices,
Have the strength to force the moment to its crisis?   80
But though I have wept and fasted, wept and prayed,
Though I have seen my head (grown slightly bald) brought in
    upon a platter,
I am no prophet—and here's no great matter;
I have seen the moment of my greatness flicker,
And I have seen the eternal Footman hold my coat, and snicker, 85
And in short, I was afraid.

And would it have been worth it, after all,
After the cups, the marmalade, the tea,
Among the porcelain, among some talk of you and me,
Would it have been worth while,   90
To have bitten off the matter with a smile,
To have squeezed the universe into a ball
To roll it toward some overwhelming question,
To say: "I am Lazarus, come from the dead,
Come back to tell you all, I shall tell you all"—   95
If one, settling a pillow by her head,
    Should say: "That is not what I meant at all.
    That is not it, at all."

And would it have been worth it, after all,
Would it have been worth while,   100
After the sunsets and the dooryards and the sprinkled streets,
After the novels, after the teacups, after the skirts that trail
    along the floor—
And this, and so much more?—
It is impossible to say just what I mean!
But as if a magic lantern threw the nerves in patterns on a
    screen: 105
Would it have been worth while
If one, settling a pillow or throwing off a shawl,

And turning toward the window, should say:
"That is not it at all,
That is not what I meant, at all."   110

      *   *   *

No! I am not Prince Hamlet, nor was meant to be;
Am an attendant lord, one that will do
To swell a progress, start a scene or two,
Advise the prince; no doubt, an easy tool,
Deferential, glad to be of use,   115
Politic, cautious, and meticulous:
Full of high sentence, but a bit obtuse;
At times, indeed, almost ridiculous—
Almost, at times, the Fool.

I grow old . . . I grow old . . .   120
I shall wear the bottoms of my trousers rolled.°   cuffed

Shall I part my hair behind? Do I dare to eat a peach?
I shall wear white flannel trousers, and walk upon the beach.
I have heard the mermaids singing, each to each.

I do not think that they will sing to me.   125

I have seen them riding seaward on the waves
Combing the white hair of the waves blown back
When the wind blows the water white and black.

We have lingered in the chambers of the sea
By sea-girls wreathed with seaweed red and brown   130
Till human voices wake us, and we drown.

T. S. Eliot (1888–1965)

QUESTIONS

1. Vocabulary: *insidious* (9), *Michelangelo* (14), *muzzle* (16), *malingers* (77), *progress* (113), *deferential* (115), *politic* (116), *meticulous* (116), *sentence* (117).
2. This poem may be for you the most difficult in the book, because it uses a "stream of consciousness" technique (that is, presents the apparently random thoughts going through a person's head within a certain time interval), in which the transitional links are psychological rather than logical, and also because it uses allusions you may be unfamiliar with. Even if you do not at first understand the poem in detail, you should be able to get from it a quite accurate picture of Prufrock's character and personality. What kind of person is he? (Answer this as fully as possible.) From what class of society is he? What one line especially well sums up the nature of his past life? A brief

initial orientation may be helpful: Prufrock is apparently on his way, at the beginning of the poem, to a late afternoon tea, at which he wishes (or does he?) to make a declaration of love to some lady who will be present. The "you and I" of the first line are divided parts of Prufrock's own nature, for he is undergoing internal conflict. Does he or does he not make the declaration? Where does the climax of the poem come? If the first half of the poem (up to the climax) is devoted to Prufrock's effort to prepare himself psychologically to make the declaration (or to postpone such effort), what is the latter half (after the climax) devoted to?

3. There are a number of striking or unusual figures of speech in the poem. Most of them in some way reflect Prufrock's own nature or his desires or fears. From this point of view discuss lines 2–3; 15–22 and 75–78; 57–58; 73–74; and 124–31. What figure of speech is lines 73–74? In what respect is the title ironic?

4. The poem makes an extensive use of literary allusion. The Italian epigraph is a passage from Dante's *Inferno* in which a man in Hell tells a visitor that he would never tell his story if there were a chance that it would get back to living ears. In line 29 the phrase "works and days" is the title of a long poem—a description of agricultural life and a call to toil—by the early Greek poet Hesiod. Line 52 echoes the opening speech of Shakespeare's *Twelfth Night*. The prophet of lines 81–83 is John the Baptist, whose head was delivered to Salome by Herod as a reward for her dancing (Matthew 14:1–11, and Oscar Wilde's play *Salome*). Line 92 echoes the closing six lines of Marvell's "To His Coy Mistress" (No. 51). Lazarus (94–95) may be either the beggar Lazarus (of Luke 16) who was not permitted to return from the dead to warn the brothers of a rich man about Hell, the Lazarus (of John 11) whom Christ raised from death, or both. Lines 111–19 allude to a number of characters from Shakespeare's *Hamlet*: Hamlet himself, the chamberlain Polonius, and various minor characters including probably Rosencrantz, Guildenstern, and Osric. "Full of high sentence" (117) echoes Chaucer's description of the Clerk of Oxford in the Prologue to *The Canterbury Tales*. Relate as many of these allusions as you can to the character of Prufrock. How is Prufrock particularly like Hamlet, and how is he unlike him? Contrast Prufrock with the speaker in "To His Coy Mistress."

5. "The Love Song of J. Alfred Prufrock," "The Canonization," and "Home Burial" are all dramatic poems. "The Canonization" is a dramatic monologue (one person is speaking to another, whose replies we do not hear). Frost's poem (though it has a slight narrative element) is largely a dialogue between two speakers who speak in their own voices. Eliot's poem is a highly allusive soliloquy, or interior monologue. In what ways do their dramatic structures facilitate what they have to say?

part 2
POEMS FOR
FURTHER
READING

189. SLIPPING

Age comes to my father as a slow
slipping: the leg that weakens, will
barely support him, the curtain of mist
that falls over one eye. Years, like
pickpockets, lift his concentration,   5
memory, fine sense of direction. The car,
as he drives, drifts from lane to lane
like a raft on a river, speeds and slows
for no reason, keeps missing turns.

As my mother says, "He's never liked   10
to talk about feelings," but tonight
out walking, as I slow to match his pace—
his left leg trailing a little like
a child who keeps pulling on your hand—he says,
"I love you so much." Darkness, and the sense   15
we always have that each visit may be
the last, have pushed away years of restraint.

A photograph taken of him teaching—
white coat, stethoscope like a pet snake
around his neck, chair tipped back   20
against the lecture-room wall—shows
a man talking, love of his work lighting
his face—in a way we seldom saw at home.
I answer that I love him, too, but
hardly knowing him, what I love   25
is the way reserve has slipped from
his feeling, like a screen suddenly
falling, exposing someone dressing or
washing: how wrinkles ring a bent neck,
how soft and mutable is the usually hidden flesh.   30

Joan Aleshire (b. 1947)

190. PROVIDENCE

To stay
bright as
if just
thought of
earth requires
only that
nothing stay

A. R. Ammons (b. 1926)

191. DOVER BEACH

The sea is calm tonight,
The tide is full, the moon lies fair
Upon the straits;—on the French coast the light
Gleams and is gone; the cliffs of England stand,
Glimmering and vast, out in the tranquil bay.   5
Come to the window, sweet is the night-air!
Only, from the long line of spray
Where the sea meets the moon-blanched land,
Listen! you hear the grating roar
Of pebbles which the waves draw back, and fling,   10
At their return, up the high strand,
Begin, and cease, and then again begin,
With tremulous cadence slow, and bring
The eternal note of sadness in.

Sophocles long ago   15
Heard it on the Aegean, and it brought
Into his mind the turbid ebb and flow
Of human misery; we
Find also in the sound a thought,
Hearing it by this distant northern sea.   20

The Sea of Faith
Was once, too, at the full, and round earth's shore
Lay like the folds of a bright girdle furled.
But now I only hear
Its melancholy, long, withdrawing roar,   25
Retreating, to the breath
Of the night-wind, down the vast edges drear
And naked shingles° of the world.   pebbled beaches

Ah, love, let us be true
To one another! for the world, which seems   30
To lie before us like a land of dreams,
So various, so beautiful, so new,
Hath really neither joy, nor love, nor light,
Nor certitude, nor peace, nor help for pain;
And we are here as on a darkling plain   35
Swept with confused alarms of struggle and flight,
Where ignorant armies clash by night.

Matthew Arnold (1822–1888)

192. MUSÉE DES BEAUX ARTS

About suffering they were never wrong,
The Old Masters: how well they understood
Its human position; how it takes place
While someone else is eating or opening a window or just
    walking dully along;
How, when the aged are reverently, passionately waiting   5
For the miraculous birth, there always must be
Children who did not specially want it to happen, skating
On a pond at the edge of the wood:
They never forgot
That even the dreadful martyrdom must run its course   10
Anyhow in a corner, some untidy spot
Where the dogs go on with their doggy life and the
    torturer's horse
Scratches its innocent behind on a tree.

In Brueghel's *Icarus*, for instance: how everything turns away
Quite leisurely from the disaster; the ploughman may   15
Have heard the splash, the forsaken cry,
But for him it was not an important failure; the sun shone
As it had to on the white legs disappearing into the green
Water; and the expensive delicate ship that must have seen
Something amazing, a boy falling out of the sky,   20
Had somewhere to get to and sailed calmly on.

W. H. Auden (1907–1973)

193. ON READING POEMS TO A SENIOR CLASS AT SOUTH HIGH

Before
I opened my mouth
I noticed them sitting there
as orderly as frozen fish
in a package.   5

Slowly water began to fill the room
though I did not notice it
till it reached
my ears

and then I heard the sounds   10
of fish in an aquarium

and I knew that though I had
tried to drown them
with my words
that they had only opened up 15
like gills for them
and let me in.

Together we swam around the room
like thirty tails whacking words
till the bell rang 20
puncturing
a hole in the door

where we all leaked out

They went to another class
I suppose and I home 25

where Queen Elizabeth
my cat met me
and licked my fins
till they were hands again.

D. C. Berry (b. 1942)

194. ONE ART

The art of losing isn't hard to master;
so many things seem filled with the intent
to be lost that their loss is no disaster.

Lose something every day. Accept the fluster
of lost door keys, the hour badly spent. 5
The art of losing isn't hard to master.

Then practice losing farther, losing faster:
places, and names, and where it was you meant
to travel. None of these will bring disaster.

I lost my mother's watch. And look! my last, or 10
next-to-last, of three loved houses went.
The art of losing isn't hard to master.

I lost two cities, lovely ones. And, vaster,
some realms I owned, two rivers, a continent.
I miss them, but it wasn't a disaster. 15

—Even losing you (the joking voice, a gesture
I love) I shan't have lied. It's evident
the art of losing's not too hard to master
though it may look like (*Write* it!) like disaster.

Elizabeth Bishop (1911–1979)

195. THE GARDEN OF LOVE

I went to the Garden of Love,
And saw what I never had seen:
A Chapel was built in the midst,
Where I used to play on the green.

And the gates of this Chapel were shut,   5
And "Thou shalt not" writ over the door;
So I turned to the Garden of Love
That so many sweet flowers bore;

And I saw it was filled with graves,
And tomb-stones where flowers should be;   10
And Priests in black gowns were walking their rounds,
And binding with briars my joys and desires.

William Blake (1757–1827)

196. THE LAMB

Little Lamb, who made thee?
Dost thou know who made thee?
Gave thee life and bid thee feed
By the stream and o'er the mead;
Gave thee clothing of delight,   5
Softest clothing wooly bright;
Gave thee such a tender voice,
Making all the vales rejoice!
Little Lamb, who made thee?
Dost thou know who made thee?   10

Little Lamb, I'll tell thee,
Little Lamb, I'll tell thee!
He is callèd by thy name,
For he calls himself a Lamb;
He is meek and he is mild,   15
He became a little child;

I a child and thou a lamb,
We are callèd by his name.
  Little Lamb, God bless thee.
  Little Lamb, God bless thee.

William Blake (1757–1827)

197. THE TIGER

Tiger! Tiger! burning bright
In the forests of the night,
What immortal hand or eye
Could frame thy fearful symmetry?

In what distant deeps or skies   5
Burnt the fire of thine eyes?
On what wings dare he aspire?
What the hand dare seize the fire?

And what shoulder, and what art,
Could twist the sinews of thy heart?   10
And when thy heart began to beat,
What dread hand forged thy dread feet?

What the hammer? what the chain?
In what furnace was thy brain?
What the anvil? what dread grasp   15
Dare its deadly terrors clasp?

When the stars threw down their spears,
And watered heaven with their tears,
Did he smile his work to see?
Did he who made the Lamb make thee?   20

Tiger! Tiger! burning bright
In the forests of the night,
What immortal hand or eye
Dare frame thy fearful symmetry?

William Blake (1757–1827)

198. GOOD TIMES

My Daddy has paid the rent
and the insurance man is gone
and the lights is back on
and my uncle Brud has hit

for one dollar straight   5
and they is good times
good times
good times

My Mama has made bread
and Grampaw has come   10
and everybody is drunk
and dancing in the kitchen
and singing in the kitchen
oh these is good times
good times   15
good times

oh children think about the
good times

Lucille Clifton (b. 1936)

199. KUBLA KHAN

In Xanadu did Kubla Khan
A stately pleasure-dome decree:
Where Alph, the sacred river, ran
Through caverns measureless to man
    Down to a sunless sea.   5
So twice five miles of fertile ground
With walls and towers were girdled round:
And here were gardens bright with sinuous rills,
Where blossomed many an incense-bearing tree;
And here were forests ancient as the hills,   10
Enfolding sunny spots of greenery.

But oh! that deep romantic chasm which slanted
Down the green hill athwart a cedarn cover!
A savage place! as holy and enchanted
As e'er beneath a waning moon was haunted   15
By woman wailing for her demon-lover!
And from this chasm, with ceaseless turmoil seething,
As if this earth in fast thick pants were breathing,
A mighty fountain momently was forced:
Amid whose swift half-intermitted burst   20
Huge fragments vaulted like rebounding hail,
Or chaffy grain beneath the thresher's flail:
And 'mid these dancing rocks at once and ever
It flung up momently the sacred river.

Five miles meandering with a mazy motion   25
Through wood and dale the sacred river ran,
Then reached the caverns measureless to man,
And sank in tumult to a lifeless ocean:
And 'mid this tumult Kubla heard from far
Ancestral voices prophesying war!   30

　　The shadow of the dome of pleasure
　　Floated midway on the waves;
　　Where was heard the mingled measure
　　From the fountain and the caves.
It was a miracle of rare device,   35
A sunny pleasure-dome with caves of ice!

　　A damsel with a dulcimer
　　In a vision once I saw:
　　It was an Abyssinian maid,
　　And on her dulcimer she played,   40
　　Singing of Mount Abora.
　　Could I revive within me
　　Her symphony and song,
To such a deep delight, 'twould win me,
That with music loud and long,   45
I would build that dome in air,
That sunny dome! those caves of ice!
And all who heard should see them there,
And all should cry, Beware! Beware!
His flashing eyes, his floating hair!   50
Weave a circle round him thrice,
And close your eyes with holy dread,
For he on honey-dew hath fed,
And drunk the milk of Paradise.

Samuel Taylor Coleridge (1772–1834)

200. BECAUSE I COULD NOT STOP FOR DEATH

　　Because I could not stop for Death,
　　He kindly stopped for me;
　　The carriage held but just ourselves
　　And Immortality.

We slowly drove; he knew no haste,   5
And I had put away
My labor and my leisure too,
For his civility.

We passed the school, where children strove,
At recess, in the ring,   10
We passed the fields of gazing grain,
We passed the setting sun,

Or rather, he passed us;
The dews drew quivering and chill;
For only gossamer, my gown;   15
My tippet, only tulle.

We paused before a house that seemed
A swelling of the ground;
The roof was scarcely visible.
The cornice, in the ground.   20

Since then, 'tis centuries, and yet
Feels shorter than the day
I first surmised the horses' heads
Were toward eternity.

Emily Dickinson (1830–1886)

201. I TASTE A LIQUOR NEVER BREWED

I taste a liquor never brewed,
From tankards scooped in pearl;
Not all the vats upon the Rhine
Yield such an alcohol!

Inebriate of air am I,   5
And debauchee of dew,
Reeling, through endless summer days,
From inns of molten blue.

When landlords turn the drunken bee
Out of the foxglove's door,   10
When butterflies renounce their drams,
I shall but drink the more!

Till seraphs swing their snowy hats,
And saints to windows run,
To see the little tippler   15
Leaning against the sun!

Emily Dickinson (1830–1886)

202. IN WINTER IN MY ROOM

In winter in my room
I came upon a worm,
Pink, lank, and warm;
But as he was a worm—
And worms presume—   5
Not quite with him at home
Secured him by a string
To something neighboring
And went along.

A trifle afterward   10
A thing occurred
I'd not believe it if I heard
But state with creeping blood.
A snake with mottles rare
Surveyed my chamber floor   15
In feature as the worm before
But ringed with power.
The very string with which
I tied him—too,
When he was mean and new,   20
That string was there.

I shrunk—"How fair you are!"
Propitiation's claw.
"Afraid," he hissed,
"Of me?"   25
"No cordiality."
He fathomed me.
Then to a rhythm *slim*
Secreted in his form
As patterns swim   30
Projected him.

That time I flew,
Both eyes his way
Lest he pursue,
Nor ever ceased to run   35
Till in a distant town,
Towns on from mine,
I set me down.
This was a dream.

Emily Dickinson (1830–1886)

203. THE GOOD-MORROW

I wonder, by my troth, what thou and I
Did till we loved? were we not weaned till then,
But sucked on country pleasures childishly?
Or snorted we in the seven sleepers' den?
'Twas so; but this, all pleasures fancies be.   5
If ever any beauty I did see,
Which I desired, and got, 'twas but a dream of thee.

And now good-morrow to our waking souls,
Which watch not one another out of fear;
For love all love of other sights controls,   10
And makes one little room an everywhere.
Let sea-discoverers to new worlds have gone;
Let maps to other,° worlds on worlds have shown;   others
Let us possess one world; each hath one, and is one.

My face in thine eye, thine in mine appears,   15
And true plain hearts do in the faces rest;
Where can we find two better hemispheres
Without sharp north, without declining west?
Whatever dies was not mixed equally;
If our two loves be one, or thou and I   20
Love so alike that none can slacken, none can die.

John Donne (1572–1631)

THE GOOD-MORROW   4. *seven sleepers' den:* a cave where, according to Christian legend, seven youths escaped persecution and slept for two centuries.

204. SONG: GO AND CATCH A FALLING STAR

Go and catch a falling star,
  Get with child a mandrake root,
Tell me where all past years are,
  Or who cleft the devil's foot,
Teach me to hear mermaids singing,   5
  Or to keep off envy's stinging,
      And find
      What wind
Serves to advance an honest mind.

If thou be'st born to strange sights,   10
  Things invisible to see,
Ride ten thousand days and nights,
  Till age snow white hairs on thee,
Thou, when thou return'st, wilt tell me
  All strange wonders that befell thee,   15
      And swear
      No where
Lives a woman true and fair.

If thou find'st one, let me know;
  Such a pilgrimage were sweet.   20
Yet do not; I would not go,
  Though at next door we might meet.
Though she were true when you met her,
  And last till you write your letter,
      Yet she   25
      Will be
False, ere I come, to two or three.

John Donne (1572–1631)

205. VERGISSMEINNICHT

Three weeks gone and the combatants gone,
returning over the nightmare ground
we found the place again, and found
the soldier sprawling in the sun.

SONG   2. *mandrake:* supposed to resemble a human being because of its forked root.

VERGISSMEINNICHT   The German title means "Forget me not." The author, an English poet, fought with a tank battalion in World War II and was killed in the invasion of Normandy.

The frowning barrel of his gun   5
overshadowing. As we came on
that day, he hit my tank with one
like the entry of a demon.

Look. Here in the gunpit spoil
the dishonored picture of his girl   10
who has put: *Steffi.° Vergissmeinnicht*   a girl's name
in a copybook gothic script.

We see him almost with content
abased, and seeming to have paid
and mocked at by his own equipment   15
that's hard and good when he's decayed.

But she would weep to see to-day
how on his skin the swart flies move;
the dust upon the paper eye
and the burst stomach like a cave.   20

For here the lover and killer are mingled
who had one body and one heart.
And death who had the soldier singled
has done the lover mortal hurt.

Keith Douglas (1920–1944)

206. THE COLONEL

What you have heard is true. I was in his house. His wife carried a tray of
coffee and sugar. His daughter filed her nails, his son went out for the
night. There were daily papers, pet dogs, a pistol on the cushion beside
him. The moon swung bare on its black cord over the house. On the televi-
sion was a cop show. It was in English. Broken bottles were embedded in
the walls around the house to scoop the kneecaps from a man's legs or cut
his hands to lace. On the windows there were gratings like those in liquor
stores. We had dinner, rack of lamb, good wine, a gold bell was on the table
for calling the maid. The maid brought green mangoes, salt, a type of
bread. I was asked how I enjoyed the country. There was a brief commer-
cial in Spanish. His wife took everything away. There was some talk then
of how difficult it had become to govern. The parrot said hello on the
terrace. The colonel told it to shut up, and pushed himself from the table.
My friend said to me with his eyes: say nothing. The colonel returned with
a sack used to bring groceries home. He spilled many human ears on the
table. They were like dried peach halves. There is no other way to say this.
He took one of them in his hands, shook it in our faces, dropped it into a

water glass. It came alive there. I am tired of fooling around he said. As for the rights of anyone, tell your people they can go fuck themselves. He swept the ears to the floor with his arm and held the last of his wine in the air. Something for your poetry, no? he said. Some of the ears on the floor caught this scrap of his voice. Some of the ears on the floor were pressed to the ground.

May 1978

Carolyn Forché (b. 1950)

207. ACQUAINTED WITH THE NIGHT

I have been one acquainted with the night.
I have walked out in rain—and back in rain.
I have outwalked the furthest city light.

I have looked down the saddest city lane.
I have passed by the watchman on his beat   5
And dropped my eyes, unwilling to explain.

I have stood still and stopped the sound of feet
When far away an interrupted cry
Came over houses from another street,

But not to call me back or say good-by;   10
And further still at an unearthly height
One luminary clock against the sky

Proclaimed the time was neither wrong nor right.
I have been one acquainted with the night.

Robert Frost (1874–1963)

208. MENDING WALL

Something there is that doesn't love a wall,
That sends the frozen-ground-swell under it
And spills the upper boulders in the sun,
And makes gaps even two can pass abreast.
The work of hunters is another thing: 5
I have come after them and made repair
Where they have left not one stone on a stone,
But they would have the rabbit out of hiding,
To please the yelping dogs. The gaps I mean,
No one has seen them made or heard them made,   10

But at spring mending-time we find them there.
I let my neighbor know beyond the hill;
And on a day we meet to walk the line
And set the wall between us once again.
We keep the wall between us as we go.　　　　　　　　15
To each the boulders that have fallen to each.
And some are loaves and some so nearly balls
We have to use a spell to make them balance:
"Stay where you are until our backs are turned!"
We wear our fingers rough with handling them.　　　20
Oh, just another kind of outdoor game,
One on a side. It comes to little more:
There where it is we do not need the wall:
He is all pine and I am apple orchard.
My apple trees will never get across　　　　　　　　25
And eat the cones under his pines, I tell him.
He only says, "Good fences make good neighbors."
Spring is the mischief in me, and I wonder
If I could put a notion in his head:
"*Why* do they make good neighbors? Isn't it　　　　30
Where there are cows? But here there are no cows.
Before I built a wall I'd ask to know
What I was walling in or walling out,
And to whom I was like to give offense.
Something there is that doesn't love a wall,　　　　35
That wants it down." I could say "Elves" to him,
But it's not elves exactly, and I'd rather
He said it for himself. I see him there,
Bringing a stone grasped firmly by the top
In each hand, like an old-stone savage armed.　　　40
He moves in darkness as it seems to me,
Not of woods only and the shade of trees.
He will not go behind his father's saying,
And he likes having thought of it so well
He says again, "Good fences make good neighbors."　　45

Robert Frost (1874–1963)

209. GIMBOLING

Nimble as dolphins to
dive leap and gimble, sleek, supple
as ripples to slip round each other to
wander and fondle on under and into
the seeking and coupling and swarming of water　　　5

compliant as sea-plants to bend with the tide
unfolding and folding to frond and to flower
a winding and twining to melt and to merge
to rock upon billowing founder in surf
and a fathom's down drowning before the sweet waking   10
the floating ashore into sleep and to morning.

Isabella Gardner (b. 1915)

210. PUSHING

Me and my brother would jump off the porch
mornings for a better view of the cars
that raced around the corner up Olds Ave.,
naming the make and year; this was '58
and his voice still young enough to wait for   5
how I'd say the names right to the air.
Cold mornings in Lansing we'd stop the mile
to school in the high-priced grocery nearly there
and the owner, maybe a decent White man
whose heavy dark hair and far Lebanese look   10
had caught too many kids at his candy,
would follow us down the aisles and say,
"I know what you boys is up to, big-eyed
and such, so you better be going your way—
buy something or else you got to leave."   15
We'd rattle the pennies we had and go
but coming home buy some nutchews to stay
and try his nerve again, because we didn't steal
but warmed ourselves till Ray would ask me why—
till, like big brothers will, one day I guessed,   20
"Some things you do because you want to.
Some things you do because you can't."
In what midwest warmth there was we'd laugh,
throw some snowballs high where the sun was
breaking up the clouds.   25

Christopher Gilbert (b. 1945)

211. DOWN, WANTON, DOWN!

Down, wanton, down! Have you no shame
That at the whisper of Love's name,
Or Beauty's, presto! up you raise
Your angry head and stand at gaze?

Poor bombard-captain, sworn to reach   5
The ravelin and effect a breach—
Indifferent what you storm or why,
So that in the breach you die!

Love may be blind, but Love at least
Knows what is man and what mere beast;   10
Or Beauty wayward, but requires
More delicacy from her squires.

Tell me, my witless, whose one boast
Could be your staunchness at the post,
When were you made a man of parts   15
To think fine and profess the arts?

Will many-gifted Beauty come
Bowing to your bald rule of thumb,
Or Love swear loyalty to your crown?
Be gone, have done! Down, wanton, down!   20

Robert Graves (1895–1985)

212. CHANNEL FIRING

That night your great guns, unawares,
Shook all our coffins as we lay,
And broke the chancel window-squares,
We thought it was the Judgment-day

And sat upright. While drearisome   5
Arose the howl of wakened hounds:
The mouse let fall the altar-crumb,
The worms drew back into the mounds,

The glebe cow drooled. Till God called, "No;
It's gunnery practice out at sea   10
Just as before you went below;
The world is as it used to be:

"All nations striving strong to make
Red war yet redder. Mad as hatters
They do no more for Christès sake   15
Than you who are helpless in such matters.

"That this is not the judgment-hour
For some of them's a blessed thing,
For if it were they'd have to scour
Hell's floor for so much threatening. . . .   20

"Ha, ha. It will be warmer when
I blow the trumpet (if indeed
I ever do; for you are men,
and rest eternal sorely need)."

So down we lay again. "I wonder,   25
Will the world ever saner be,"
Said one, "than when He sent us under
In our indifferent century!"

And many a skeleton shook his head.
"Instead of preaching forty year,"   30
My neighbor Parson Thirdly said,
"I wish I had stuck to pipes and beer."

Again the guns disturbed the hour,
Roaring their readiness to avenge,
As far inland as Stourton Tower,   35
And Camelot, and starlit Stonehenge.

April 1914

Thomas Hardy (1840–1928)

213. BREDON HILL

In summertime on Bredon
    The bells they sound so clear;
Round both the shires they ring them
    In steeples far and near,
    A happy noise to hear.   5

Here of a Sunday morning
    My love and I would lie,
And see the colored counties,
    And hear the larks so high
    About us in the sky.   10

The bells would ring to call her
    In valleys miles away:
"Come all to church, good people;
    Good people, come and pray."
    But here my love would stay.   15

CHANNEL FIRING   35–36. *Stourton Tower:* memorial at the spot where Alfred the Great
resisted the invading Danes in 879; *Camelot:* legendary capital of Arthur's kingdom;
Stonehenge: mysterious circle of huge stones erected in Wiltshire by very early inhabitants
of Britain. The three references move backward in time through the historic, the legendary, and the prehistoric.

And I would turn and answer
  Among the springing thyme,
"Oh, peal upon our wedding,
  And we will hear the chime,
  And come to church in time."   20

But when the snows at Christmas
  On Bredon top were strown,
My love rose up so early
  And stole out unbeknown
  And went to church alone.   25

They tolled the one bell only,
  Groom there was none to see,
The mourners followed after,
  And so to church went she,
  And would not wait for me.   30

The bells they sound on Bredon,
  And still the steeples hum.
"Come all to church, good people,"—
  Oh, noisy bells, be dumb;
  I hear you, I will come.   35

A. E. Housman (1859–1936)

214. TO AN ATHLETE DYING YOUNG

The time you won your town the race
We chaired you through the market-place;
Man and boy stood cheering by,
And home we brought you shoulder-high.

To-day, the road all runners come,   5
Shoulder-high, we bring you home,
And set you at your threshold down,
Townsman of a stiller town.

Smart lad, to slip betimes away
From fields where glory does not stay   10
And early though the laurel grows
It withers quicker than the rose.

Eyes the shady night has shut
Cannot see the record cut,
And silence sounds no worse than cheers   15
After earth has stopped the ears:

Now you will not swell the rout
Of lads that wore their honors out,
Runners whom renown outran
And the name died before the man.   20

So set, before its echoes fade,
The fleet foot on the sill of shade,
And hold to the low lintel up
The still-defended challenge-cup.

And round that early-laureled head   25
Will flock to gaze the strengthless dead,
And find unwithered on its curls
The garland briefer than a girl's.

A. E. Housman (1859–1936)

215. THE DEATH OF THE BALL TURRET GUNNER

From my mother's sleep I fell into the State,
And I hunched in its belly till my wet fur froze.
Six miles from earth, loosed from its dream of life,
I woke to black flak and the nightmare fighters.
When I died they washed me out of the turret with a hose.

Randall Jarrell (1914–1965)

216. PATHEDY OF MANNERS

At twenty she was brilliant and adored,
Phi Beta Kappa, sought for every dance;
Captured symbolic logic and the glance
Of men whose interest was their sole reward.

She learned the cultured jargon of those bred   5
To antique crystal and authentic pearls,
Scorned Wagner, praised the Degas dancing girls,
And when she might have thought, conversed instead.

PATHEDY OF MANNERS   *Pathedy:* a coined word formed from the Greek root *path-* (as in *pathetic, pathology*) plus the suffix *-edy* (as in *tragedy, comedy*).

She hung up her diploma, went abroad,
Saw catalogues of domes and tapestry,   10
Rejected an impoverished marquis,
And learned to tell real Wedgwood from a fraud.

Back home her breeding led her to espouse
A bright young man whose pearl cufflinks were real.
They had an ideal marriage, and ideal   15
But lonely children in an ideal house.

I saw her yesterday at forty-three,
Her children gone, her husband one year dead,
Toying with plots to kill time and re-wed
Illusions of lost opportunity.   20

But afraid to wonder what she might have known
With all that wealth and mind had offered her,
She shuns conviction, choosing to infer
Tenets of every mind except her own.

A hundred people call, though not one friend,   25
To parry a hundred doubts with nimble talk.
Her meanings lost in manners, she will walk
Alone in brilliant circles to the end.

Ellen Kay (b. 1931)

217. LA BELLE DAME SANS MERCI

A BALLAD

O, what can ail thee, knight-at-arms,
    Alone and palely loitering?
The sedge has withered from the lake,
    And no birds sing.

O, what can ail thee, knight-at-arms,   5
    So haggard and so woe-begone?
The squirrel's granary is full,
    And the harvest's done.

I see a lily on thy brow,
    With anguish moist and fever dew;   10
And on thy cheeks a fading rose
    Fast withereth too.

LA BELLE DAME SANS MERCI   The title means "The beautiful lady without pity."

I met a lady in the meads,
    Full beautiful—a faery's child
Her hair was long, her foot was light,   15
    And her eyes were wild.

I made a garland for her head,
    And bracelets too, and fragrant zone;
She looked at me as she did love,
    And made sweet moan.   20

I set her on my pacing steed,
    And nothing else saw all day long;
For sidelong would she bend, and sing
    A faery's song.

She found me roots of relish sweet,   25
    And honey wild, and manna dew,
And sure in language strange she said—
    "I love thee true."

She took me to her elfin grot,
    And there she wept and sighed full sore,   30
And there I shut her wild wild eyes
    With kisses four.

And there she lullèd me asleep
    And there I dreamed—Ah! woe betide!
The latest dream I ever dreamed   35
    On the cold hill side.

I saw pale kings and princes too,
    Pale warriors, death-pale were they all;
They cried—"La Belle Dame sans Merci
    Hath thee in thrall!"   40

I saw their starved lips in the gloam
    With horrid warning gapèd wide,
And I awoke and found me here
    On the cold hill's side.

And this is why I sojourn here   45
    Alone and palely loitering,
Though the sedge has withered from the lake,
    And no birds sing.

John Keats (1795–1821)

218. ODE ON A GRECIAN URN

Thou still unravished bride of quietness,
　　Thou foster-child of silence and slow time,
Sylvan historian, who canst thus express
　　A flowery tale more sweetly than our rhyme:
What leaf-fringed legend haunts about thy shape　　　5
　　Of deities or mortals, or of both,
　　　　In Tempe or the dales of Arcady?
　　What men or gods are these? What maidens loth?
What mad pursuit? What struggle to escape?
　　　　What pipes and timbrels? What wild ecstasy?　　10

Heard melodies are sweet, but those unheard
　　Are sweeter; therefore, ye soft pipes, play on;
Not to the sensual ear, but, more endeared,
　　Pipe to the spirit ditties of no tone:
Fair youth, beneath the trees, thou canst not leave　　15
　　Thy song, nor ever can those trees be bare;
　　　　Bold lover, never, never canst thou kiss,
Though winning near the goal—yet, do not grieve;
　　She cannot fade, though thou hast not thy bliss,
　　For ever wilt thou love, and she be fair!　　　　20

Ah, happy, happy boughs! that cannot shed
　　Your leaves, nor ever bid the spring adieu;
And, happy melodist, unwearièd,
　　For ever piping songs for ever new;
More happy love! more happy, happy love!　　　　25
　　For ever warm and still to be enjoyed,
　　　　For ever panting and for ever young;
All breathing human passion far above,
　　That leaves a heart high-sorrowful and cloyed,
　　A burning forehead, and a parching tongue.　　30

Who are these coming to the sacrifice?
　　To what green altar, O mysterious priest,
Lead'st thou that heifer lowing at the skies,
　　And all her silken flanks with garlands drest?
What little town by river or sea shore,　　　　35
　　Or mountain-built with peaceful citadel,
　　　　Is emptied of its folk, this pious morn?
And, little town, thy streets for evermore
　　Will silent be; and not a soul to tell
　　　　Why thou art desolate, can e'er return.　　40

O Attic shape! Fair attitude! with brede
   Of marble men and maidens overwrought,
With forest branches and the trodden weed;
   Thou, silent form, dost tease us out of thought
As doth eternity: Cold Pastoral!   45
   When old age shall this generation waste,
      Thou shalt remain, in midst of other woe
Than ours, a friend to man, to whom thou say'st,
Beauty is truth, truth beauty,—that is all
   Ye know on earth, and all ye need to know.   50

John Keats (1795–1821)

219. ODE TO A NIGHTINGALE

My heart aches, and a drowsy numbness pains
   My sense, as though of hemlock° I had drunk,   *a poisonous*
Or emptied some dull opiate to the drains   *drink*
   One minute past, and Lethe-wards had sunk:
'Tis not through envy of thy happy lot,   5
   But being too happy in thine happiness,—
      That thou, light-wingèd Dryad° of the trees,   *wood nymph*
      In some melodious plot
Of beechen green, and shadows numberless,
   Singest of summer in full-throated ease.   10

O for a draught of vintage! that hath been
   Cooled a long age in the deep-delvèd earth,
Tasting of Flora° and the country green,   *goddess of flowers*
   Dance, and Provençal song, and sunburnt mirth!
O for a beaker full of the warm South,   15
   Full of the true, the blushful Hippocrene,
      With beaded bubbles winking at the brim,
      And purple-stainèd mouth;
That I might drink, and leave the world unseen,
   And with thee fade away into the forest dim: 20

Fade far away, dissolve, and quite forget
    What thou among the leaves hast never known,
The weariness, the fever, and the fret
    Here, where men sit and hear each other groan;
Where palsy shakes a few, sad, last gray hairs,   25
    Where youth grows pale, and specter-thin, and dies;
        Where but to think is to be full of sorrow
            And leaden-eyed despairs,
    Where Beauty cannot keep her lustrous eyes,
        Or new Love pine at them beyond to-morrow.   30

Away! away! for I will fly to thee,
    Not charioted by Bacchus and his pards,
But on the viewless° wings of Poesy,   invisible
    Though the dull brain perplexes and retards:
Already with thee! tender is the night,   35
    And haply the Queen-Moon is on her throne,
        Clustered around by all her starry Fays;
            But here there is no light,
    Save what from heaven is with the breezes blown
        Through verdurous glooms and winding mossy ways.   40

I cannot see what flowers are at my feet,
    Nor what soft incense hangs upon the boughs,
But, in embalmèd° darkness, guess each sweet   perfumed
    Wherewith the seasonable month endows
The grass, the thicket, and the fruit-tree wild;   45
    White hawthorn, and the pastoral eglantine;
        Fast fading violets covered up in leaves;
            And mid-May's eldest child,
    The coming musk-rose, full of dewy wine,
        The murmurous haunt of flies on summer eves.   50

Darkling° I listen; and, for many a time   in darkness
    I have been half in love with easeful Death,
Called him soft names in many a musèd rhyme,
    To take into the air my quiet breath;
Now more than ever seems it rich to die,   55
    To cease upon the midnight with no pain,
        While thou art pouring forth thy soul abroad
            In such an ecstasy!
    Still wouldst thou sing, and I have ears in vain—
        To thy high requiem become a sod.   60

32. *Bacchus . . . pards:* Bacchus, god of wine, had a chariot drawn by leopards.

Thou wast not born for death, immortal Bird!
  No hungry generations tread thee down;
The voice I hear this passing night was heard
  In ancient days by emperor and clown:
Perhaps the self-same song that found a path   65
  Through the sad heart of Ruth, when, sick for home,
    She stood in tears amid the alien corn;
      The same that oft-times hath
Charmed magic casements, opening on the foam
  Of perilous seas, in faery lands forlorn.   70

Forlorn! the very word is like a bell
  To toll me back from thee to my sole self!
Adieu! the fancy cannot cheat so well
  As she is famed to do, deceiving elf.
Adieu! adieu! thy plaintive anthem fades   75
  Past the near meadows, over the still stream,
    Up the hill-side; and now 'tis buried deep
      In the next valley-glades:
Was it a vision, or a waking dream?
  Fled is that music:—Do I wake or sleep?   80

John Keats (1795–1821)

220. BLACKBERRY EATING

I love to go out in late September
among fat, overripe, icy, black blackberries
to eat blackberries for breakfast,
the stalks very prickly, a penalty
they earn for knowing the black art   5
of blackberry-making; and as I stand among them
lifting the stalks to my mouth, the ripest berries
fall almost unbidden to my tongue,
as words sometimes do, certain peculiar words
like *strengths* or *squinched*,   10
many-lettered, one-syllabled lumps,
which I squeeze, squinch open, and splurge well
in the silent, startled, icy, black language
of blackberry-eating in late September.

Galway Kinnell (b. 1927)

66. *Ruth:* see Bible, Ruth 2.

221. THE WARDEN SAID TO ME

The warden said to me the other day
(innocently, I think), "Say, etheridge,
why come the black boys don't run off
like the white boys do?"
I lowered my jaw and scratched my head
and said (innocently, I think), "Well, suh,
I ain't for sure, but I reckon it's cause
we ain't got no wheres to run to."

Etheridge Knight (b. 1933)

222. BEDTIME STORY

Long long ago when the world was a wild place
Planted with bushes and peopled by apes, our
Mission Brigade was at work in the jungle.
    Hard by the Congo

Once, when a foraging detail was active   5
Scouting for green-fly, it came on a grey man, the
Last living man, in the branch of a baobab
    Stalking a monkey.

Earlier men had disposed of, for pleasure,
Creatures whose names we scarcely remember—   10
Zebra, rhinoceros, elephants, wart-hog,
    Lion, rats, deer. But

After the wars had extinguished the cities
Only the wild ones were left, half-naked
Near the Equator: and here was the last one,   15
    Starved for a monkey.

By then the Mission Brigade had encountered
Hundreds of such men: and their procedure,
History tells us, was only to feed them:
    Find them and feed them;   20

Those were the orders. And this was the last one.
Nobody knew that he was, but he was. Mud
Caked on his flat grey flanks. He was crouched, half-
    Armed with a shaved spear

Glinting beneath broad leaves. When their jaws cut   25
Swathes through the bark and he saw fine teeth shine,
Round eyes roll round and forked arms waver
    Huge as the rough trunks

Over his head, he was frightened. Our workers
Marched through the Congo before he was born, but   30
This was the first time perhaps that he'd seen one.
    Staring in hot still

Silence, he crouched there: then jumped. With a long swing
Down from his branch, he had angled his spear too
Quickly, before they could hold him, and hurled it   35
    Hard at the soldier

Leading the detail. How could he know Queen's
Orders were only to help him? The soldier
Winced when the tipped spear pricked him. Unsheathing his
    Sting was a reflex.   40

Later the Queen was informed. There were no more
Men. An impetuous soldier had killed off,
Purely by chance, the penultimate primate.
    When she was certain,

Squadrons of workers were fanned through the Congo   45
Detailed to bring back the man's picked bones to be
Sealed in the archives in amber. I'm quite sure
    Nobody found them

After the most industrious search, though.
Where had the bones gone? Over the earth, dear,   50
Ground by the teeth of the termites, blown by the
    Wind, like the dodo's.

George MacBeth (b. 1932)

223. MIDWAY

I've come this far to freedom and I won't turn back.
I'm climbing to the highway from my old dirt track.
    I'm coming and I'm going
    And I'm stretching and I'm growing
And I'll reap what I've been sowing or my skin's not black.   5

I've prayed and slaved and waited and I've sung my song.
You've bled me and you've starved me but I've still grown strong.
    You've lashed me and you've treed me
    And you've everything but freed me
But in time you'll know you need me and it won't be long.   10

I've seen the daylight breaking high above the bough.
I've found my destination and I've made my vow;
  So whether you abhor me
  Or deride me or ignore me,
Mighty mountains loom before me and I won't stop now.   15

Naomi Long Madgett (b. 1923)

224. A DIALOGUE BETWEEN THE SOUL AND BODY

SOUL: Oh, who shall from this dungeon raise
  A soul enslaved so many ways?
  With bolts of bones, that fettered stands
  In feet, and manacled in hands;
  Here blinded with an eye, and there
  Deaf with the drumming of an ear;
  A soul hung up, as 'twere, in chains
  Of nerves, and arteries, and veins;
  Tortured, besides each other part,
  In a vain head, and double heart.   10

BODY: Oh, who shall me deliver whole
  From bonds of this tyrannic soul?
  Which, stretched upright, impales me so,
  That mine own precipice I go;
  And warms and moves this needless frame   15
  (A fever could but do the same)
  And, wanting where its spite to try,
  Has made me live to let me die;
  A body that could never rest,
  Since this ill spirit it possessed.   20

SOUL: What magic could me thus confine
  Within another's grief to pine?
  Where, whatsoever it complain,
  I feel, that cannot feel, the pain,
  And all my care itself employs,   25
  That to preserve, which me destroys;
  Constrained not only to endure
  Diseases, but, what's worse, the cure;
  And ready oft the port to gain,
  Am shipwrecked into health again.   30

BODY: But physic° yet could never reach   medicine
      The maladies thou me dost teach;
      Whom first the cramp of hope does tear,
      And then the palsy shakes of fear;
      The pestilence of love does heat,   35
      Or hatred's hidden ulcer eat;
      Joy's cheerful madness does perplex,
      Or sorrow's other madness vex,
      Which madness forces me to know,
      And memory will not forgo.   40
      What but a soul could have the wit
      To build me up for sin so fit?
      So architects do square and hew
      Green trees that in the forest grew.

                           Andrew Marvell (1621–1678)

225. GETTING OUT

That year we hardly slept, waking like inmates
who beat the walls. Every night
another refusal, the silent work
of tightening the heart.
Exhausted, we gave up; escaped   5
to the apartment pool, swimming those laps
until the first light relieved us.

Days were different: FM and full-blast   10
blues, hours of guitar "you gonna miss me
when I'm gone." Think how you tried
to pack up and go, for weeks stumbling
over piles of clothing, the unstrung tennis rackets.
Finally locked into blame, we paced   15
that short hall, heaving words like furniture.

I have the last unshredded pictures
of our matching eyes and hair. We've kept
to separate sides of the map,
still I'm startled by men who look like you.   20
And in the yearly letter, you're sure to say
you're happy now. Yet I think of the lawyer's bewilderment
when we cried, the last day. Taking hands
we walked apart, until our arms stretched
between us. We held on tight, and let go.   25

                           Cleopatra Mathis (b. 1947)

226. NEVERTHELESS

you've seen a strawberry
    that's had a struggle; yet
    was, where the fragments met,

a hedgehog or a star-
    fish for the multitude   5
    of seeds. What better food

than apple seeds—the fruit
    within the fruit—locked in
    like counter-curved twin

hazelnuts? Frost that kills   10
    the little rubber-plant-
    leaves of *kok-saghyz*-stalks, can't

harm the roots; they still grow
    in frozen ground. Once where
    there was a prickly-pear-   15

leaf clinging to barbed wire,
    a root shot down to grow
    in the earth two feet below;

as carrots form mandrakes
    or a ram's-horn root some-   20
    times. Victory won't come

to me unless I go
    to it; a grape tendril
    ties a knot in knots till

knotted thirty times—so   25
    the bound twig that's under-
    gone and over-gone, can't stir.

The weak overcomes its
    menace, the strong over-
    comes itself. What is there   30

NEVERTHELESS   12. *kok-saghyz:* a perennial dandelion native to south central U.S.S.R., cultivated for its fleshy roots, which contain a high rubber content.   15. *prickly-pear:* a flat-jointed cactus with edible fruit.   19. *mandrakes:* The root of the carrot sometimes is forked, resembling the root of the mandrake plant, the subject of superstition because it may look like a human being.

like fortitude! What sap
went through that little thread
to make the cherry red!

Marianne Moore (1887–1972)

227. I DO, I WILL, I HAVE

How wise I am to have instructed the butler to instruct the first
    footman to instruct the second footman to instruct the door-
    man to order my carriage;
I am about to volunteer a definition of marriage.
Just as I know that there are two Hagens, Walter and Copen,
I know that marriage is a legal and religious alliance entered into
    by a man who can't sleep with the window shut and a woman
    who can't sleep with the window open.
Moreover just as I am unsure of the difference between flora and
    fauna and flotsam and jetsam   5
I am quite sure that marriage is the alliance of two people one of
    whom never remembers birthdays and the other never for-
    getsam,
And he refuses to believe there is a leak in the water pipe or
    the gas pipe and she is convinced she is about to asphyx-
    iate or drown,
And she says Quick get up and get my hairbrushes off the window
    sill, it's raining in, and he replies Oh they're all right, it's
    only raining straight down.
That is why marriage is so much more interesting than divorce,
Because it's the only known example of the happy meeting of the
    immovable object and the irresistible force.   10
So I hope husbands and wives continue to debate and combat
    over everything debatable and combatable,
Because I believe a little incompatibility is the spice of life, par-
    ticularly if he has income and she is pattable.

Ogden Nash (1902–1971)

I DO, I WILL, I HAVE   3. *Walter:* After Bobby Jones, Walter Hagen was the world's most successful and most celebrated golfer during the decades 1910–1930.

228. GRACE TO BE SAID AT THE SUPERMARKET

That God of ours, the Great Geometer,
Does something for us here, where He hath put
(if you want to put it that way) things in shape,
Compressing the little lambs in orderly cubes,
Making the roast a decent cylinder,   5
Fairing the tin ellipsoid of a ham,
Getting the luncheon meat anonymous
In squares and oblongs with the edges bevelled
Or rounded (streamlined, maybe, for greater speed).

Praise Him, He hath conferred aesthetic distance   10
Upon our appetites, and on the bloody
Mess of our birthright, our unseemly need,
Imposed significant form. Through Him the brutes
Enter the pure Euclidean kingdom of number,
Free of their bulging and blood-swollen lives   15
They come to us holy, in cellophane
Transparencies, in the mystical body,

That we may look unflinchingly on death
As the greatest good, like a philosopher should.

Howard Nemerov (b. 1920)

229. FAMOUS

The river is famous to the fish.

The loud voice is famous to silence,
which knew it would inherit the earth
before anybody said so.

The cat sleeping on the fence is famous to the birds   5
watching him from the birdhouse.

The tear is famous, briefly, to the cheek.

The idea you carry close to your bosom
is famous to your bosom.

The boot is famous to the earth,   10
more famous than the dress shoe,
which is famous only to floors.

The bent photograph is famous to the one who carries it
and not at all famous to the one who is pictured.

I want to be famous to shuffling men   15
who smile while crossing streets,
sticky children in grocery lines,
famous as the one who smiled back.

I want to be famous in the way a pulley is famous,
or a buttonhole, not because it did anything spectacular,   20
but because it never forgot what it could do.

Naomi Shihab Nye (b. 1952)

230. THE CONNOISSEUSE OF SLUGS

When I was a connoisseuse of slugs
I would part the ivy leaves, and look for the
naked jelly of those gold bodies,
translucent strangers glistening along the
stones, slowly, their gelatinous bodies   5
at my mercy. Made mostly of water, they would shrivel
to nothing if they were sprinkled with salt,
but I was not interested in that. What I liked
was to draw aside the ivy, breathe the
odor of the wall, and stand there in silence   10
until the slug forgot I was there
and sent its antennae up out of its
head, the glimmering umber horns
rising like telescopes, until finally the
sensitive knobs would pop out the ends,   15
delicate and intimate. Years later,
when I first saw a naked man,
I gasped with pleasure to see that quiet
mystery reenacted, the slow
elegant being coming out of hiding and   20
gleaming in the dark air, eager and so
trusting you could weep.

Sharon Olds (b. 1942)

231. THE LANDLADY

Through sepia air the boarders come and go,
impersonal as trains. Pass silently
the craving silence swallowing her speech;
click doors like shutters on her camera eye.

Because of her their lives become exact: 5
their entrances and exits are designed;
phone calls are cryptic. Oh, her ticklish ears
advance and fall back stunned.

Nothing is unprepared. They hold the walls
about them as they weep or laugh. Each face   10
is dialed to zero publicly. She peers
stippled with curious flesh;

pads on the patient landing like a pulse,
unlocks their keyholes with the wire of sight,
searches their rooms for clues when they are out,   15
pricks when they come home late.

Wonders when they are quiet, jumps when they move,
dreams that they dope or drink, trembles to know
the traffic of their brains, jaywalks their street
in clumsy shoes.   20

Yet knows them better than their closest friends:
their cupboards and the secrets of their drawers,
their books, their private mail, their photographs
are theirs and hers.

Knows when they wash, how frequently their clothes   25
go to the cleaners, what they like to eat,
their curvature of health, but even so
is not content.

And like a lover must know all, all, all.
Prays she may catch them unprepared at last   30
and palm the dreadful riddle of their skulls—
hoping the worst.

                                    P. K. Page (b. 1917)

232. ETHICS

In ethics class so many years ago
our teacher asked this question every fall:
if there were a fire in a museum
which would you save, a Rembrandt painting
or an old woman who hadn't many   5
years left anyhow? Restless on hard chairs
caring little for pictures or old age
we'd opt one year for life, the next for art
and always half-heartedly. Sometimes

the woman borrowed my grandmother's face   10
leaving her usual kitchen to wander
some drafty, half-imagined museum.
One year, feeling clever, I replied
why not let the woman decide herself?
Linda, the teacher would report, eschews   15
the burdens of responsibility.
This fall in a real museum I stand
before a real Rembrandt, old woman,
or nearly so, myself. The colors
within this frame are darker than autumn,   20
darker even than winter—the browns of earth,
though earth's most radiant elements burn
through the canvas. I know now that woman
and painting and season are almost one
and all beyond saving by children.   25

Linda Pastan (b. 1932)

233. BALLAD OF BIRMINGHAM

(On the bombing of a church in Birmingham, Alabama, 1963)

"Mother dear, may I go downtown
Instead of out to play,
And march the streets of Birmingham
In a Freedom March today?"

"No, baby, no, you may not go,   5
For the dogs are fierce and wild,
And clubs and hoses, guns and jails
Aren't good for a little child."

"But, mother, I won't be alone.
Other children will go with me,   10
And march the streets of Birmingham
To make our country free."

"No, baby, no, you may not go,
For I fear those guns will fire.

BALLAD OF BIRMINGHAM   The poem is based on a historical incident. On September 15, 1963, a dynamite bomb exploded in a black church in Birmingham, killing four children.

But you may go to church instead 15
And sing in the children's choir."

She has combed and brushed her night-dark hair,
And bathed rose petal sweet,
And drawn white gloves on her small brown hands,
And white shoes on her feet. 20

The mother smiled to know her child
Was in the sacred place,
But that smile was the last smile
To come upon her face.

For when she heard the explosion, 25
Her eyes grew wet and wild.
She raced through the streets of Birmingham
Calling for her child.

She clawed through bits of glass and brick,
Then lifted out a shoe. 30
"O, here's the shoe my baby wore,
But, baby, where are you?"

Dudley Randall (b. 1914)

234. NANI

Sitting at her table, she serves
the sopa de arroz° to me   rice soup
instinctively, and I watch her,
the absolute *mamá*, and eat words
I might have had to say more   5
out of embarrassment. To speak,
now-foreign words I used to speak,
too, dribble down her mouth as she serves
me albóndigas.° No more   spiced meatballs
than a third are easy to me.   10
By the stove she does something with words
and looks at me only with her
back. I am full. I tell her
I taste the mint, and watch her speak
smiles at the stove. All my words   15
make her smile. Nani° never serves   granny
herself, she only watches me
with her skin, her hair. I ask for more.

I watch the *mamá* warming more
tortillas for me. I watch her   20
fingers in the flame for me.
Near her mouth, I see a wrinkle speak
of a man whose body serves
the ants like she serves me, then more words
from more wrinkles about children, words   25
about this and that, flowing more
easily from these other mouths. Each serves
as a tremendous string around her,
holding her together. They speak
nani was this and that to me   30
and I wonder just how much of me
will die with her, what were the words
I could have been, was. Her insides speak
through a hundred wrinkles, now, more
than she can bear, steel around her,   35
shouting, then, What is this thing she serves?

She asks me if I want more.
I own no words to stop her.
Even before I speak, she serves.

Alberto Ríos (b. 1952)

235. MR. FLOOD'S PARTY

Old Eben Flood, climbing alone one night
Over the hill between the town below
And the forsaken upland hermitage
That held as much as he should ever know
On earth again of home, paused warily.   5
The road was his with not a native near;
And Eben, having leisure, said aloud,
For no man else in Tilbury Town to hear:

"Well, Mr. Flood, we have the harvest moon
Again, and we may not have many more;   10
The bird is on the wing, the poet says,
And you and I have said it here before.

MR. FLOOD'S PARTY   11. *bird:* Mr. Flood is quoting from *The Rubáiyát of Omar Khayyám*,
"The bird of Time . . . is on the wing."

Drink to the bird." He raised up to the light
The jug that he had gone so far to fill,
And answered huskily: "Well, Mr. Flood,   15
Since you propose it, I believe I will."

Alone, as if enduring to the end
A valiant armor of scarred hopes outworn,
He stood there in the middle of the road
Like Roland's ghost winding a silent horn.   20
Below him, in the town among the trees,
Where friends of other days had honored him,
A phantom salutation of the dead
Rang thinly till old Eben's eyes were dim.

Then, as a mother lays her sleeping child   25
Down tenderly, fearing it may awake,
He set the jug down slowly at his feet
With trembling care, knowing that most things break;
And only when assured that on firm earth
It stood, as the uncertain lives of men   30
Assuredly did not, he paced away,
And with his hand extended paused again:

"Well, Mr. Flood, we have not met like this
In a long time; and many a change has come
To both of us, I fear, since last it was   35
We had a drop together. Welcome home!"
Convivially returning with himself,
Again he raised the jug up to the light;
And with an acquiescent quaver said:
"Well, Mr. Flood, if you insist, I might.   40

"Only a very little, Mr. Flood—
For auld lang syne. No more, sir; that will do."
So, for the time, apparently it did,
And Eben evidently thought so too;
For soon amid the silver loneliness   45
Of night he lifted up his voice and sang,
Secure, with only two moons listening,
Until the whole harmonious landscape rang—

20. *Roland*: hero of the French epic poem *The Song of Roland*. He died fighting a rear-
guard action for Charlemagne against the Moors in Spain; before his death he sounded a
call for help on his famous horn, but the king's army arrived too late.

"For auld lang syne." The weary throat gave out,
The last word wavered, and the song was done.   50
He raised again the jug regretfully
And shook his head, and was again alone.
There was not much that was ahead of him,
And there was nothing in the town below—
Where strangers would have shut the many doors   55
That many friends had opened long ago.

Edwin Arlington Robinson (1869–1935)

236. I KNEW A WOMAN

I knew a woman, lovely in her bones,
When small birds sighed, she would sigh back at them;
Ah, when she moved, she moved more ways than one:
The shapes a bright container can contain!
Of her choice virtues only gods should speak,   5
Or English poets who grew up on Greek
(I'd have them sing in chorus, cheek to cheek).

How well her wishes went! She stroked my chin,
She taught me Turn, and Counter-turn, and Stand;
She taught me Touch, that undulant white skin;   10
I nibbled meekly from her proffered hand;
She was the sickle; I, poor I, the rake,
Coming behind her for her pretty sake
(But what prodigious mowing we did make).

Love likes a gander, and adores a goose: 15
Her full lips pursed, the errant note to seize;
She played it quick, she played it light and loose;
My eyes, they dazzled at her flowing knees;
Her several parts could keep a pure repose,
Or one hip quiver with a mobile nose   20
(She moved in circles, and those circles moved).

Let seed be grass, and grass turn into hay:
I'm martyr to a motion not my own;
What's freedom for? To know eternity.
I swear she cast a shadow white as stone.   25
But who would count eternity in days?
These old bones live to learn her wanton ways:
(I measure time by how a body sways).

Theodore Roethke (1908–1963)

237. THE WAKING

I wake to sleep, and take my waking slow.
I feel my fate in what I cannot fear.
I learn by going where I have to go.

We think by feeling. What is there to know?
I hear my being dance from ear to ear.   5
I wake to sleep, and take my waking slow.

Of those so close beside me, which are you?
God bless the Ground! I shall walk softly there,
And learn by going where I have to go.

Light takes the Tree; but who can tell us how?   10
The lowly worm climbs up a winding stair;
I wake to sleep, and take my waking slow.

Great Nature has another thing to do
To you and me; so take the lively air,
And, lovely, learn by going where to go.   15

This shaking keeps me steady. I should know.
What falls away is always. And is near.
I wake to sleep, and take my waking slow.
I learn by going where I have to go.

Theodore Roethke (1908–1963)

238. FEAR NO MORE

Fear no more the heat o' the sun,
   Nor the furious winter's rages;
Thou thy worldly task hast done,
   Home art gone, and ta'en thy wages.
Golden lads and girls all must,   5
As chimney-sweepers, come to dust.

Fear no more the frown o' the great;
   Thou art past the tyrant's stroke;
Care no more to clothe and eat;
   To thee the reed is as the oak.   10
The scepter, learning, physic,° must   *art of healing*
All follow this, and come to dust.

Fear no more the lightning-flash,
   Nor the all-dreaded thunder-stone;°   *thunderbolt*

Fear not slander, censure rash;   15
   Thou hast finished joy and moan.
All lovers young, all lovers must
   Consign to thee,° and come to dust.   yield to your condition

William Shakespeare (1564–1616)

239. LET ME NOT TO THE MARRIAGE OF TRUE MINDS

Let me not to the marriage of true minds
Admit impediments. Love is not love
Which alters when it alteration finds,
Or bends with the remover to remove.
O no! it is an ever-fixèd mark   5
That looks on tempests and is never shaken;
It is the star to every wandering bark,
Whose worth's unknown, although his height be taken.
Love's not Time's fool, though rosy lips and cheeks
Within his bending sickle's compass come;   10
Love alters not with his brief hours and weeks,
But bears it out even to the edge of doom.
If this be error and upon me proved,
I never writ, nor no man ever loved.

William Shakespeare (1564–1616)

240. MY MISTRESS' EYES

My mistress' eyes are nothing like the sun;
Coral is far more red than her lips' red:
If snow be white, why then her breasts are dun;
If hairs be wires, black wires grow on her head.
I have seen roses damasked,° red and white,   of different colors 5
But no such roses see I in her cheeks;
And in some perfumes is there more delight
Than in the breath that from my mistress reeks.°   exhales
I love to hear her speak, yet well I know
That music hath a far more pleasing sound: 10
I grant I never saw a goddess go,—
My mistress, when she walks, treads on the ground.
And yet, by heaven, I think my love as rare
As any she belied with false compare.

William Shakespeare (1564–1616)

241. SMALL TOWN WITH ONE ROAD

We could be here. This is the valley
And its black strip of highway, big-eyed
With rabbits that won't get across.
Kids could make it, though.
They leap barefoot to the store—   5
Sweetness on their tongues, red stain of laughter.
They are the spectators of fun.
Hot dimes fall from their palms,
Chinks of light, and they eat
Candies all the way home   10
Where there's a dog for each hand,
Cats, chickens in the yard.
A pot bangs and water runs in the kitchen.
Beans, they think, and beans it will be,
Brown soup that's muscle for the field   15
And crippled steps to a ladder.
Okie or Mexican, Jew that got lost,
It's a hard life where the sun looks.
The cotton gin stands tall in the money dream
And the mill is a paycheck for   20
A wife—and perhaps my wife
Who, when she was a girl,
Boxed peaches and plums, hoed
Papa's field that wavered like a mirage
That wouldn't leave. We could go back.   25
I could lose my job, this easy one
That's only words, and pick up a shovel,
Hoe, broom that takes it away.
Worry is my daughter's story.
She touches my hand. We suck roadside   30
Snowcones in the shade
And look about. Behind sunglasses
I see where I stood: a brown kid
Getting across. "He's like me,"
I tell my daughter, and she stops her mouth.   35
He looks both ways and then leaps
Across the road where riches
Happen on a red tongue.

Gary Soto (b. 1952)

242. THE DEATH OF A SOLDIER

Life contracts and death is expected,
As in a season of autumn.
The soldier falls.

He does not become a three-days personage,
Imposing his separation,   5
Calling for pomp.

Death is absolute and without memorial,
As in a season of autumn,
When the wind stops,

When the wind stops and, over the heavens,   10
The clouds go, nevertheless,
In their direction.

Wallace Stevens (1879–1955)

243. THE SNOW MAN

One must have a mind of winter
To regard the frost and the boughs
Of the pine-trees crusted with snow;

And have been cold a long time
To behold the junipers shagged with ice,   5
The spruces rough in the distant glitter

Of the January sun; and not to think
Of any misery in the sound of the wind,
In the sound of a few leaves,

Which is the sound of the land   10
Full of the same wind
That is blowing in the same bare place

For the listener, who listens in the snow,
And, nothing himself, beholds
Nothing that is not there and the nothing that is.   15

Wallace Stevens (1879–1955)

244. QUESTION

Body my house
my horse my hound
what will I do
when you are fallen

Where will I sleep 5
How will I ride
What will I hunt

Where can I go
without my mount
all eager and quick 10
How will I know
in thicket ahead
is danger or treasure
when Body my good
bright dog is dead 15

How will it be
to lie in the sky
without roof or door
and wind for an eye

With cloud for shift 20
how will I hide?

May Swenson (b. 1919)

245. A DESCRIPTION OF THE MORNING

Now hardly here and there a hackney-coach
Appearing, showed the ruddy morn's approach.
Now Betty from her master's bed had flown,
And softly stole to discompose her own.
The slip-shod 'prentice from his master's door 5
Had pared the dirt, and sprinkled round the floor.
Now Moll had whirled her mop with dextrous airs,
Prepared to scrub the entry and the stairs.
The youth with broomy stumps began to trace
The kennel's edge, where wheels had worn the place. 10
The small-coal man was heard with cadence deep,
Till drowned in shriller notes of chimney-sweep.
Duns at his lordship's gate began to meet;
And Brickdust Moll had screamed through half the street.
The turnkey now his flock returning sees, 15

A DESCRIPTION OF THE MORNING   9. *youth*: he is apparently searching for salvage.
10. *kennel:* gutter.   14. *Brickdust:* red-complexioned.

Duly let out a-nights to steal for fees.
The watchful bailiffs take their silent stands;
And schoolboys lag with satchels in their hands.

Jonathan Swift (1667–1745)

246. DO NOT GO GENTLE INTO THAT GOOD NIGHT

Do not go gentle into that good night,
Old age should burn and rave at close of day;
Rage, rage against the dying of the light.

Though wise men at their end know dark is right,
Because their words had forked no lightning they   5
Do not go gentle into that good night.

Good men, the last wave by, crying how bright
Their frail deeds might have danced in a green bay,
Rage, rage against the dying of the light.

Wild men who caught and sang the sun in flight,   10
And learn, too late, they grieved it on its way
Do not go gentle into that good night.

Grave men, near death, who see with blinding sight
Blind eyes could blaze like meteors and be gay,
Rage, rage against the dying of the light.   15

And you, my father, there on the sad height,
Curse, bless, me now with your fierce tears, I pray.
Do not go gentle into that good night.
Rage, rage against the dying of the light.

Dylan Thomas (1914–1953)

247. FERN HILL

Now as I was young and easy under the apple boughs
About the lilting house and happy as the grass was green,
 The night above the dingle starry,
  Time let me hail and climb
 Golden in the heydays of his eyes,   5

And honored among wagons I was prince of the apple towns
And once below a time I lordly had the trees and leaves
    Trail with daisies and barley
Down the rivers of the windfall light.

And as I was green and carefree, famous among the barns   10
About the happy yard and singing as the farm was home,
    In the sun that is young once only,
        Time let me play and be
Golden in the mercy of his means,
And green and golden I was huntsman and herdsman, the calves   15
Sang to my horn, the foxes on the hills barked clear and cold,
    And the sabbath rang slowly
    In the pebbles of the holy streams.

All the sun long it was running, it was lovely, the hay
Fields high as the house, the tunes from the chimneys, it was air   20
    And playing, lovely and watery
        And fire green as grass.
    And nightly under the simple stars
As I rode to sleep the owls were bearing the farm away,
All the moon long I heard, blessed among stables, the nightjars   25
    Flying with the ricks, and the horses
        Flashing into the dark.

And then to awake, and the farm, like a wanderer white
With the dew, come back, the cock on his shoulder: it was all
    Shining, it was Adam and maiden,   30
        The sky gathered again
    And the sun grew round that very day.
So it must have been after the birth of the simple light
In the first, spinning place, the spellbound horses walking warm
    Out of the whinnying green stable   35
        On to the fields of praise.

And honored among foxes and pheasants by the gay house
Under the new made clouds and happy as the heart was long,
    In the sun born over and over,
        I ran my heedless ways,   40
    My wishes raced through the house high hay
And nothing I cared, at my sky blue trades, that time allows
In all his tuneful turning so few and such morning songs
    Before the children green and golden
        Follow him out of grace,   45

Nothing I cared, in the lamb white days, that time would take me
Up to the swallow thronged loft by the shadow of my hand,
   In the moon that is always rising,
      Nor that riding to sleep
I should hear him fly with the high fields   50
And wake to the farm forever fled from the childless land.
Oh as I was young and easy in the mercy of his means,
    Time held me green and dying
Though I sang in my chains like the sea.

Dylan Thomas (1914–1953)

248. REAPERS

Black reapers with the sound of steel on stones
Are sharpening scythes. I see them place the hones
In their hip-pockets as a thing that's done,
And start their silent swinging, one by one.
Black horses drive a mower through the weeds,
And there, a field rat, startled, squealing bleeds,
His belly close to ground. I see the blade,
Blood-stained, continue cutting weeds and shade.

Jean Toomer (1894–1967)

249. EX-BASKETBALL PLAYER

Pearl Avenue runs past the high-school lot,
Bends with the trolley tracks, and stops, cut off
Before it has a chance to go two blocks,
At Colonel McComsky Plaza. Berth's Garage
Is on the corner facing west, and there,   5
Most days, you'll find Flick Webb, who helps Berth out.

Flick stands tall among the idiot pumps—
Five on a side, the old bubble-head style,
Their rubber elbows hanging loose and low.
One's nostrils are two S's, and his eyes   10
An E and O. And one is squat, without
A head at all—more of a football type.

EX-BASKETBALL PLAYER   10–11. *two S's . . . E and O:* The brand of gasoline now called
EXXON was called ESSO prior to 1972.

Once Flick played for the high-school team, the Wizards.
He was good: in fact, the best. In '46
He bucketed three hundred ninety points,   15
A county record still. The ball loved Flick.
I saw him rack up thirty-eight or forty
In one home game. His hands were like wild birds.

He never learned a trade, he just sells gas,
Checks oil, and changes flats. Once in a while,   20
As a gag, he dribbles an inner tube,
But most of us remember anyway.
His hands are fine and nervous on the lug wrench.
It makes no difference to the lug wrench, though.

Off work, he hangs around Mae's luncheonette.   25
Grease-gray and kind of coiled, he plays pinball,
Smokes those thin cigars, nurses lemon phosphates.
Flick seldom says a word to Mae, just nods
Beyond her face toward bright applauding tiers
Of Necco Wafers, Nibs, and Juju Beads.   30

John Updike (b. 1932)

250. RETURN TO THE SWAMP

To begin again, I come back to the swamp,
To its rich decay, its calm disorder,
To alders with their reddening catkins, to hummocks
Of marsh grass floating on their own living and dead
Abundance, and wait on the shore. From my shallow angle,   5
Even shallows turn solid: a castoff sky,
A rough sketching of clouds, a bearable version
Of the sun in a mist, the upside-down redoubling
Of cattails, and my eyes, shiftless,
Depending on surface tension like water striders.   10

What did I hope to find? This crystal-gazing
Brings me no nearer what the mergansers know
Or the canvasbacks keeping their distance or the snipes
Whirring away from me, cackling, their beaks down-turned,
Heads cocked for my false alarm as they swivel   15
Loudly and jaggedly into the next bog.

27. *lemon phosphates:* soft drinks.   29–30. *tiers . . . Juju beads:* display rack of candies.

Here among shotgun shells and trampled blackberries,
How can I shape, again, something from nothing?

Edgy and mute, I wait at the edge,
And a bass taking a fly—a splashing master,   20
Ringmaster of refracted light—remakes the world,
Rippling out beautiful exchanges of stress
And yield, upheaval and rearrangement, scattering
And then regathering the shards of the day,
And suddenly near, there, near in the water   25
Where he's been floating motionless all this hour,
The hump-browed bullfrog staring at me closemouthed,
Fixing on me his green, princely attention.

David Wagoner (b. 1926)

251. THE VIRGINS

Down the dead streets of sun-stoned Frederiksted,
the first free port to die for tourism,
strolling at funeral pace, I am reminded
of life not lost to the American dream;
but my small-islander's simplicities   5
can't better our new empire's civilized
exchange of cameras, watches, perfumes, brandies
for the good life, so cheaply underpriced
that only the crime rate is on the rise
in streets blighted with sun, stone arches   10
and plazas blown dry by the hysteria
of rumor. A condominium drowns
in vacancy; its bargains are dusted,
but only a jeweled housefly drones
over the bargains. The roulettes spin   15
rustily to the wind—the vigorous trade
that every morning would begin afresh
by revving up green water round the pierhead
heading for where the banks of silver thresh.

Derek Walcott (b. 1930)

THE VIRGINS   1. *Frederiksted:* chief port of St. Croix, largest of the American Virgin Islands, is a free port where goods can be bought without payment of customs duties and therefore at bargain prices. The economy of St. Croix, once based on sugar cane, is now chiefly dependent on tourism. Like the other American Virgin Islands, it has suffered from uncontrolled growth, building booms, unevenly distributed prosperity, destruction of natural beauty, and pollution.   5. *my . . . simplicities:* The poet is a native of St. Lucia in the West Indies.   16. *trade:* cf. trade wind.

252. OLD BIBLES

I throw things away
usually, but there's
this whole shelf
of Bibles in my house.
Old Bibles, with pages missing   5
or scribbled by children
and black covers chewed by puppies.
I believe in euthanasia,
but I can't get rid of them.
It's a sin,   10
like stepping on a crack
or not crossing your fingers
or dropping the flag.

I did that once,
and for weeks   15
a gaunt bearded stranger
in tricolored clothes
came to get me,
moaning,
Give me my flag.   20
And Bibles are worse,
they maybe have souls
like little birds fluttering
over the dump
when the wind blows their pages.   25
Bibles are holy, blessed,
they're like
kosher.

So I keep them,
a row of solemn apostles   30
doomed to life,
and I wait for the great collection
and conflagration,
when they'll all burn together
with a sound like the wings   35
of a flock of doves:
little ash ascensions
of the Word.

Marilyn Nelson Waniek (b. 1946)

253. BOY WANDERING IN SIMMS' VALLEY

Through brush and love-vine, well blooded by blackberry thorn
Long dry past prime, under summer's late molten light
And past the last rock-slide at ridge-top and stubborn,
Raw tangle of cedar, I clambered, breath short and spit white

From lung-depth. Then down the lone valley, called Simms' Valley
    still,   5
Where Simms, long back, had nursed a sick wife till she died.
Then turned out his spindly stock to forage at will,
And took down his twelve-gauge, and simply lay down by her side.

No kin they had, and nobody came just to jaw.
It was two years before some straggling hunter sat down   10
On the porch-edge to rest, then started to prowl. He saw
What he saw, saw no reason to linger, so high-tailed to town.

A dirt-farmer needs a good wife to keep a place trim,
So the place must have gone to wrack with his old lady sick.
And when I came there, years later, old furrows were dim,   15
And dimmer in fields where grew maples and such, a span thick.

So for years the farm had contracted: now barn down, and all
The yard back to wilderness gone, and only
The house to mark human hope, but ready to fall.
No buyer at tax-sale, it waited, forgotten and lonely.   20

I stood in the bedroom upstairs, in lowering sun,
And saw sheets hang spiderweb-rotten, and blankets a mass
Of what weather and leaves from the broken window had done,
Not to mention the rats. And thought what had there come to pass.

But lower was sinking the sun. I shook myself,   25
Flung a last glance around, then suddenly
Saw the old enameled bedpan, high on a shelf.
I stood still again, as the last sun fell on me,

And stood wondering what life is, and love, and what they may be.

Robert Penn Warren (b. 1905)

254. A NOISELESS PATIENT SPIDER

A noiseless patient spider,
I marked where on a little promontory it stood isolated,
Marked how to explore the vacant vast surrounding,

It launched forth filament, filament, filament, out of itself,
Ever unreeling them, ever tirelessly speeding them.   5

And you O my soul where you stand,
Surrounded, detached, in measureless oceans of space,
Ceaselessly musing, venturing, throwing, seeking the spheres to
    connect them,
Till the bridge you will need be formed, till the ductile anchor hold,
Till the gossamer thread you fling catch somewhere, O my soul.   10

Walt Whitman (1819–1892)

255. THERE WAS A CHILD WENT FORTH

There was a child went forth every day,
And the first object he looked upon, that object he became,
And that object became part of him for the day or a
    certain part of the day,
Or for many years or stretching cycles of years.

The early lilacs became part of this child,   5
And grass and white and red morning-glories, and white and red
    clover, and the song of the phoebe-bird,
And the Third-month lambs and the sow's pink-faint litter, and the
    mare's foal and the cow's calf,
And the noisy brood of the barnyard or by the mire of the
    pond-side,
And the fish suspending themselves so curiously below there,
    and the beautiful curious liquid,
And the water-plants with their graceful flat heads, all became
    part of him.   10

The field-sprouts of Fourth-month and Fifth-month became
    part of him,
Winter-grain sprouts and those of the light-yellow corn, and the
    esculent roots of the garden,
And the apple-trees covered with blossoms and the fruit afterward,
    and wood-berries, and the commonest weeds by the road,
And the old drunkard staggering home from the outhouse of the
    tavern whence he had lately risen,
And the schoolmistress that passed on her way to the school,   15
And the friendly boys that passed, and the quarrelsome boys,
And the tidy and fresh-cheeked girls, and the barefoot negro boy
    and girl,
And all the changes of city and country wherever he went.

His own parents, he that had fathered him and she that had
   conceived him in her womb and birthed him,
They gave this child more of themselves than that,   20
They gave him afterward every day, they became part of him.

The mother at home quietly placing the dishes on the supper-table,
The mother with mild words, clean her cap and gown, a wholesome
   odor falling off her person and clothes as she walks by,
The father, strong, self-sufficient, manly, mean, angered, unjust,
The blow, the quick loud word, the tight bargain, the crafty lure,   25
The family usages, the language, the company, the furniture,
   the yearning and swelling heart,
Affection that will not be gainsayed, the sense of what is real,
   the thought if after all it should prove unreal,
The doubts of day-time and the doubts of night-time, the curious
   whether and how,
Whether that which appears so is so, or is it all flashes and specks?
Men and women crowding fast in the streets, if they are not
   flashes and specks what are they?   30
The streets themselves and the façades of houses, and goods
   in the windows,
Vehicles, teams, the heavy-planked wharves, the huge crossing
   at the ferries,
The village on the highland seen from afar at sunset, the river
   between,
Shadows, aureola and mist, the light falling on roofs and gables
   of white or brown two miles off,
The schooner near by sleepily dropping down the tide, the little
   boat slack-towed astern,   35
The hurrying tumbling waves, quick-broken crests, slapping,
The strata of colored clouds, the long bar of maroon-tint away
   solitary by itself, the spread of purity it lies motionless in,
The horizon's edge, the flying sea-crow, the fragrance of salt marsh
   and shore mud,
These became part of that child who went forth every day, and who
   now goes, and will always go forth every day.

Walt Whitman (1819–1892)

256. WHEN I HEARD THE LEARN'D ASTRONOMER

When I heard the learn'd astronomer,
When the proofs, the figures, were ranged in columns before me,
When I was shown the charts and diagrams, to add, divide,
   and measure them,

When I sitting heard the astronomer where he lectured with much
    applause in the lecture-room,
How soon unaccountable I became tired and sick,
Till rising and gliding out I wandered off by myself,
In the mystical moist night-air, and from time to time,
Looked up in perfect silence at the stars.

Walt Whitman (1819–1892)

257. THE MILL

The spoiling daylight inched along the bar-top,
Orange and cloudy, slowly igniting lint,
And then that glow was gone, and still your voice,
Serene with failure and with the ease of dying,
Rose from the shades that more and more became you.   5
Turning among its images, your mind
Produced the names of streets, the exact look
Of lilacs, 1903, in Cincinnati,
—Random, as if your testament were made,
The round sums all bestowed, and now you spent   10
Your pocket change, so as to be rid of it.
Or was it that you half-hoped to surprise
Your dead life's sound and sovereign anecdote?
What I remember best is the wrecked mill
You stumbled on in Tennessee; or was it   15
Somewhere down in Brazil? It slips my mind
Already. But there it was in a still valley
Far from the towns. No road or path came near it.
If there had been a clearing now it was gone,
And all you found amidst the choke of green   20
Was three walls standing, hurdled by great vines
And thatched by height on height of hushing leaves.
But still the mill-wheel turned! its crazy buckets
Creaking and lumbering out of the clogged race
And sounding, as you said, as if you'd found   25
Time all alone and talking to himself
In his eternal rattle.
                How should I guess
Where they are gone to, now that you are gone,
Those fading streets and those most fragile lilacs,
Those fragmentary views, those times of day?   30
All that I can be sure of is the mill-wheel.
It turns and turns in my mind, over and over.

Richard Wilbur (b. 1921)

258. A WREATH TO THE FISH

Who is this fish, still wearing its wealth,
flat on my drainboard, dead asleep,
its suit of mail proof only against the stream?
What is it to live in a stream,
to dwell forever in a tunnel of cold,   5
never to leave your shining birthsuit,
never to spend your inheritance of thin coins?
And who is the stream, who lolls all day
in an unmade bed, living on nothing but weather,
singing, a little mad in the head,   10
opening her apron to shells, carcasses, crabs,
eyeglasses, the lines of fishermen begging for
news from the interior—oh, who are these lines
that link a big sky to a small stream,
that go down for great things: 15
the cold muscle of the trout,
the shining scrawl of the eel in a difficult passage,
hooked—but who is this hook, this cunning
and faithful fanatic who will not let go
but holds the false bait and the true worm alike   20
and tears the fish, yet gives it up to the basket
in which it will ride to the kitchen
of someone important, perhaps the Pope
who rejoices that his cook has found such a fish
and blesses it and eats it and rises, saying,   25
"Children, what is it to live in the stream,
day after day, and come at last to the table,
transfigured with spices and herbs,
a little martyr, a little miracle;
children, children, who is this fish?"   30

Nancy Willard (b. 1936)

259. A POEM FOR EMILY

Small fact and fingers and farthest one from me,
a hand's width and two generations away,
in this still present I am fifty-three.
You are not yet a full day.

A WREATH TO THE FISH   *Wreath:* a poem in the shape of a circle, that ends where it began
(author's note).

When I am sixty-three, when you are ten,   5
and you are neither closer nor as far,
your arms will fill with what you know by then,
the arithmetic and love we do and are.

When I by blood and luck am eighty-six
and you are some place else and thirty-three   10
believing in sex and god and politics
with children who look not at all like me,

some time I know you will have read them this
so they will know I love them and say so
and love their mother. Child, whatever is   15
is always or never was. Long ago,

a day I watched a while beside your bed,
I wrote this down, a thing that might be kept
a while, to tell you what I would have said
when you were who knows what and I was dead   20
which is I stood and loved you while you slept.

Miller Williams (b. 1930)

260. I WANDERED LONELY AS A CLOUD

I wandered lonely as a cloud
That floats on high o'er vales and hills,
When all at once I saw a crowd,
A host, of golden daffodils;
Beside the lake, beneath the trees,   5
Fluttering and dancing in the breeze.

Continuous as the stars that shine
And twinkle on the milky way,
They stretched in never-ending line
Along the margin of a bay: 10
Ten thousand saw I at a glance,
Tossing their heads in sprightly dance.

The waves beside them danced; but they
Outdid the sparkling waves in glee;
A poet could not but be gay,   15
In such a jocund company;
I gazed—and gazed—but little thought
What wealth the show to me had brought:

For oft, when on my couch I lie
In vacant or in pensive mood,   20
They flash upon that inward eye
Which is the bliss of solitude;
And then my heart with pleasure fills,
And dances with the daffodils.

William Wordsworth (1770–1850)

261. THE SOLITARY REAPER

Behold her, single in the field,
Yon solitary Highland lass!
Reaping and singing by herself;
Stop here, or gently pass!
Alone she cuts and binds the grain,   5
And sings a melancholy strain;
O listen! for the vale profound
Is overflowing with the sound.

No nightingale did ever chaunt
More welcome notes to weary bands   10
Of travelers in some shady haunt
Among Arabian sands.
A voice so thrilling ne'er was heard
In springtime from the cuckoo-bird,
Breaking the silence of the seas   15
Among the farthest Hebrides.

Will no one tell me what she sings?—
Perhaps the plaintive numbers° flow   measures
For old, unhappy, far-off things,
And battles long ago.   20
Or is it some more humble lay,°   song
Familiar matter of today?
Some natural sorrow, loss, or pain,
That has been, and may be again?

Whate'er the theme, the maiden sang   25
As if her song could have no ending;
I saw her singing at her work,
And o'er the sickle bending—

THE SOLITARY REAPER   2. *Highland:* Scottish upland. The girl is singing in the Highland
language, a form of Gaelic, quite different from English.   16. *Hebrides:* islands off the
northwest tip of Scotland.

I listened, motionless and still;
And, as I mounted up the hill,   30
The music in my heart I bore
Long after it was heard no more.

William Wordsworth (1770–1850)

262. SAILING TO BYZANTIUM

That is no country for old men. The young
In one another's arms, birds in the trees
—Those dying generations—at their song,
The salmon-falls, the mackerel-crowded seas,
Fish, flesh, or fowl, commend all summer long   5
Whatever is begotten, born, and dies.
Caught in that sensual music all neglect
Monuments of unaging intellect.

An aged man is but a paltry thing,
A tattered coat upon a stick, unless   10
Soul clap its hands and sing, and louder sing
For every tatter in its mortal dress,
Nor is there singing school but studying
Monuments of its own magnificence;
And therefore I have sailed the seas and come   15
To the holy city of Byzantium.

O sages standing in God's holy fire
As in the gold mosaic of a wall,
Come from the holy fire, perne° in a gyre,   spin
And be the singing-masters of my soul.   20
Consume my heart away; sick with desire
And fastened to a dying animal
It knows not what it is; and gather me
Into the artifice of eternity.

Once out of nature I shall never take   25
My bodily form from any natural thing,
But such a form as Grecian goldsmiths make
Of hammered gold and gold enameling

SAILING TO BYZANTIUM *Byzantium:* Ancient eastern capital of the Roman Empire; here
symbolically a holy city of the imagination.   1. *That:* Ireland, or the ordinary sensual
world.   27–31. *such . . . Byzantium:* The Byzantine Emperor Theophilus had made
for himself mechanical golden birds which sang upon the branches of a golden tree.

To keep a drowsy Emperor awake;
Or set upon a golden bough to sing   30
To lords and ladies of Byzantium
Of what is past, or passing, or to come.

William Butler Yeats (1865–1939)

263. THE SECOND COMING

Turning and turning in the widening gyre
The falcon cannot hear the falconer;
Things fall apart; the center cannot hold;
Mere anarchy is loosed upon the world,
The blood-dimmed tide is loosed, and everywhere   5
The ceremony of innocence is drowned;
The best lack all conviction, while the worst
Are full of passionate intensity.

Surely some revelation is at hand;
Surely the Second Coming is at hand.   10
The Second Coming! Hardly are those words out
When a vast image out of *Spiritus Mundi*
Troubles my sight: somewhere in sands of the desert
A shape with lion body and the head of a man,
A gaze blank and pitiless as the sun,   15
Is moving its slow thighs, while all about it
Reel shadows of the indignant desert birds.
The darkness drops again; but now I know
That twenty centuries of stony sleep   ₚₑₛᵤₛ
Were vexed to nightmare by a rocking cradle,   20
And what rough beast, its hour come round at last,
Slouches towards Bethlehem to be born?

William Butler Yeats (1865–1939)

THE SECOND COMING   In Christian legend the prophesied "Second Coming" may refer
either to Christ or to Antichrist. Yeats believed in a cyclical theory of history in which one
historical era would be replaced by an opposite kind of era every two thousand years.
Here, the anarchy in the world following World War I (the poem was written in 1919)
heralds the end of the Christian era.   12. *Spiritus Mundi:* the racial memory or collec-
tive unconscious mind of mankind (literally, world spirit).

264. THE WILD SWANS AT COOLE

The trees are in their autumn beauty,
The woodland paths are dry,
Under the October twilight the water
Mirrors a still sky;
Upon the brimming water among the stones   5
Are nine-and-fifty swans.

The nineteenth autumn has come upon me
Since I first made my count;
I saw, before I had well finished,
All suddenly mount   10
And scatter wheeling in great broken rings
Upon their clamorous wings.

I have looked upon those brilliant creatures,
And now my heart is sore,
All's changed since I, hearing at twilight,   15
The first time on this shore,
The bell-beat of their wings above my head,
Trod with a lighter tread.

Unwearied still, lover by lover,
They paddle in the cold   20
Companionable streams or climb the air;
Their hearts have not grown old;
Passion or conquest, wander where they will,
Attend upon them still.

But now they drift on the still water,   25
Mysterious, beautiful;
Among what rushes will they build,
By what lake's edge or pool
Delight men's eyes when I awake some day
To find they have flown away?   30

William Butler Yeats (1865–1939)

THE WILD SWANS AT COOLE   Coole Park, in County Galway, Ireland, was the estate of
Lady Augusta Gregory, Yeats's patroness and friend. Beginning in 1897, Yeats regularly
summered there for many years.

Glossary of Poetic Terms

The definitions in this glossary sometimes repeat and sometimes differ in language from those in the text. Where they differ, the intention is to give a fuller sense of the term's meaning by allowing the reader a double perspective on it. Page numbers refer to discussion in the text, which in most but not all cases is fuller than that in the glossary.

Accent   In this book, the same as *stress*. A syllable given more prominence in pronunciation than its neighbors is said to be accented. 169–79

Allegory   A narrative or description having a second meaning beneath the surface one. 87–88

Alliteration   The repetition at close intervals of the initial consonant sounds of accented syllables or important words (for example, *m*ap-*m*oon, *k*ill-*c*ode, *p*reach-ap*p*rove). Important words and accented syllables beginning with vowels may also be said to alliterate with each other inasmuch as they all have the same lack of an initial consonant sound (for example, "*I*nebri*a*te of *a*ir am *I*"). 157–61

Allusion   A reference, explicit or implicit, to something in previous literature or history. (The term is reserved by some writers for implicit references only, such as those in "On His Blindness," 122, and "In the Garden," 128; but the distinction between the two kinds of reference is not always clear-cut.) 117–21

Anapest   A metrical foot consisting of two unaccented syllables followed by one accented syllable (for example, ŭn-dĕr-stānd). 170, 177

Anapestic meter   A meter in which a majority of the feet are anapests. (But see *Triple meter.*) 170, 178

Apostrophe   A figure of speech in which someone absent or dead or something nonhuman is addressed as if it were alive and present and could reply. 63–65

Approximate rime (also known as *imperfect rime, near rime, slant rime,* or *oblique rime*)   A term used for words in a riming pattern that have some kind of sound correspondence but are not perfect rimes. See *Rime.* Approximate rimes occur occasionally in patterns where most of the rimes are perfect (for example, arrayed-said in "Richard Cory," 39), and sometimes are used systematically in place of perfect rime (for example, "Mr. Z," 113). 158

Assonance   The repetition at close intervals of the vowel sounds of accented syllables or important words (for example, h*a*t-r*a*n-*a*mber, v*ei*n-m*a*de). 157–60

Aubade   A poem about dawn; a morning love song; or a poem about the parting of lovers at dawn. 49–50, 138–39

Ballad   A fairly short narrative poem written in a songlike stanza form. Examples: "Edward," 219; "La Belle Dame sans Merci," 275; "Ballad of Birmingham," 290. Also see *Folk ballad.*

Blank verse   Unrimed iambic pentameter. 179

Cacophony   A harsh, discordant, unpleasant-sounding choice and arrangement of sounds. 191–92

Caesura   See *Grammatical pause* and *Rhetorical pause.*

Connotation   What a word suggests beyond its basic definition; a word's overtones of meaning. 33–38

Consonance   The repetition at close intervals of the final consonant sounds of accented syllables or important words (for example, boo*k*-pla*que*-thi*ck*er). 157–60

Continuous form   That form of a poem in which the lines follow each other without formal grouping, the only breaks being dictated by units of meaning. 206

Couplet   Two successive lines, usually in the same meter, linked by rime. 180 (Exercise 2a), 210

Dactyl   A metrical foot consisting of one accented syllable followed by two unaccented syllables (for example, mḗr-r̆i-l̆y). 170

Dactylic meter   A meter in which a majority of the feet are dactyls. (But see *Triple meter.*) 170, 177

Denotation   The basic definition or dictionary meaning of a word. 33–38

Didactic poetry   Poetry having as a primary purpose to teach or preach. 227–28

Dimeter   A metrical line containing two feet. 170

Dipodic foot   The basic foot of *dipodic verse,* consisting (when complete) of an unaccented syllable, a lightly accented syllable, an unaccented syllable, and a heavily accented syllable, in that succession. However, dipodic verse accommodates a tremendous amount of variety, as shown by the examples in the text. 184–85

Dipodic verse   A meter in which there is a perceptible alternation between light and heavy stresses. See *Dipodic foot.* 185

Double rime   A rime in which the repeated vowel is in the second last syllable of the words involved (for example, politely-rightly-spritely); one form of *feminine rime.* 165 (Question 5)

Dramatic framework   The situation, whether actual or fictional, realistic or fanciful, in which an author places his or her characters in order to express the theme. 20–21

Dramatic irony   See *Irony.*

Duple meter   A meter in which a majority of the feet contain two syllables. Iambic and trochaic are both duple meters. 170

End rime   Rimes that occur at the ends of lines. 158

End-stopped line   A line that ends with a natural speech pause, usually marked by punctuation. 179

English (or *Shakespearean*) *sonnet*   A sonnet riming *ababcdcdefefgg.* Its content or structure ideally parallels the rime scheme, falling into three coordinate quatrains and a concluding couplet; but it is often structured, like the Italian sonnet, into octave and sestet, the principal break in thought coming at the end of the eighth line. 210–11, 212 (Exercise 1)

Euphony   A smooth, pleasant-sounding choice and arrangement of sounds. 191–92

Expected rhythm   The metrical expectation set up by the basic meter of a poem. 176

Extended figure (also known as *sustained figure*)   A figure of speech (usually metaphor, simile, personification, or apostrophe) sustained or developed through a considerable number of lines or through a whole poem. 70

Feminine rime   A rime in which the repeated accented vowel is in either the second or third last syllable of the words involved (for example, ceiling-appealing, hurrying-scurrying). 158, 165 (Question 5)

Figurative language   Language employing figures of speech; language that cannot be taken literally or only literally. 59–69, 78–88, 98–107

Figure of speech   Broadly, any way of saying something other than the ordinary way; more narrowly (and for the purposes of this book) a way of saying one thing and meaning another. 59–69, 78–88, 98–107

Fixed form   Any form of poem in which the length and pattern are prescribed by previous usage or tradition, such as *sonnet, limerick, villanelle, haiku,* and so on. 208–12

Folk ballad   A narrative poem designed to be sung, composed by an anonymous author, and transmitted orally for years or generations before being written down. It has usually undergone modification through the process of oral transmission. "Edward," 219

Foot   The basic unit used in the scansion or measurement of verse. A foot usually contains one accented syllable and one or two unaccented syllables, but the *monosyllabic foot,* the *spondaic foot (spondee),* and the *dipodic foot* are all modifications of this principle. 169–70, 185

Form   The external pattern or shape of a poem, describable without reference to its content, as *continuous form, stanzaic form, fixed form* (and their varieties), *free verse,* and *syllabic verse.* 205–12, 216. See *Structure.*

Free verse   Non-metrical verse. Poetry written in free verse is arranged in lines, may be more or less rhythmical, but has no fixed metrical pattern or expectation. 178–79

Grammatical pause (also known as *caesura*)   A pause introduced into the reading of a line by a mark of punctuation. Grammatical pauses do not affect scansion. 176

Haiku   A three-line poem, Japanese in origin, narrowly conceived of as a fixed form in which the lines contain respectively 5, 7, and 5 syllables (in American practice this requirement is frequently dispensed with). Haiku are generally concerned with some aspect of nature and present a single image or two juxtaposed images without comment, relying on suggestion rather than on explicit statement to communicate their meaning. 216

Heard rhythm   The actual rhythm of a metrical poem as we hear it when it is read naturally. The heard rhythm mostly conforms to but sometimes departs from or modifies the *expected rhythm.* 176

Heptameter   A metrical line containing seven feet. 170

Hexameter   A metrical line containing six feet. 170

Hyperbole   See *Overstatement.*

Iamb   A metrical foot consisting of one unaccented syllable followed by one accented syllable (for example, rĕ-hēarse). 170

Iambic meter   A meter in which the majority of feet are iambs. The most common English meter. 170, 177–78

Iambic-anapestic meter   A meter which freely mixes iambs and anapests, and in which it might be difficult to determine which foot prevails without actually counting. 178

Imagery   The representation through language of sense experience. 46–49

Internal rime   A rime in which one or both of the rime-words occur *within* the line. 158

Irony   A situation, or a use of language, involving some kind of incongruity or discrepancy. 104. Three kinds of irony are distinguished in this book:

Verbal irony   A figure of speech in which what is meant is the opposite of what is said. 102–104

Dramatic irony   A device by which the author implies a different meaning from that intended by the speaker (or by *a* speaker) in a literary work. 104–106

Irony of situation (or *situational irony*)   A situation in which there is an incongruity between actual circumstances and those that would seem appropriate or between what is anticipated and what actually comes to pass. 106–107

Italian (or *Petrarchan*) *sonnet*   A sonnet consisting of an octave riming *abbaabba* and of a sestet using any arrangement of two or three additional rimes, such as *cdcdcd* or *cdecde*. 209–10, 212 (Exercise 1).

Limerick   A fixed form consisting of five lines of anapestic meter, the first two trimeter, the next two dimeter, the last line trimeter, riming *aabba;* used exclusively for humorous or nonsense verse. 208–209, 212–13

Masculine rime (also known as *single rime*)   A rime in which the repeated accented vowel sound is in the final syllable of the words involved (for example, dance-pants, scald-recalled). 158, 165 (Question 5).

Metaphor   A figure of speech in which an implicit comparison is made between two things essentially unlike. It may take one of four forms: (1) that in which the literal term and the figurative term are both *named;* (2) that in which the literal term is *named* and the figurative term *implied;* (3) that in which the literal term is *implied* and the figurative term *named;* (4) that in which both the literal and the figurative terms are *implied.* 59–62, 67–69

Meter   Regularized rhythm; an arrangement of language in which the accents occur at apparently equal intervals in time. 168

Metonymy   A figure of speech in which some significant aspect or detail of an experience is used to represent the whole experience. In this book the single term *metonymy* is used for what are sometimes distinguished as two separate figures: *synecdoche* (the use of the part for the whole) and *metonymy* (the use of something closely related for the thing actually meant). 65–66

Metrical pause   A pause that supplies the place of an expected accented syllable. Unlike *grammatical* and *rhetorical pauses*, metrical pauses affect scansion. 185

Monometer   A metrical line containing one foot. 170

Monosyllabic foot   A foot consisting of a single accented syllable (for example, shine). 170

Octameter   A metrical line containing eight feet. 170

Octave   (1) An eight-line stanza. (2) The first eight lines of a sonnet, especially one structured in the manner of an Italian sonnet. 209

Onomatopoeia   The use of words that supposedly mimic their meaning in their sound (for example, boom, click, plop). 189

Onomatopoetic language   Language employing *onomatopoeia*.

Overstatement (or *hyperbole*)   A figure of speech in which exaggeration is used in the service of truth. 99–102

Paradox   A statement or situation containing apparently contradictory or incompatible elements. 98–99

Paradoxical situation   A situation containing apparently but not actually incompatible elements. The celebration of a fifth birthday anniversary by a twenty-year-old man is paradoxical but explainable if the man was born on February 29. The Christian doctrines that Christ was born of a virgin and is both God and man are, for a Christian believer, paradoxes (that is, apparently impossible but true). 98

Paradoxical statement (or *verbal paradox*)   A figure of speech in which an apparently self-contradictory statement is nevertheless found to be true. 98–99

Paraphrase   A restatement of the content of a poem designed to make its *prose meaning* as clear as possible. 25–26

Pentameter   A metrical line containing five feet. 170

Personification   A figure of speech in which human attributes are given to an animal, an object, or a concept. 62–64

Petrarchan sonnet   See *Italian sonnet*.

Phonetic intensive   A word whose sound, by an obscure process, to some degree suggests its meaning. As differentiated from *onomatopoetic* words, the meanings of phonetic intensives do not refer to sounds. 189–90

Prose   Non-metrical language; the opposite of *verse*. 168

Prose meaning   That part of a poem's *total meaning* that can be separated out and expressed through paraphrase. 129–33

Prose poem   Usually a short composition having the intentions of poetry but written in prose rather than verse. 179

Quatrain   (1) A four-line stanza. (2) A four-line division of a sonnet marked off by its rime scheme. 210

Refrain   A repeated word, phrase, line, or group of lines, normally at some fixed position in a poem written in stanzaic form. 159, 208

Rhetorical pause (also known as *caesura*)   A natural pause, unmarked by punctuation, introduced into the reading of a line by its phrasing or syntax. Rhetorical pauses do not affect scansion. 176

Rhetorical poetry   Poetry using artificially eloquent language, that is, language too high-flown for its occasion and unfaithful to the full complexity of human experience. 227

Rhythm   Any wavelike recurrence of motion or sound. 168

Rime (or *rhyme*)   The repetition of the accented vowel sound and all succeeding sounds in important or importantly positioned words (for example, old-cold, vane-reign, court-report, order-recorder). The above definition applies to *perfect rime* and assumes that the accented vowel sounds involved are preceded by differing consonant sounds. If the preceding consonant sound is the same (for example, manse-romance, style-stile), or if there is no preceding consonant sound in either word (for example, aisle-isle, alter-altar), or if the same word is repeated in the riming position (for example, hill-hill), the words are called *identical rimes*. Both *perfect rimes* and *identical rimes* are to be distinguished from *approximate rimes*. 158

Rime scheme   Any fixed pattern of rimes characterizing a whole poem or its stanzas. 208

Run-on line   A line which has no natural speech pause at its end, allowing the sense to flow uninterruptedly into the succeeding line. 179

Sarcasm   Bitter or cutting speech; speech intended by its speaker to give pain to the person addressed. 102

Satire   A kind of literature that ridicules human folly or vice with the purpose of bringing about reform or of keeping others from falling into similar folly or vice. 102–103

Scansion The process of measuring verse, that is, of marking accented and unaccented syllables, dividing the lines into feet, identifying the metrical pattern, and noting significant variations from that pattern. 170

Sentimental poetry Poetry aimed primarily at stimulating the emotions rather than at communicating experience honestly and freshly. 226–27

Sestet (1) A six-line stanza. (2) The last six lines of a sonnet structured on the Italian model. 209

Shakespearean sonnet See *English sonnet*.

Simile A figure of speech in which an explicit comparison is made between two things essentially unlike. The comparison is made explicit by the use of some such word or phrase as *like, as, than, similar to, resembles,* or *seems*. 59

Single rime See *Masculine rime*.

Situational irony See *Irony*

Sonnet A fixed form of fourteen lines, normally iambic pentameter, with a rime scheme conforming to or approximating one of two main types—the *Italian* or the *English*. 209–12

Spondee A metrical foot consisting of two syllables equally or almost equally accented (for example, trūe-blūe). 170

Stanza A group of lines whose metrical pattern (and usually its rime scheme as well) is repeated throughout a poem. 170, 206–208

Stanzaic form The form taken by a poem when it is written in a series of units having the same number of lines and usually other characteristics in common, such as metrical pattern or rime scheme. 206–208

Stress In this book, the same as *Accent*. But see 169 (footnote).

Structure The internal organization of a poem's content. See *Form*.

Sustained figure See *Extended figure*.

Syllabic verse Verse measured by the number of syllables rather than the number of feet per line. 216 (Question 4). Also see *Haiku*.

Symbol A figure of speech in which something (object, person, situation, or action) means more than what it is. A symbol, in other words, may be read both literally and metaphorically. 78–87

Synecdoche A figure of speech in which a part is used for the whole. In this book it is subsumed under the term *Metonymy*. 65–66

Tetrameter A metrical line containing four feet. 170

Theme The central idea of a literary work. 25

Tone The writer's or speaker's attitude toward his subject, his audience, or himself; the emotional coloring, or emotional meaning, of a work. 141–45

Total meaning   The total experience communicated by a poem. It includes all those dimensions of experience by which a poem communicates—sensuous, emotional, imaginative, and intellectual—and it can be communicated in no other words than those of the poem itself. 129–33

Trimeter   A metrical line containing three feet. 170

Triple meter   A meter in which a majority of the feet contain three syllables. (Actually, if more than 25 percent of the feet in a poem are triple, its effect is more triple than duple, and it ought perhaps to be referred to as triple meter.) Anapestic and dactylic are both triple meters. 170

Triple rime   A rime in which the repeated accented vowel sound is in the third last syllable of the words involved (for example, gainfully-disdainfully); one form of *feminine rime*. 165 (Question 5)

Trochaic meter   A meter in which the majority of feet are trochees. 170, 175–76

Trochee   A metrical foot consisting of one accented syllable followed by one unaccented syllable (for example, bär-tĕr). 170

Understatement   A figure of speech that consists of saying less than one means, or of saying what one means with less force than the occasion warrants. 100–102

Verbal irony   See *Irony*.

Verse   Metrical language; the opposite of *prose*. 168

Villanelle   See 212 (Exercise 2).

COPYRIGHTS AND ACKNOWLEDGMENTS

by Ellen Kay. Reprinted with the permission of The Ohio University Press, Athens.

GALWAY KINNELL "Blackberry Eating" © 1983 *Saturday Review* magazine. Reprinted by permission.

ETHERIDGE KNIGHT "The warden said to me" from *Poems from Prison* © 1968 by Broadside Press. Reprinted by permission of Broadside Press.

MAXINE KUMIN "400-Meter Freestyle" from *Our Ground Time Here Will Be Brief* by Maxine Kumin. Copyright © 1959 by Maxine Kumin. Reprinted by permission of Viking Penguin, Inc.

PHILIP LARKIN "Toads" by Philip Larkin is reprinted from *The Less Deceived* by permission of The Marvell Press, England. "A Study of Reading Habits" from *The Whitsun Weddings* by Philip Larkin. Reprinted by permission of Faber and Faber, Ltd. "Aubade" from the *Times Literary Supplement*, December 23, 1977, by permission of the author.

GEORGE MACBETH "Bedtime Story" from *The Broken Places* by George Macbeth (Scorpion Press, 1963). Reprinted by permission of the author.

DAVID MCCORD Limerick "Well, it's partly the shape of the thing" from *What Cheer* (New York: Coward-McCann, 1945). Reprinted by courtesy of the author.

ARCHIBALD MACLEISH "Ars Poetica" and "You, Andrew Marvell" from *New and Collected Poems 1917–1976* by Archibald MacLeish. Copyright © 1976 by Archibald MacLeish. Reprinted by permission of Houghton Mifflin Company.

NAOMI LONG MADGETT "Midway" from *Star by Star* by Naomi Long Madgett. (Detroit: Harlo Press, 1965; Evenill, Inc., 1970). By permission of the author.

CLEOPATRA MATHIS "Getting Out" reprinted from *Aerial View of Louisiana*, The Sheep Meadow Press, 1979.

EDNA ST. VINCENT MILLAY "Counting-Out Rhyme" from *Collected Poems*, Harper & Row. Copyright 1928, 1955 by Edna St. Vincent Millay and Norma Millay Ellis.

MARIANNE MOORE "Nevertheless," reprinted with permission of Macmillan Publishing Co., Inc. from *Collected Poems* by Marianne Moore. Copyright 1944 by Marianne Moore, renewed by Marianne Moore.

OGDEN NASH "The Turtle" from *Verses from 1929 On*. Copyright 1940 by Ogden Nash. By permission of Little, Brown and Company. "I Do, I Will, I Have" from *Verses from 1929 On* by Ogden Nash. Copyright 1948 by The Curtis Publishing Company. First appeared in *The Saturday Evening Post*. By permission of Little, Brown and Company.

HOWARD NEMEROV "Grace To Be Said at the Supermarket" from *The Collected Poems of Howard Nemerov* (The University of Chicago Press, 1977). Reprinted by permission of the author.

JOHN FREDERICK NIMS "Love Poem" from *The Iron Pastoral* by John Frederick Nims. Reprinted by permission of the author.

NAOMI SHIHAB NYE "Famous" from *Hugging the Jukebox*, E. P. Dutton, 1982. © 1982 by Naomi Shihab Nye. Reprinted with permission of the author.

SHARON OLDS "The Connoisseuse of Slugs" from *The Dead and the Living*, by Sharon Olds. Copyright © 1983 by Sharon Olds. Reprinted by permission of Alfred A. Knopf, Inc.

WILFRED OWEN "Dulce et Decorum Est" and "Anthem for Doomed Youth" from *The Collected Poems of Wilfred Owen*. Copyright © 1963 by Chatto & Windus, Ltd. Reprinted by permission of New Directions Publishing Corporation.

P. K. PAGE "The Landlady" from *Poems, Selected and New* by P. K. Page. Reprinted by permission of the author.

LINDA PASTAN   "Ethics" is reprinted from *Waiting for My Life, Poems by Linda Pastan*, by permission of W. W. Norton & Company, Inc. Copyright © 1981 by Linda Pastan.

SYLVIA PLATH   "Mirror" from *The Collected Poems of Sylvia Plath*, edited by Ted Hughes. Copyright © 1963 by Ted Hughes. "Metaphors" from *The Collected Poems of Sylvia Plath*, edited by Ted Hughes. Copyright © 1971 by Ted Hughes. Reprinted by permission of Harper & Row, Publishers, Inc.

RALPH POMEROY   "Row" from *Stills and Movies* (Gesture Books). © 1956, 1984 by Ralph Pomeroy. Originally appeared in *The New Yorker*, September 1956.

EZRA POUND   "Portrait d'une Femme" from *Personae*. Copyright 1926 by Ezra Pound. Reprinted by permission of New Directions Publishing Corporation.

DUDLEY RANDALL   "Ballad of Birmingham" by Dudley Randall reprinted by permission of Third World Press.

JOHN CROWE RANSOM   "Parting, Without a Sequel" copyright 1927 by Alfred A. Knopf, Inc. and renewed 1955 by John Crowe Ransom. "Bells for John Whiteside's Daughter" copyright 1924 by Alfred A. Knopf, Inc. and renewed 1952 by John Crowe Ransom. Reprinted from *Selected Poems*, Third Edition, Revised and Enlarged, by John Crowe Ransom, by permission of Alfred A. Knopf, Inc.

HENRY REED   "Naming of Parts" from *A Map of Verona* by Henry Reed. Reprinted by permission of Jonathan Cape Ltd.

ALASTAIR REID   "Curiosity" from *Passwords* by Alastair Reid. Copyright © 1959 by Alastair Reid; originally published in *The New Yorker*. Reprinted by permission of the author.

ADRIENNE RICH   "Living in Sin" is reprinted from *The Fact of a Doorframe, Poems Selected and New, 1950–1984*, by Adrienne Rich, by permission of W. W. Norton & Company, Inc. Copyright © 1984 by Adrienne Rich. Copyright © 1975, 1978, by W. W. Norton & Company, Inc. Copyright © 1981 by Adrienne Rich.

DOROTHY LEE RICHARDSON   "At Cape Bojeador" from *The Half-Seen Face* by Dorothy Lee Richardson. (Dublin, New Hampshire: William L. Bauhan, Publisher, 1979). Reprinted with permission of the author.

ALBERTO RÍOS   "Nani" reprinted from *Whispering to Fool the Wind*, The Sheep Meadow Press, 1983.

EDWIN ARLINGTON ROBINSON   "Mr. Flood's Party," "Miniver Cheevy," "The Mill," and "The Dark Hills," from *Collected Poems* by Edwin Arlington Robinson. "Richard Cory" from *The Children of the Night*. Reprinted courtesy of Charles Scribner's Sons.

THEODORE ROETHKE   "The Waking" and "I Knew a Woman" copyright 1948, 1954 by Theodore Roethke from *The Collected Poems of Theodore Roethke*. Reprinted by permission of Doubleday & Company, Inc.

CARL SANDBURG   "The Harbor" from *Chicago Poems* by Carl Sandburg, copyright 1916 by Holt, Rinehart and Winston, Inc.; renewed 1944 by Carl Sandburg. Reprinted by permission of Harcourt Brace Jovanovich, Inc. "Splinter" from *Good Morning, America*, copyright 1928, 1956 by Carl Sandburg. Reprinted by permission of Harcourt Brace Jovanovich, Inc.

SIEGFRIED SASSOON   "Base Details" from *Collected Poems* by Siegfried Sassoon. Copyright 1918 by E. P. Dutton & Co., copyright 1946 by Siegfried Sassoon. Reprinted by permission of Viking Penguin Inc. and G. T. Sassoon.

MARTIN BRISTOW SMITH   "A goat on a stroll near a brook" from *Five-Line Frolics* © 1982 Exposition Press. Reprinted with permission of Exposition Press of Florida, Inc.

GARY SOTO   "Small Town with One Road" first appeared in *Poetry* © November 1985 by

Index of Authors, Titles, and First Lines

Authors' names appear in capitals, titles of poems in italics, and first lines of poems in roman type. Numbers in roman type indicate the page of the selection and italic numbers indicate discussion of the poem.

A bird came down the walk 12
"A cold coming we had of it 125
A decrepit old gas man named Peter 213
A goat on a stroll near a brook 213
A lightning gleam 216
A narrow fellow in the grass 52
A noiseless patient spider 306
A poem should be palpable and mute 140
A route of evanescence 66
A sudden blow: the great wings beating still 124
A tutor who tooted the flute 213
About suffering they were never wrong 257
Abraham to kill him 127
Acquainted with the Night 268
After Apple-Picking 50
Age comes to my father as a slow 255
Aim Was Song, The 186
ALESHIRE, JOAN
Slipping 255
All day I hear the noise of waters 202

AMMONS, A. R.
Providence 255
An ant on the tablecloth 112
And here face down beneath the sun 83, *84–85*
"And if I did what then? 29
ANONYMOUS
A decrepit old gas man named Peter 213
Edward 219
God's Will for You and Me 229
I sat next the duchess at tea 208
In the garden there strayed 128
Little Jack Horner 129
Love 154
My Church 235
Pease porridge hot 188, *188*
There was a young lady from Niger 212
There was a young lady of Lynn 213
There was a young maid who said, "Why 213
"Why dois your brand sae drap wi bluid 219

Anthem for Doomed Youth 201
Apparently with no surprise 143,
 144–45
Apparition, The 151
ARNOLD, MATTHEW
 Dover Beach 256
Ars Poetica 140
As a dare-gale skylark scanted in a dull
 cage 137
As he lay dying, two fat crows 219
As imperceptibly as grief 162
As virtuous men pass mildly away 72
At Cape Bojeador 80, *81*
At twenty she was brilliant and adored
 274
Aubade 138
AUDEN, W. H.
 Musée des Beaux Arts 257
 That night when joy began 158
 The Unknown Citizen 111

BAKER, DONALD W.
 Formal Application 110
Ballad of Birmingham 290
Barter 131, *132*
Base Details 45
BASHŌ, MATSUO
 A lightning gleam 216
 The lightning flashes! 216
Batter my heart, three-personed God;
 for you 108
Because I could not stop for Death 262
Bedtime Story 281
Before 257
Before man came to blow it right 186
Behold her, single in the field 312
Bells for John Whiteside's Daughter 234
Belshazzar had a letter 127
Bent double, like old beggars under
 sacks 8
Bereft 60
BERRY, D. C.
 *On Reading Poems to a Senior Class
 at South High* 257
BISHOP, ELIZABETH
 One Art 258
Black reapers with the sound of steel
 on stones 302
Blackberry Eating 280
BLAKE, WILLIAM
 A Poison Tree 233
 "Introduction" to *Songs of Innocence*
 180

Soft Snow 97
The Chimney Sweeper 105
The Garden of Love 259
The Lamb 259
The Sick Rose 81, *82–83*
The Tiger 260
Body my house 298
Both robbed of air, we both lie in one
 ground 122
Boy Wandering in Simms' Valley 306
Break of Day 26
Breathes there the man, with soul so
 dead 236
Bredon Hill 272
BROOKE, RUPERT
 The Dead 89
BROOKS, GWENDOLYN
 We Real Cool 162
BROWNING, ROBERT
 Meeting at Night 47, *47–48*
 My Last Duchess 114
 Parting at Morning 48
BRYANT, WILLIAM CULLEN
 To a Waterfowl 133
BURFORD, WILLIAM
 A Christmas Tree 223
Busy old fool, unruly sun 100

Caged Skylark, The 137
CAMPION, THOMAS
 There is a garden in her face 69
Canonization, The 241
Channel Firing 271
Chimney Sweeper, The 105
Christmas Eve, and twelve of the clock
 150
Christmas Tree, A 223
CLIFTON, LUCILLE
 Good Times 260
COLERIDGE, SAMUEL TAYLOR
 Kubla Khan 261
 Metrical Feet 187
COLLINS, MARTHA
 The Story We Know 218
Colonel, The 267
Come up from the fields father, here's
 a letter from our Pete 230
Coming of Wisdom with Time, The 145
Connoisseuse of Slugs, The 288
Constantly risking absurdity 11
CORNFORD, FRANCES
 The Guitarist Tunes Up 59
Counting-Out Rhyme 166

COWLEY, MALCOLM
The Long Voyage 236
Cross 42
Crossing the Bar 149
CULLEN, COUNTEE
Incident 101
CUMMINGS, E. E.
if everything happens that can't be done 182
in Just- 121
the greedy the people 207
Curiosity 92

Dance, The 203
Dark Hills, The 64
Dark hills at evening in the west 64
Darkling Thrush, The 54
DAVIES, W. H.
The Villain 143, 144–45
Dead, The 89
Death of a Soldier, The 298
Death of the Ball Turret Gunner, The 274
Death, be not proud, though some have called thee 217
Departmental 112
Description of the Morning, A 299
Design 134
Dialogue Between the Soul and Body, A 283
DICKINSON, EMILY
A bird came down the walk 12
A Hummingbird 66
A narrow fellow in the grass 52
Abraham to kill him 127
Apparently with no surprise 143, 144–45
As imperceptibly as grief 162
Because I could not stop for Death 262
Belshazzar had a letter 127
I heard a fly buzz when I died 203
I like to see it lap the miles 198
I taste a liquor never brewed 263
In winter in my room 264
It sifts from leaden sieves 61
My life closed twice before its close 99
One dignity delays for all 148
Some keep the Sabbath going to church 235
There is no frigate like a book 34, 34

There's been a death in the opposite house 27
'Twas warm at first like us 149
Do Not Go Gentle into that Good Night 300
Does the road wind uphill all the way? 96
DONNE, JOHN
A Hymn to God the Father 44
A Valediction: Forbidding Mourning 72
Batter my heart, three-personed God; for you 108
Break of Day 26
Death, be not proud, though some have called thee 217
Hero and Leander 122
Hymn to God My God, in My Sickness 95
Love's Deity 136
Song: Go and catch a falling star 266
The Apparition 151
The Canonization 241
The Flea 152
The Good-Morrow 265
The Indifferent 135
The Sun Rising 100
The Triple Fool 13
DOUGLAS, KEITH
Vergissmeinnicht 266
Dover Beach 256
Down by the salley gardens my love and I did meet 185
Down the dead streets of sun-stoned Frederiksted 304
Down, wanton, down! Have you no shame 270
DRAYTON, MICHAEL
Since there's no help 146
Dream Deferred 77
DUGAN, ALAN
Love Song: I and Thou 93
Dulce et Decorum Est 8
Dust of Snow 97

Eagle, The 5
Edward 219
Eight O'Clock 201
ELIOT, T. S.
Journey of the Magi 125
The Love Song of J. Alfred Prufrock 247
Engraved on the Collar of a Dog Which I Gave to His Royal Highness 153

Epitaph on an Army of Mercenaries 181
Ethics 289
EVANS, MARI
   When in Rome 28
Ex-Basketball Player 302

Faded Coat of Blue, The 232
Famous 287
Fear no more the heat o' the sun 295
FERLINGHETTI, LAWRENCE
   Constantly risking absurdity 11
Fern Hill 300
FIELD, EUGENE
   Little Boy Blue 237
Fire and Ice 88
Flea, The 152
For God's sake, hold your tongue, and
   let me love! 241
For me, the naked and the nude 36
FORCHÉ, CAROLYN
   The Colonel 267
Formal Application 110
400-Meter Freestyle 221
FRANCIS, ROBERT
   The Hound 60
   Pitcher 229
From my mother's sleep I fell into the
   State 274
FROST, ROBERT
   Acquainted with the Night 268
   After Apple-Picking 50
   Bereft 60
   Departmental 112
   Design 134
   Dust of Snow 97
   Fire and Ice 88
   Home Burial 243
   It takes all sorts 181
   Mending Wall 268
   Mowing 25, *25*
   Nothing Gold Can Stay 167
   "Out, Out—" 118, *119*
   Stopping by Woods on a Snowy Eve-
     ning 131, *132*
   The Aim Was Song 186
   The Road Not Taken 78, *79–80*
   The Span of Life 195, *195–96*
   The Silken Tent 70
   The Telephone 146

Garden of Love, The 259
GARDNER, ISABELLA
   Gimboling 269

GASCOIGNE, GEORGE
   And if I did what then? 29
Gather ye rosebuds while ye may 86
Getting Out 284
GILBERT, CHRISTOPHER
   Pushing 270
Gimboling 269
Glory be to God for dappled things
   229
Go and catch a falling star 266
God's Grandeur 160
God's Will for You and Me 229
Good-Morrow, The 265
Good Times 260
Grace To Be Said at the Supermarket
   287
GRAVES, ROBERT
   Down, wanton, down! have you no
     shame 270
   The Naked and the Nude 36
Guitarist Tunes Up, The 59

Had he and I but met 19, *20–21*
Had I the choice to tally greatest bards
   186
Had we but world enough, and
   time 74
Handful of Limericks, A 212
Harbor, The 163
HARDY, THOMAS
   Channel Firing 271
   The Darkling Thrush 54
   The Man He Killed 19, *20–21*
   The Oxen 150
Hark, hark! 189
HARINGTON, SIR JOHN
   On Treason 110
Having been tenant long to a rich
   Lord 88
HAYDEN, ROBERT
   Those Winter Sundays 54
He clasps the crag with crooked hands
   5
He saw her from the bottom of the
   stairs 243
He stood, and heard the steeple 201
He was found by the Bureau of Statis-
   tics to be 111
Heaven-Haven 200
HERBERT, GEORGE
   Redemption 88
   The Quip 63
   Virtue 170, *171–76*
Hero and Leander 122

HERRICK, ROBERT
To the Virgins, to Make Much of
Time 86
Upon Julia's Voice 191, 191–92
His art is eccentricity, his aim 229
HOLMAN, M. CARL
Mr. Z 113
Home Burial 243
HOPKINS, GERARD MANLEY
God's Grandeur 160
Heaven-Haven 200
Pied Beauty 229
Spring 56
The Caged Skylark 137
Hound, The 60
HOUSMAN, A. E.
Bredon Hill 272
Eight O'Clock 201
Epitaph on an Army of Mercenaries
181
Is my team ploughing 21, 23
Loveliest of trees, the cherry now
76
Oh who is that young sinner 184
Terence, this is stupid stuff 14
To an Athlete Dying Young 273
With rue my heart is laden 161
How dear to my heart was the old-
fashioned hurler 230
How wise I am to have instructed the
butler to instruct the first 286
HUGHES, LANGSTON
Cross 42
Dream Deferred 77
HUGHES, TED
Wind 199
Hummingbird, A 66
Hymn to God My God, in My Sickness
95
Hymn to God the Father, A 44

I am his Highness' dog at Kew 153
I am silver and exact. I have no pre-
conceptions 31
I am two fools, I know 13
I can love both fair and brown 135
I Do, I Will, I Have 286
I found a dimpled spider, fat and
white 134
I have been one acquainted with the
night 268
I have desired to go 200
I heard a fly buzz when I died 203

I knew a woman, lovely in her bones
294
I know the thing that's most uncom-
mon 103
I leant upon a coppice gate 54
I like to see it lap the miles 198
I long to talk with some old lover's
ghost 136
I love to go out in late September 280
"I love you, Horowitz," he said, and
blew his nose 147
I met a traveler from an antique land
106
I sat next the duchess at tea 208
I shall begin by learning to throw 110
I taste a liquor never brewed 263
I throw things away 305
I wake to sleep, and take my waking
slow 295
I walked abroad in a snowy day 97
I wandered lonely as a cloud 311
I was angry with my friend 233
I went to the Garden of Love 259
I wonder, by my troth, what thou and
I 265
I work all day, and get half drunk at
night 138
if everything happens that can't be
done 182
If I profane with my unworthiest hand
216
If I were fierce, and bald, and short of
breath 45
I'm a riddle in nine syllables 70
In Breughel's great picture, The
Kermess 203
In ethics class so many years ago 289
in Just- 121
In summertime on Bredon 272
In the garden there strayed 128
In Xanadu did Kubla Khan 261
In winter in my room 264
Incident 101
Indifferent, The 135
"Introduction" to Songs of Innocence
180
"Is my team ploughing 21, 23
It little profits that an idle king 90
It sifts from leaden sieves 61
It takes all sorts of in- and outdoor
schooling 181
It was my thirtieth year to heaven 214
I've come this far to freedom and I
won't turn back 282

JARRELL, RANDALL
  The Death of the Ball Turret Gunner
  274
JENNISON, KEITH
  Last Stand 123
Journey of the Magi 125
JOYCE, JAMES
  All day I hear 202
Just to be tender, just to be true 229

KAY, ELLEN
  Pathedy of Manners 274
KEATS, JOHN
  La Belle Dame sans Merci 275
  Ode on a Grecian Urn 277
  Ode to a Nightingale 278
  On First Looking into Chapman's
    Homer 209
  To Autumn 56
  To Sleep 76
KINNELL, GALWAY
  Blackberry Eating 280
KLEISER, GRANFIELD
  The Most Vital Thing in Life 233
KNIGHT, ETHERIDGE
  The warden said to me 281
Kubla Khan 261
KUMIN, MAXINE
  400-Meter Freestyle 221

La Belle Dame sans Merci 275
Lamb, The 259
Landlady, The 288
LARKIN, PHILIP
  A Study of Reading Habits 31
  Aubade 138
  Toads 71
Last Stand 123
Late Aubade, A 49
Leda and the Swan 124
Let me not to the marriage of true
  minds 296
Let us go then, you and I 247
Life contracts and death is expected
  298
Life has loveliness to sell 131, 132
Life the hound 60
Little Boy Blue 237
Little Jack Horner 129
Little Lamb, who made thee? 259
Living in Sin 53
Long long ago when the world was a
  wild place 281

Long Voyage, The 236
Love 154
Love Poem 109
Love Song: I and Thou 93
Love Song of J. Alfred Prufrock, The
  247
Love in Brooklyn 147
Love's Deity 136
Loveliest of trees, the cherry now 76

MACBETH, GEORGE
  Bedtime Story 281
MCCORD, DAVID
  Well, it's partly the shape of the
    thing 213
MACLEISH, ARCHIBALD
  Ars Poetica 140
  You, Andrew Marvell 83, 84–85
MCNAUGHTON, J. M.
  The Faded Coat of Blue 232
MADGETT, NAOMI LONG
  Midway 282
Man He Killed, The 19
Man proposes, God in His time dis-
  poses 234
Mark but this flea, and mark in this
  152
MARVELL, ANDREW
  To His Coy Mistress 74
  A Dialogue Between the Soul and
    Body 283
MATHIS, CLEOPATRA
  Getting Out 284
Mattie dear 28
may have killed the cat; more likely
  92
Me and my brother would jump off
  the porch 270
Meeting at Night 47, 47–48
Mending Wall 268
Metaphors 70
Metrical Feet 187
MIDDLETON, RICHARD
  On a Dead Child 234
Midway 282
Mill, The (Robinson) 30
Mill, The (Wilbur) 309
MILLAY, EDNA ST. VINCENT
  Counting-Out Rhyme 166
MILTON, JOHN
  On His Blindness 122
Miniver Cheevy, child of scorn 123
Mirror 31

MOORE, MARIANNE
  Nevertheless 285
MORITAKE
  The falling flower 216
  Fallen flowers rise 216
Most Vital Thing in Life, The 233
"Mother dear, may I go downtown 290
Mowing 25, 25
Mr. Flood's Party 292
Mr. Z 113
Much have I traveled in the realms of
  gold 209
Musée des Beaux Arts 257
My brave lad he sleeps in his faded
  coat of blue 232
My Church 235
My church has but one temple 235
My clumsiest dear, whose hands ship-
  wreck vases 109
My Daddy has paid the rent 260
My heart aches, and a drowsy numb-
  ness pains 278
My Last Duchess 114
My life closed twice before its close 99
My little Son, who looked from
  thoughtful eyes 238
My long two-pointed ladder's sticking
  through a tree 50
My mistress' eyes are nothing like the
  sun 296
My old man's a white old man 42

Naked and the Nude, The 36
Naming of Parts 40
Nani 291
NASH, OGDEN
  I Do, I Will, I Have 286
  The Turtle 156, 157
Nature's first green is gold 167
NEMEROV, HOWARD
  Grace To Be Said at the Supermarket
  287
Nevertheless 285
Nimble as dolphins to 269
NIMS, JOHN FREDERICK
  Love Poem 109
Not that the pines were darker there
  236
Nothing Gold Can Stay 167
Nothing is plumb, level or square 93
Nothing is so beautiful as spring 56
Now as I was young and easy under
  the apple boughs 300
Now hardly here and there a hackney-
  coach 299

NYE, NAOMI SHIHAB
  Famous 287

O Rose, thou art sick! 81, 82–83
O soft embalmer of the still mid-
  night 76
O, what can ail thee, knight-at-arms
  275
Ode on a Grecian Urn 277
Ode to a Nightingale 278
Oh who is that young sinner with the
  handcuffs on his wrists? 184
Oh, who shall from this dungeon raise
  283
Old Bibles 305
Old Eben Flood, climbing alone one
  night 292
Old-Fashioned Pitcher, The 230
OLDS, SHARON
  The Connoisseuse of Slugs 288
On a Certain Lady at Court 103
On a Dead Child 234
On First Looking into Chapman's Homer
  209
On His Blindness 122
On Reading Poems to a Senior Class at
  South High 257
On Treason 110
Once riding in old Baltimore 101
One Art 258
One dignity delays for all 148
One must have a mind of winter 298
"Out, Out—" 118, 119
OWEN, WILFRED
  Anthem for Doomed Youth 201
  Dulce et Decorum Est 8
Oxen, The 150
Ozymandias 106

PAGE, P. K.
  The Landlady 288
Parting at Morning 48
Parting, Without a Sequel 164
Passing through huddled and ugly
  walls 163
PASTAN, LINDA
  Ethics 289
Pathedy of Manners 274
PATMORE, COVENTRY
  The Toys 238
Pearl Avenue runs past the high-school
  lot 302
Pease porridge hot 188

PHAIR, GEORGE E.
   The Old-Fashioned Pitcher 230
Pied Beauty 229
Piping down the valleys wild 180
Pitcher 229
PLATH, SYLVIA
   Metaphors 70
   Mirror 31
Poem for Emily, A 310
Poem in October 214
Poison Tree, A 233
POMEROY, RALPH
   Row 165
POPE, ALEXANDER
   Engraved on the Collar of a Dog
     Which I Gave to His Royal High-
     ness 153
   On a Certain Lady at Court 103
   Sound and Sense 198
Portrait d'une Femme 41
POUND, EZRA
   Portrait d'une Femme 41
Providence 255
Pushing 270

Question 298
Quip, The 63

RANDALL, DUDLEY
   Ballad of Birmingham 290
RANSOM, JOHN CROWE
   Bells for John Whiteside's Daughter
     234
   Parting, Without a Sequel 164
Reapers 302
Redemption 88
Red Wheelbarrow, The 14
REED, HENRY
   Naming of Parts 40
REID, ALASTAIR
   Curiosity 92
Return to the Swamp 303
RICH, ADRIENNE
   Living in Sin 53
Richard Cory 39
RICHARDSON, DOROTHY LEE
   At Cape Bojeador 80, 81
RÍOS, ALBERTO
   Nani 291
Road Not Taken, The 78, 79–80
ROBINSON, EDWIN ARLINGTON
   Miniver Cheevy 123
   Mr. Flood's Party 292

Richard Cory 39
The Dark Hills 64
The Mill 30
ROETHKE, THEODORE
   I Knew a Woman 294
   The Waking 295
ROSSETTI, CHRISTINA
   Uphill 96
Round the cape of a sudden came the
   sea 48
Row 165

Sailing to Byzantium 313
SANDBURG, CARL
   Splinter 190
   The Harbor 163
SASSOON, SIEGFRIED
   Base Details 45
SCOTT, SIR WALTER
   Breathes there the man 236
Season of mists and mellow fruitful-
   ness 56
Second Coming, The 314
SHAKESPEARE, WILLIAM
   Fear no more 295
   If I profane with my unworthiest
     hand (from *Romeo and Juliet*) 216
   Let me not to the marriage of true
     minds 296
   My mistress' eyes are nothing like
     the sun 296
   She should have died hereafter (from
     Macbeth) 68, 120, *120*
   Song: Hark, hark! 189
   That time of year 210
   When my love swears that she is
     made of truth 35
   Winter 6, 7
She had thought the studio would keep
   itself 53
She has finished and sealed the letter
   164
She is as in a field a silken tent 70
She should have died hereafter 68,
   120, *120*
SHELLEY, PERCY BYSSHE
   Ozymandias 106
Sick Rose, The 81, *82–83*
Silken Tent, The 70
Silver bark of beech, and sallow 166
Since I am coming to that holy
   room 95
Since there's no help, come let us kiss
   and part 146

Sitting at her table, she serves 291
Slap. Clap. 165
Slipping 255
Small Town with One Road 297
Small fact and fingers and farthest one
from me 310
SMITH, MARTIN BRISTOW
A goat on a stroll near a brook 213
Snow Man, The 298
Solitary Reaper, The 312
so much depends 14
So smooth, so sweet, so silvery is thy
voice 191, *191–92*
Soft Snow 97
Some keep the Sabbath going to
church 235
Some say the world will end in fire 88
Something there is that doesn't love a
wall 268
Song: Go and catch a falling star 266
Song: Hark, hark! 189
SOTO, GARY
Small Town with One Road 297
Sound and Sense 198
Span of Life, The 195, *195–96*
Splinter 190
Spring 56
STAFFORD, WILLIAM
Traveling Through the Dark 166
Star 223
STEVENS, WALLACE
The Death of a Soldier 298
The Snow Man 298
Stopping by Woods on a Snowy Evening
131, *132*
Story We Know, The 218
STOW, RANDOLPH
As he lay dying, two fat crows 219
Study of Reading Habits, A 31
Sun Rising, The 100
Sundays too my father got up early 54
Sunset and evening star 149
Sweet day, so cool, so calm, so bright
170, *171–76*
SWENSON, MAY
Question 298
SWIFT, JONATHAN
A Description of the Morning 299

Taught early that his mother's skin
was the sign of error 113
TEASDALE, SARA
Barter 131, *132*

Telephone, The 146
TENNYSON, ALFRED, LORD
Crossing the Bar 149
The Eagle 5
Ulysses 90
"Terence, this is stupid stuff 14
That God of ours, the Great Geometer
287
That is no country for old men. The
young 313
That night when joy began 158
That night your great guns, unawares
271
That time of year thou mayst in me
behold 210
That year we hardly slept, waking like
inmates 284
That's my last duchess painted on the
wall 114
The art of losing isn't hard to master
258
The buzz-saw snarled and rattled in
the yard 118, *119*
The falling flower 216
The gray sea and the long black land
47, *47–48*
the greedy the people 207
THE GUN full swing the swimmer
catapults and cracks 221
The lightning flashes! 216
The little toy dog is covered with dust
237
The merry world did on a day 63
The miller's wife had waited long 30
The old dog barks backward without
getting up 195, *195–96*
The river is famous to the fish 287
The sea is calm tonight 256
The spoiling daylight inched along the
bar-top 309
The time you won your town the race
273
The trees are in their autumn beauty
315
The turtle lives 'twixt plated decks
156, *157*
The voice of the last cricket 190
The warden said to me the other day
281
The way a crow 97
The way to begin is always the same.
Hello 218
The world is charged with the gran-
deur of God 160

The world is too much with us; late and soon 43
There is a garden in her face 69
There is no frigate like a book 34, *34*
There was a child went forth every day 307
There was a young lady from Niger 212
There was a young lady of Lynn 213
There was a young maid who said, "Why 213
There was never a sound beside the wood but one 25, *25*
There was such speed in her little body 234
There's been a death in the opposite house 27
There's the wonderful love of a beautiful maid 154
These hearts were woven of human joys and cares 89
These, in the day when heaven was falling 181
This house has been far out at sea all night 199
THOMAS, DYLAN
   Do Not Go Gentle into that Good Night 300
   Fern Hill 300
   Poem in October 214
Those Winter Sundays 54
Thou still unravished bride of quietness 277
Though leaves are many, the root is one 145
Three weeks gone and the combatants gone 266
Through brush and love-vine, well blooded by blackberry thorn 306
Through sepia air the boarders come and go 288
Tiger, The 260
Tiger! Tiger! burning bright 260
'Tis true, 'tis day; what though it be? 26
To a Waterfowl 133
To an Athlete Dying Young 273
To Autumn 56
To begin again, I come back to the swamp 303
To His Coy Mistress 74
To Sleep 76
To stay 255

To the Virgins, to Make Much of Time 86
Toads 71
To-day we have naming of parts. Yesterday 40
TOOMER, JEAN
   Reapers 302
Toys, The 238
Traveling through the dark I find a deer 166
Treason doth never prosper: what's the reason? 110
Triple Fool, The 13
Trochee trips from long to short 187
True ease in writing comes from art, not chance 198
Turning and turning in the widening gyre 314
Turtle, The 156, *157*
'Twas warm at first like us 149
Two Japanese Haiku 216
Two roads diverged in a yellow wood 78, *79–80*

Ulysses 90, *192*
Unknown Citizen, The 111
UPDIKE, JOHN
   Ex-Basketball Player 302
Uphill 96
Upon Julia's Voice 191, *191–92*

Valediction: Forbidding Mourning, A 72
Vergissmeinnicht 266
Villain, The 143, *144–45*
Virgins, The 304
Virtue 170, *171–76*

WAGONER, DAVID
   Return to the Swamp 303
WAKEMAN, JOHN
   Love in Brooklyn 147
Waking, The 295
WALCOTT, DEREK
   The Virgins 304
Walking the beach at daybreak I came on a violet sea urchin 80, *81*
WANIEK, MARILYN NELSON
   Old Bibles 305
WARREN, ROBERT PENN
   Boy Wandering in Simms' Valley 306
We could be here. This is the valley 297

We real cool. We 162
Well, it's partly the shape of the thing
213
WELLS, CAROLYN
A tutor who tooted the flute 213
What happens to a dream deferred? 77
What passing-bells for these who die as
cattle? 210
What you have heard is true. I was in
his house. 267
When by thy scorn, O murderess, I
am dead 151
When getting my nose in a book 31
When I consider how my light is spent
122
When I heard the learn'd astronomer
308
When I was a connoisseuse of slugs
288
"When I was just as far as I could
walk 146
When icicles hang by the wall 6
When in Rome 28
When my love swears that she is made
of truth 35
When my mother died I was very
young 105
When the alarm came 123
When you feel like saying something
233
Whenever Richard Cory went down
town 39
Where had I heard this wind before 60
While joy gave clouds the light of stars
143, 144–45
Whither, midst falling dew 133
WHITMAN, WALT
A Noiseless Patient Spider 306
Come up from the fields father 230
Had I the Choice 186
There Was a Child Went Forth 307
When I Heard the Learn'd Astrono-
mer 308
Who is this fish, still wearing its
wealth 310
Whose woods these are I think I know
131, 132
"Why dois your brand sae drap wi
bluid 219
Why should I let the toad work 71
WILBUR, RICHARD
A Late Aubade 49
The Mill 309
Wild Swans at Coole, The 315

WILLARD, NANCY
A Wreath to the Fish 310
WILLIAMS, MILLER
A Poem for Emily 310
WILLIAMS, WILLIAM CARLOS
The Dance 203
The Red Wheelbarrow 14
Wilt thou forgive that sin where I
begun 44
Wind 199
Winter 6, 7
With rue my heart is laden 161
With what attentive courtesy he
bent 59
WORDSWORTH, WILLIAM
I wandered lonely as a cloud 311
The Solitary Reaper 312
The world is too much with us 43
Wreath to the Fish, A 310

YEATS, WILLIAM BUTLER
Down by the Salley Gardens 185
Leda and the Swan 124
Sailing to Byzantium 313
The Coming of Wisdom with Time 145
The Second Coming 314
The Wild Swans at Coole 315
You, Andrew Marvell 83, 84–85
You could be sitting now in a carrel 49
Your mind and you are our Sargasso
Sea 41
you've seen a strawberry 285

A 6
B 7
C 8
D 9
E 0
F 1
G 2
H 3
I 4
J 5

Life has loveliness to sell 131, 132
Life the hound 60
Little Boy Blue 237
Little Jack Horner 129
Little Lamb, who made thee? 259
Living in Sin 53
Long, long ago when the world was a / ... wild place 281

JARRELL, RANDALL
  The Death of the Ball Turret Gunner 274
JENNISON, KEITH
  Last Stand 123
Journey of the Magi 125
JOYCE, JAMES
  All day I hear 202
Just to be tender, just to be true 229

KAY, ELLEN
  Pathedy of Manners 274
KEATS, JOHN
  La Belle Dame sans Merci 275
  Ode on a Grecian Urn 277
  Ode to a Nightingale 278
  On First Looking into Chapman's Homer 209
  To Autumn 56
  To Sleep 76
KINNELL, GALWAY
  Blackberry Eating 280
KLEISER, GRANFIELD
  The Most Vital Thing in Life 233
KNIGHT, ETHERIDGE
  The warden said to me 291
Kubla Khan 261
KUMIN, MAXINE
  400-Meter Freestyle 221

La Belle Dame sans Merci 275
Lamb, The 259
Landlady, The 288
LARKIN, PHILIP
  A Study of Reading Habits 31
  Aubade 138
  Toads 71
Last Stand 123
Late Aubade, A 49
Leda and the Swan 124
Let me not to the marriage of true minds 296
Let us go then, you and I 247
Life contracts and death is expected 298
Life has loveliness to sell 131, 132
Life the hound 60
Little Boy Blue 237
Little Jack Horner 129
Little Lamb, who made thee? 259
Living in Sin 53

Long Voyage, The 236
Love 154
Love Poem 109
Love Song: I and Thou 93
Love Song of J. Alfred Prufrock, The 247
Love in Brooklyn 147
Love's Deity 136
Loveliest of trees, the cherry now 76

MACBETH, GEORGE
  Bedtime Story 281
MCCORD, DAVID
  Well, it's partly the shape of the thing 213
MACLEISH, ARCHIBALD
  Ars Poetica 140
  You, Andrew Marvell 94-5
MCNAUGHTON, J. M.
  The Faded Coat of Blue 32
MADGETT, NAOMI LONG
  Midway 282
Man He Killed, The 19
Man proposes, God disposes 234
Mark but this flea, and 152
MARVELL, ANDREW
  To His Coy Mistress 74
  A Dialogue Between ... Body 283
MATHIS, CLEOPATRA
  Getting Out 284
Mattie dear 28
may have killed the cat 92
Me and my brother ... the porch 270
Meeting at Night 47
Mending Wall 268
Metaphors 70
Metrical Feet 187
MIDDLETON, RICHARD
  On a Dead Child 234
Midway 282
Mill, The (Robinson) 30
Mill, The (Wilbur) 309
MILLAY, EDNA ST. VINCENT
  Counting-Out Rhyme 166
MILTON, JOHN
  On His Blindness 122

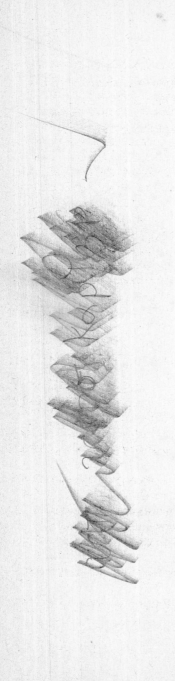